CW00762594

Made in Belfast

By Fra McCartney

SHANWAY PRESS

All rights reserved. No part of this publication may be reproduced, distributed or transmitted in any form or by any means, including photocopying, recording, or other electronic or mechanical methods, without the prior written permission of the author. Permission requests can be sent either directly to the author or to the publisher at the address below.

Copyright © 2023 Fra McCartney

ISBN 978-1-910044-55-1

Shanway Press
15 Crumlin Road
Belfast
www.shanway.com

I'd like to thank my sisters Bernadette and Marian and my brother in law Sean Mc Erlean for their help with the editing and advice on this book and any others for their input.

My thoughts dictated my actions then my actions ignited my thoughts.

Chapter 1

My view of Belfast

This book is about Belfast and the sum of all its parts. It's not really about one particular district and if you're a Belfast person you should be able to identify yourself or your parents. I was born in the Falls, so that's the part I know best and this is my story.

This book is dedicated to all my family and friends who have left this world before me. Especially my mother and father, my sister Brigit brother Paddy, and the sister I later knew as, Philomena, the baby in the drawer. The raison detre for this book is for my children to find out what life was like in my early life. It's also my way of trying to enlighten them as to whom, or what I was and the person I have become.

Lots of times I've thought about my life and times on the Falls Road and living in Belfast and what impact it had on my life. I asked myself how could I share my experience with others from this great city. I then thought about putting pen to paper, or getting the keyboard going. As usual procrastination set in and I would tell myself, "I will do it tomorrow" or I'll wait for the long cold winter, wrap myself up and get down to business. Then I'd bump into an old friend, Jim O'Riley and he would ask " When are you going to write that book your always talking about?" which wasn't entirely true as I never told anyone I was writing a book. But after a lot of thought I took up the gauntlet, so to speak, or maybe I took a bit of resentment and then put pen to paper metaphorically. It's now a lot easier to use the modern tools, the keyboard with the screen and all the effects it provides. What a hard task it must have been back in the day when one had to use a typewriter and no cut and paste. People do speculate and like myself can be presumptuous and in a way this is my answer to all Jim's and others goading which was taken in the best possible taste.

Two others have been instrumental in the writing of this book. Hughie Clarke I imagine would have the memory for a great book of times gone past. Another wee friend of mine who would say to me, " Did you do any writing today"? In some way again that got me to get the head down and proceed when I was in a negative state of mind. In between all the talk and slagging I had started writing some poetry and had a web site called "Old Belfast News" which I couldn't sustain financially so I closed it down and then I started trying my hand at writing stage and screenplays. As Babe Ruth said, "If your not in pitching you cant score a home run" and that's what its all about, doing rather than dreaming. A big farmer friend once said to me, "you can't turn a field in your mind you need to get up and do it".

Lots of people presume that when you write, you should or have to write a book about where you're from, in my case the Falls Road in Belfast. Maybe they're right and I'm taking that road, pun intended.

I believe that everyone has a book in them and it could serve as very good therapy for one living a troubled life. It's the best therapy I have known or met in my long trudged road in life and my quest for happiness or contentment. One day I sat down and wondered. Would a book about the road be of any great interest to its residents? Or would it be of any interest to people who lived in other parts of Belfast. More importantly, how would those that have never experienced the joy of living, in or around the place, what way would they react?

So I made a decision to write this book about the Falls Road and Belfast. I had somehow downed tools on this book and wrote another book called Silver's City, which for some reason took precedence and the Falls was lost for the Market area of Belfast. I then asked myself why should I and what would the outcome be and I came up with a simple answer. You can't please all the people all of the time, not even some of the time. Why bother then I asked my self again, do I need the flak that comes with this type of book. The answer came to me right there and then and I came to this conclusion. I was born there, I love the place and its history and maybe, just maybe, it could make some others happy as they escape into the past and relive the good times of long ago that wont be coming back unfortunately.

The Falls Road was the making of who and what I am today; I'm not making any statements, I'm just an ordinary guy who loves most of the things about this great city of Belfast without any pretence. I know that the snap shot I shall give is more heartfelt than pictures painted by people who wouldn't know a Falls Road man at a ten yards, not alone the road at a hundred yards. In fact in some cases they never even lived here, or visited on any occasion. You have to have lived there to experience the whole package, the atmosphere, the people and the craic.

The most important thing about areas in Belfast is territory and this was a big thing on the road. In fact it's difficult to comprehend its importance so lets set the scene for a journey of nostalgia through the working class streets of the Falls often in modern terms referred to as the Lower Falls and the Lower Whack the fore-mentioned being a Brit term so we will give it the high level of credence it deserves, none. We shall confine it to the dustbin. The first person I remember using the term Lower Whack was from the Pound Loney but I'm sure someone will argue so lets begin our story or stories.

The things you have to have to do to be classed as a Falls Road man are, firstly to be born there, then the dander, attitude and dress code and that's before your half way there. You could also be the quiet man who just got on with his life without the aforementioned and still be from the road and there were lots of people like that. It isn't a given that you have to have had all the previously mentioned things but it helped. Most young lads dressed and portrayed themselves as American kids, mimicked from films they watched in the cinemas or read in comics. They also wore clothes that were in some cases sent by relatives who lived in America, or brought by their peers who sailed the world in the Merchant Navy and came home dressed like those that acted in films. Yes the ones we watched with great joy in the Arcadian and Clonard picture houses were becoming a reality in dress sense at least. Bomber Jackets, P Jackets, Wranglers, Lee and Levi jeans and the ostentatious High Boy Roll shirt, a must have for you to fulfil the American dream. Girls in some cases followed suit and wore American jeans and the odd one even wore a bomber jacket, but years ago that was unusual. Unfortunately my writing wont please everyone but then that's

3

normal and one has to take criticism but on the other hand you don't have to listen to it, unless its constructive. Then it would be more than welcome and taken under consideration.

Some people on the Falls had a real pronounced dander, a good friend comes to mind, Patrick Tohill, unlike say the Carrickhill dander or swagger. I remember in later years being in a pub in London having a coffee when a guy went by the frosted window. I said to the guys I was with, "that's a friend of mine". Big Dominic replied, "every where you go you think you know somebody". By this time I was calling Patrick back and he came in for a pint to the amazement of my friends. I couldn't see him through the frosted window but he had a unique Falls road dander and there was no betting as we say in racing terms. Our walk was more of tuck the shoulders up and shuffle along with a step in our toes and hands stuck in your jeans pockets or later in the side pockets of you're newfound friend, the American bomber or flying jacket. If you had one in green or the even more popular blue you had arrived. If you had an Schott leather jacket you were in a league of your own. They first company to put a zip fastener on a leather jacket just like the one I got in Speckmans.

Then there was also a dance hall dress code, the mohair suit, the snap tab, pinned, or button down collar shirt. You were really going places if you had one of the afore-mentioned in short sleeves or indeed the piece de résistance a pair of white or cream coloured Lee jeans or a pair of K, Dees for casual wear. The scene was now set for a bunch of fellows who thought, if it wasn't American it wasn't it. Peer pressure was such that you had to acquire these items of apparel to be part of the team. As I got older I set out my own stall and in some ways I formulated my own style for me not others. If you wore something special, which may have been a Frank Sinatra style mac and a pork pie style hat you were a cool dude.

The Falls Road has now metamorphosed into a place barely recognisable to the place I remember as a child or a youth. It's an entirely different district, to the one I lived in. Not the one I loved and all I can do is to set out to do is try and recapture the places, some of its characters and the people that times have forgotten. In this journey through time some other events took precedence hence some characters got lost, died or were just forgotten. I will try to tell the stories about those people, places, things, that time and death has taken from us. The linen mills had gone, as had many factories, stabling yards, small builders yards that were all once a common sight in the Falls but not today. All but a couple have disappeared and I hope the small yards that remain will be treasured. The horses and carts, the camaraderie, the neighbours, that stayed friends for a lifetime in the days when everyone knew each other and were like a large extended family. It wasn't all good but some say give me the good old days back to which some reply, "What good old days?" and in a way that bears some truth, as it wasn't all *Sweet Lorraine* you know, the words of a famous Belfast balladeer. There were hard times: cold winters, damp housing, good Christmases and bad in the respect that money was tight. But is there such a thing as a bad Christmas if taken in its correct connotation, a religious event. I dare say no but give me the people and the old days anytime: People places and the things have the power to make you or break you, as we learn and struggle through life and place our dependence on the fore mentioned three.

Then we had the war or troubles as its euphemistically called. It came along and lasted thirty years, from nineteen sixty-nine until nineteen Ninety-nine. That's at least; one may ask is it ever over or just waiting on a new beginning. In among those years of turmoil some of our best-loved characters became less important, or decided to join one of the armies that where formed, just like their fathers, mothers, sisters, brothers and grand parents before them. In doing so they lost their character and became attached to something more important to them as they donned the persona of a soldier rather than a character. Being in one of these armies was not a place to portray one's character as these where secret armies and subtly was the order off the day. It subdued the character within, as he or she became a serious player and displayed a more private attitude to life.

Chapter 2

Nick name

In Belfast a nickname usually denotes a character and in some cases was self-descriptive or described a characteristic that was synonymous with their nickname. Some of these people where oblivious to their nicknames and I wont mention those but here are some examples of commonly known and used by all and sundry and some that just retained their own name. Cheeky Charlie McKenna, Sean Buster Crossin, Gerard Digus Mc Custer, Daniel Ghosty Mc Areavey, Peter Gaskin Dempsey, Gerry Spit Clarke, Dominic Sudden Darling, Glocky, Vinty Bendo Boyle, Thomas Yacko Hughes, Bunny Rice, Doggie and Funky May, Joe Dirty-Eyes McCabe, Gerry Peezer Ward, Tommy Skee Skelly, Big Josie Walsh, Paddy Yankee Trotter Cummings, Paddy Comanche Cummings, Peter Kelly, Neddy Docherty, Jimmy Frog Mooney, Tacky Mc Cluskey, Frankie Mouse Eyes Short, Docky, Mulanto, Molser, Micky Boolavouge Walsh, Vinegar Bottle, Nugget, Leaf, Go Go Riley one and two, Plum Duffy, and Lazy Tom Clarke who was a contradiction to my previous statement about character names being self descriptive, as he was a great worker. Just to add a proviso, or caveat. I'm not saying any of the above named characters where involved in any of the armies formed in the Falls or anywhere else for that matter. Some other characters come to mind, like shopkeepers and publicans and the people that frequented the places owned by those people. All of the fore mentioned would have stories to tell us and I hope to tell some of those stories through sympathetic eyes. Alas most of the aforementioned are dead which in itself is sad because they are never mentioned in dispatches. As we would say now, the three-day wonder of death has arrived. Not like years ago when someone was mentioned long after they had died.

Stories were told and retold about the characters mentioned, their exploits then turned into dare devil stories, added to, subtracted from and exaggerated in some cases beyond belief. But some say great stories need a bit of embroidery, or is the truth the real deal. Sometime someone will write the definitive book about the Falls Road, but this is my attempt to open an avenue for that to happen. Perhaps some bright spark or some old-timer will put pen to paper and I really hope they do, maybe someone may even collaborate with me or someone else. I'm here and opened to all interested parties. Here's my story sit back relax and hopefully you will enjoy the journey.

Most people in Belfast use colloquial terms to describe where they where born and reared and to a man or woman they like their district to be called as they call it, or see it. That's only but right I presume, after all it's their area so let them decide. Lets take a look at some of them in an objective way if that's at all possible. The Falls Road is the main arterial road running through West Belfast and carries most of the traffic. You may ask, is it the main road? I can assure you that to the people of the Falls it's not only the main road; it's the only road. It's the only place on Gods earth as far as they and me are concerned. A vibrant, and thriving road with grocery and sweetie shops, public houses, butchers, bakers and even the odd tailor, one Willie John Clarke and they all thrived. Most got a good living but some were foolish and their fortunes disappeared like snow off a ditch. Life went on idyllically for most of the residents and of course some others who didn't get it so good had to visit the pawnshops and for them it may not have been so idyllic. In fairness though most families visited the pawn on one or more occasion. These were times when people shared a cup of sugar or even a drop of milk to make a cup of tea. That was called helping out or doing a neighbour a wee turn and that was the norm.

Biddy my granny told a story of a wee woman rapping her door one day and telling here she had a cabbage boiling in the pot but had done the money in for the pork ribs in and her husband was coming home from work and he would beat the living daylights out of her. As everyone usually made the same dinners on the day Biddy asked her what could she do. She knew Biddy was cooking cabbage and ribs because she could smell them boiling and she asked her could she borrow the ribs to taste her cabbage and she could tell her husband that the ribs boiled through the cabbage. Biddy duly obliged and the woman's husband arrived home with a few drinks taken and he was none the wiser and ate the plate of cabbage and potatoes without complaint. There was never a hall door locked in daylight hours and everyone was friendly and helpful and it was all, *"Our own little Idaho"*. But there were other districts that thought and acted exactly the same: here is a snapshot of some of them.

Carrickhill: was a small district later rebuilt and renamed Unity Flats much to they annoyance of its residents. How dare you call it by that name when in the company of the people from the Hill as it's colloquially called. It would be like taking the Lords name in vain. I'm glad to say that it has now returned to its original name, "Carrickhill" much to the delight of its residents and enjoys a very vibrant community. My own father was born there in a street called California Street, but you can conjure up all the thoughts and ideas in your minds eye that you like, it in no way resembled the sunshine state it was named after in America. It was a real working class area that thrived with Dealers, Dockers general tradesmen and builder's labourer's. It was were my grannies family, the Walsh's came from twenty two Arnon street which we will talk about later.

Then there's Ballymacarrett, parts of which is in the Short Strand but dare you say to Ballymacarrett man that's he's a Short Strand man or vice versa. These people are usually called collectively, in a friendly way, the Wise Men and Women from the East. This once thriving place is now a shadow of itself with most of the small shops all but disappeared. This happened either through regeneration or shear vandalism brought about by redevelopment with little or no other input. The authorities may have provided better housing, but very little else. The result being that many areas lost their identity and in some cases they're very soul. Most shops on the Newtownards road are gone and it was one of the busiest roads in the town a few years ago.

The Market is another place that's a bit touchy about its name. Firstly, it's located in the heart of Belfast beside the Markets but don't call it the Markets, it's the Market and they are called Market men and women. The **S** is removed and that's the way it is. If you lived on the Hamilton Street part of the district there is always debate as to whether you are a real Market man or not. Just because you live on the other side of the street, but then you'd have to ask Harry The Wave McDermott for his opinion on that, as I'm not qualified to answer that, I only wear the brown boots.

This was the place where the men wore brown dealer boots and there was a chicken or fowl shops on most street corners running off Cromac Street. It was the main street, which carried all the wee streets, which amounted to what was and is the Market area. A very vibrant area, with all kinds of business, that included a bicycle shop, a dental technicians, which made the false teeth for most of the community and others far and near, barbers and some other small shops. It also had like the rest of Belfast plenty of public houses. Most people in the Market nearly put an *S* in there, where dealers of sorts. The Murdock's, where horse and fruit dealers and Barney Ross also dealt in horses and owned a rag store. Then there was Big George Stow an English man who owned the scrap yard and was a rubber dealer; well that's what it said on his billheads anyway.

Lots of the women folk were what we called black bag women, who traded in the Belfast Variety markets and further afield. Every bit of their wares was carried in a large silk bag similar to what a barrister of the day carried. The variety markets was situated next door to the high courts and it's questionable as to whom it was started to carry the first black bag, or the silk hold all, the barrister or the Markets trading woman?

Ardoyne was to me the countryside when I was young. Some people call it **The Ardoyne** much to the annoyance of its residents who call it Ardoyne and that's it. Others who lived close by in Glenbryn or upper Ardoyne call it the same. Is Glenbryn part of Ardoyne, well it's as close to Ardoyne as a chicken is to its egg, but is it Ardoyne? The people of Belfast all love their districts and are very protective of where they were born and bred. This large area almost disappeared as a result of rows and rows of houses being burned in sectarian trouble that wasn't only reserved for Ardoyne. Most public housing districts in this great city suffered some form of wrecking and burning during our turbulent years the Falls included.

The Bone is another place. It's called the Marrow Bone by some of its elder residents and woe betides you if you just address it as The Bone. Again the local term given to it as time went by and it remains that way. And as they say, that's life in Belfast. One person from The Bone I knew, as a kid was a man called Baldo Walker who drove a wee van for Paddy McFarlane who was my mate Chips Da, and was as wee say, " a wee rag man." Baldo's name lived on for years, as I called a mate of mine Baldo after him. His real name was John Hinds who recently passed away.

The Shankill or The Heel and Ankle as it is lovingly called by some of its residents is no more than one hundred yards from the Falls but during troubled times it may as well have been a million miles away and geographically its literally on the doorstep. But it remains as if it's in another county or country even. A great shopping place in its day where people from all walks of life went on Saturday for their rations or messages as they where called. I think the word rations stems from the war years when food was rationed and the people had ration books. This probably came from world war two and it remains the term used by all Belfast colloquially versed people. Some might say " going for the messages." It's one or the other. My own grandfather was from the Shankill and was called Robert Law Mc McCartney. He was killed at the battle of **Neuve Chapelle** in 1914. He married my granny Biddy whose brother Joseph and child Michael were later murdered in the Arnon Street murders in nineteen twenty two after having received a commendation in the first world war for bravery when fighting for king and country. And who killed him? The very people he fought for. It's ironic and can be funny at times, but also a very tragic world we live in, then it's not so funny.

The Pound Loney is another well-known district, also called The Pound, named after an animal pound back in the 19th century, which is definitely based on truth. It did evidently exist. Lots of the people from the Pound actually would call themselves Falls Road men but there are others who are Pound Loney men through and through and rightly so. It was a place where the residents worked hard and a lot of people sold flowers, chopped sticks, made and sold candy apples and so on. There were always plenty of handcarts in most streets, evidence that a dealer lived in the house. Their cart was parked outside of the house indicating that they usually owned it. That was a big thing back in the day. The Conway's were one such family, who always had a cart outside their door; they were fruit traders and a great family of characters.

If you love where you where born why not be territorial and guard your heritage with pride. "You're only born once you know". Every district has or had small pockets of people who to others in that district looked upon them as if they were different. They maybe felt isolated from the epicentre of the district and where called colloquial names. One that comes to mind is the **Coreekions** who lived in a part of the Falls. In fact it was right on the Falls but alas they got this name and it was more of a playful thing but that's what they where called whether they liked it or not. That district consisted of about ten streets and probably the best known were Mary and Ross Street and before anyone starts complaining about my description my mother was born and reared on Ross Street.

The Donegal Road was divided into two distinct areas not by a border but by the people who lived there and was defined by their religion to be honest. There was the Falls Road end and then there was the Village end. I could go on and on about people places and things but this book is about all of Belfast but focuses on the Falls Road. Bear in mind and I'm sure people will identify themselves in here some where and give a little chuckle as memories coming flooding by. It's about nostalgia and the love of this great city. No matter where you came from, one thing can be said about us all, "You can take the man out of Belfast but you can't take Belfast out of the man". I always pride myself as others do as being from Belfast no matter where I went and I went to a lot of places. Some good, some not so good, but I was a Belfast man no matter what part of the world I was in.

Never forget where you come from, because it probably was the making of you as a person. Just in case you may have forgotten where you came from, I hope this book reminds you. If it doesn't I'm sure there's always someone waiting to say "I remember you when you hadn't an arse in your trousers."

"My answer to that is, no one remembers it better than me!" with a chuckle. Another story I heard in a joke fashion, a wee man from sailor town another district were most of the residents went to sea was invited up to his sons house for a barbeque. After enjoying some food being cooked in the sons large garden the wee man asked could he use the toilet. The son t gave his da directions and the man replied, "I remember when you ate inside and went to the toilet outside' the son looked at him in silence. Another night I went to see a friend of mine Liam Baker in hospital and as I walked into the ward I couldn't see him and I asked one of the fellows was he in this ward and he replied, ' he'll be back in a minute he's just away to the yard" and that says it all. Sailor town was a real hive of industry and was always full of traffic coming or going with cargo for the boats.

Chapter 3

Growing up

One day of the week, I think it may have been Tuesday, Cows where walked to market, not driven in big lorry's or trucks but walked down the Grosvenor Road in herd fashion. This wasn't unlike a scene from a Wild West film without the Technicolor or the main protagonists the cowboys. That's up to the individual to formulate in his or her own minds eye, his own western. If the cattle didn't sell they had to do the return journey back up again, lead by a group of drovers carrying large ash plants, used more for guiding the cattle than anything else. It was a great sight and sometimes cows would take off down the opposite way causing mayhem. It was all in a days work for the drovers. But you could imagine John Wayne or Randolph Scott riding in front of the herd and the outriders chasing the cattle on to their new destination in the open planes of Kanas. Alas they were only going back to what is now known as Turf Lodge.

Dogs in Belfast had an identification all of there own and wandered about in every street and carried the name of the families that owned them. Very much like an extra member of the family. Here are a few that come too mind. Shelia Darling, Rebel Clarke, Shamrock Ward, Rinty Fox, Marty Daly who got lost one day in Ardglass and after a frantic search the Daly's left for Belfast without their beloved Marty only for the poor dog to walk home a week later much to the delight of its owners. His poor paws in raw flesh but after a rest and some Vaseline applied to his paws he was right as rain in a few days.

There was also a big Alsatian called Sooty Quinn, just like his master, he was a giant. His owner was also the tallest man in our district at the time but then big Paul Mc Corry came along and he may just have taken that title in later years.

Hoops and cleeks were a plaything made out of an old bicycle wheel with no tyre or spokes and a lump of strong wire to guide it on its endless journey to nowhere or anywhere you wanted to go in your dreams. It was straightforward with no electronic complication, batteries, gears, or anything else for that matter, other than ingenuity from days gone by. This piece of mechanical wonder was one of the greatest forms of entertainment and fun ever to be made by local lads and what fun it provided as you raced around the district as if you were driving a car.

Guiders were another source of simple entertainment and consisted of a simple plank of wood, two pram wheels and two ball bearings roughly knocked up as the materials came to hand. No one ever disclosed where they got the ball bearings from, but one day Liam Boyle and myself came across a small engineering firm in Wellington Street right plum in the centre of Belfast and they dumped ball bearings on a regular basis into large packing cases. They were also full of rubbish. You then had to search through the rubbish and the remains of the workers lunches among other things to find the Holy Grail, a set of ball bearings. This was our big secret now, but the old adage applies, when two know, everyone soon knows. They became even scarcer after the disclosure as a lot of the lads searched to get two of the main components for their own guider.

Our guider was built with one plank of wood, a wooden back axle, with two ball bearings on each end and two pram wheels up front. A large bolt and a piece of rope or string formed the steering mechanism and plenty of nails held it all together. Jamesy Kane would have come in handy, as we shall read later. The bigger the guider usually meant is was the best and whoever had it usually had the fastest and they were king. That's until it fell apart after a week or two after been used constantly day and night.

Seasonal games, winter, summer, and autumn come to mind. For the real cold winters, a few of us got bottles of water and poured the water on the ground and watched as it froze to a shinning finish. Then we slide up and down on it until it shone even more and you could see the reflection of the moon in it. Not unlike a Christmas card of the day. It really was a work of art and everyone prided him or herself in making the biggest slide. After the preparation and a lot of bumming and blowing about who had the best, we then waited for a few hours to find out. We thought we were operating our own bob sleigh run, not unlike the Olympic games. At least that's what we thought or imagined as we slide down it.

Perries and whips where a favourite toy of mine, if they can be called that but they provided the fun that a lot of toys couldn't and it was a very cheap way to have endless happiness. They consisted of a large whip and a peerie, sometimes called a spinning top. The whip in my case was made out of one of the wooden rods from an old baby's cot my mother had thrown out prematurely. Thinking she would have no further use for it. Was she mistaken? So here's how it worked. You put the perrie in a bit of soft muck between the kerb and the flagstone outside some ones house. Then you carefully wrapped the whip, string, or lash around the perrie. You then launched it and it spun in the middle of the street. You just whipped the perrie to keep it spinning, great times and what memories. I lashed my perrie for hours on end. I can actually see it spinning in my minds eye. I'm just reminiscing on how many windows I broke when I launched the peerie through some neighbour's window and into their kitchen. Which was what we called the now the renamed living room. This always caused a bit of confusion because to a man we all described the front and only sitting room in our houses as the kitchen. Alas if you asked a young person what any of the aforementioned where or meant they'd have no idea. They'd probably own a real car or a drone, but to repeat myself that was life in Belfast, any part of it, on any road.

Rallyo in our district was a bit different from other places as our boundaries stretched as far as Windsor Park in the Village area. It was really out of bounds but no one played by the rules and it was par for the course. Down town was definitely out of bounds as was Ballymurphy and the surrounding area. These were just a step too far but it was a very loosely ruled game that went on for hours. The game might have been just about to end and everyone caught and in the gaol, or jail. This was a part of the footpath designated to hold the captives. Then someone would run through, count to ten and it started all over again as everyone made good their escape.

Someone who may have evaded the opposing team the night before may have been accosted the following morning as they made their way to

15

school. They were then told they were caught. It was endless. Some also captured people who had evaded them the night before, as they went to the shops for the baps early in the morning, they never relented. It was taken so seriously and that was the game. It was never really over.

Street games where high on the agenda and were taken very seriously. One guy was called stinker for the rest of his life because he wouldn't take his turn at getting down in a game of Mossycock. Our team had been down all night, well I was only the banks man who stood with my back to the wall and three or four other bent down and the other team jumped on their backs and I counted to ten and if our team didn't collapse we won and the other team had to get down for their turn. Many times the number one guy would pull your strides down as he tried every which way but which to hold on to me before collapsing in a heap. This went on for about an hour and our team was down most of the night as the other boys where bigger and heavier and really jumped on us in a savage way forcing the team to collapse. Finally we done it, we stood up for the count and it was their turn to get down and be the recipients of our team when one of them called Brendan said he was going home, as it was dark. He never lived it down and I bet he would have changed his mind later given half a chance. He became Stinker in no way associated to greenwoods shop, which held a different connotation all together. Then Mossycock fell out of favour for Heinzy that involved guys jumping singularly over each other's backs. Back to the daddy of them all the longest game of them all Rallyo. This was a game of hide and seek, with a big difference. A game of boundaries that may have stretched for miles in fact one team caught a member of the opposing team at Windsor Park one night, which in those days was a million miles away and in dangerous territory. Rallyo would start at about eight o'clock at night and would go on to about midnight and later and it was based on catch us if you can with a den. The den was like a prison and had a guard whose job it was to guard the guys who got caught but if any of the opposing team ran through the den and shouted Rallyo counted to ten they could all escape. A very simplistic game but taken with the utmost seriousness and caused numerous fights when opposing teams argued over rules and the rights and wrongs of the game. Caught out of bounds was one rule that springs to mind. Before a game boundaries where set like a war zone you could go there but not there and it was usually about a square mile that turned into a square ten miles as people interpreted the boundaries in their own way. Some games where even halted and resumed the next night and the teams reformed some guys even switching teams.

Our district wasn't your normal soccer and Gaelic football type place. It was all about being different, horses, Rallyo, making small bombs or fireworks that banged in tins of carbine bought in Gases bicycle shop in King Street. One such story comes to light about a tin with a pop of lid filled with carbine and spat on and put in a small stopcock in the middle of the street as we waited until it exploded with a loud bang blowing the lid off and causing people to complain about such activity. In a way it was a simple improvisation to use something cheap for a bit of excitement that it provided. That activity died out as Gasses bicycle shop was blown up and carbine became a listed substance. That was the end of that until some bright spark; pun intended started taking the heads of red head matches and placing them in between two large iron bolts joined together by a large nut. You then threw the bolts filed with match heads up in the air and if it landed properly it gave a very loud bang so we where back to square one. So this was our new fireworks and life continued.

Chapter 4

Biddy's surgery

I was born in the Falls Road in sixty-six Servia Street in my granny Biddy Mc Cartney's front bedroom from where two days later I was removed across the street to thirty nine Servia Street to join five other siblings, the children of Lily and Robert McCartney. My Da worked in Andrew's Flour Mill in Percy Street and my Ma worked in Sarah Moss's shop at the corner of Servia Street, "Our Street" as we called it covetously. It was a longish street that ran from Albert to Cyprus Street.

My granny Biddy McCartney nee Walsh lived across the street from us. Her house doubled as a maternity ward when my Ma was having a baby and she had plenty of them, ten living children and a couple that didn't survive at birth. So it was a busy house. Biddy also washed the dead and prepared them for the here after, as did Big May Clarke. Biddy had cures for everything from a sore throat to closing a person's head. You could say her house doubled as a doctor's surgery. Her nephew Paddens Walsh was a regular patient as was his son Francey in later years.

Invariably on Saturdays Paddens Walsh usually visited his aunt Biddy, his father Francey's sister to have his head closed. Now for all of the sceptics, before you get all hot headed, pun intended, I have asked people who suffered this pain and they did and to this day say that Biddy could sort it out. Having watched my granny perform this piece of wizardry on Paddens; I am also convinced that she did have the cure.

First of all she sat him down on a good chair. Then she got her medical equipment: a gentleman's tie, yes the thing you put around your neck and put in a knot. She firstly measured the circumference of his head with the tie and then copied that by measuring from forehead to crown. Then the operation began in earnest. She then centred on the forehead, the tie wrapped around it, holding the two ends she squeezes with all her might. She was a hardy wee woman and I can remember her getting her knee and

18

placing it on Padden's chest and squeezing for all she was worth. She then held her marker on the tie and began the same process all over again until the marker moved to being a bit smaller and this was showing to her that his head was closing. She then went to the crown of the head and began the same operation. Padden's was in terrible pain but he was a tough guy and Biddy was as tough as him and she used all her might to relieve his pain, which he described to me as excruciating.

After about a half an hour or so the job was done and Biddy would then show him how much she closed it by the tie markings. Padden's eldest son Francey would have the same thing done on him in later life by an aging Biddy who had cures for eye, ears, nose and throat and I can assure you they all worked whether they were a placebo or not, does it really matter? Imagine you had a real bad migraine and this simple process cured it. How many would be queuing at her door for the cure. I remember her telling me on another occasion that my Da had been born with a coating over his eyes and she and a friend licked the coating off. I later I knew them to be cataracts, but was it true? I don't know but my own daughter Biddy called after her great granny was born with the same affliction and they are genetic and that sort of hardens my opinion on the previous statement being true.

One Saturday Paddens called to my house after having his head closed and then having a livener in the Long Bar. I was married and living in Abyssinia Street at the time and he had let's say one too many. After settling him down I decided to walk him up to the black taxi stand at the corner of Springfield Road to get a taxi to Lenadoon. On arrival a taxi driver pointed to his cab. I then decided to travel up with him so I put him in first in the front seat and I got in along side him. The taxi drivers usually left there cabs running as they where hard to start. Some drivers used bad old batteries and in some cases no battery so they had to keep them running. Just incase someone asks, once you got a diesel car going it didn't need a battery until late on when it needed lights and most were of the road at night. As we sat waiting for the cab to pack up with customers Paddens got impatient and jumped over into the drivers seat and we took off. As I struggled to get the taxi to stop and him with a little too much drink taken he fortunately stalled the black taxi. The driver ran up and was becoming a bit hot and bothered over the whole affair, which was understandable and was getting very angry with Paddens. I took the driver aside and explained that he would be backing a loser if he pursued the affair, as Paddens was a real rough house and the driver took my advice. The driver actually knew Paddens family so he settled down after getting the taxi started again he then ran us both right to the Walsh's front door, which was very unusual to say the least.

A couple of years later Paddens was out with a friend. It was a warm summers day and they both decided to go in for a swim in the Half Moon Lake. Paddens, who was a very good swimmer, drowned that day, probably becoming entangled in weeds, or debris. One of the good guys in life, generous to a fault, that are sometimes forgotten but I can assure you not by their family or friends.

Biddy's cure for a sore throat was simplicity, she made a lotion of butter mixed with salt that was then applied it to the patients neck. Then she got a proper silk scarf and wrapped it around the persons neck went to the back door made a sign of the cross on the step and that was it. She also made a sign of the cross on the neck and I suppose said a few prayers. Her cure for warts was again simple. She cut a potato in half, made a sign of the cross on the wart with one half and then I was sent to bury it on the Far Hill. The other half of the potato was cooked and then eaten. She had the mind-set to waste not wants not and in ways very frugal.

Our district and our family included had more cases of TB, chest and respiratory problems than most places, Glasgow only outdoing it on the score sheet. Unfortunately Biddy didn't have a cure for this but her daughter my Aunt Lily had a cure for whooping cough, as she was born after her fathers death and is was accepted that she had the cure and all she done was breath into the child's mouth and the cough abated. People brought their children from miles around to get this cure. But TB would linger into future generations and some cases they carried the symptoms for years to come. It eventually lead to my own father's death at the ripe young age of fifty-two.

Chapter 5

Bad housing

Back to the streets in the district that ran diagonally and horizontally along side each other and were named after the Balkan countries but that's where the resemblance ends except on a cold, wet, or snowy wintry morning when this place could be any of the aforementioned countries. Winter in the Falls was similar to most districts and countries in these isles. It was cold, damp, miserable, coupled with bouts of fog, smog and every now and then the *pea souper*. That was the name given to fog or smog when you couldn't see a hand in front of you, making this a very bleak place to live in. We had frozen water taps in winter, leaking roofs and in some cases no electricity. This made these houses probably some of the worst living conditions in Europe. The streets where lined with terraced houses, clad in Bangor blue slates, which in later years would become a great source of income. Brightly painted hall doors made the bad housing take some semblance of normality. The residents took pride in their homes and tried their best to make them liveable with some colour added in. In some other cases the sign of a family having a little more money than their neighbours was the pebble dashed walls. These were adorned with small seashells and bits of mirrored glass and a range of coloured glass giving the impression of wealth or pride, "take your pick," but it did serve its purpose and it made the owners house stand out from the rest.

A gas lamp was strategically placed every fifty yards or so and shone like a beacon on a dark winter's night and gave a little comfort to the somewhat dark and dingy streets. They also doubled as a place for the girls and us boys to swing from in most cases by ropes, but some lads myself included would speedy up the lamp and swing from it's cross bars and then turn the lamp out causing the street to fall into partial darkness. It gave us cover to rap doors, have a smoke, or just have our nightly singsong at the corner of Osman Street outside Raymond O'Neil's butchers shop.

The lamplighters would come around the next day to repair the damage, which was very regular. One was a big man called Walsh from Ross Street. He would arrive about dusk on his bicycle, which doubled as his ladder. Some others lamplighters used a small ladder carried on the cross bar of their bikes to scale the heights of the lamppost. He had no difficulty, as he was tall so he just stood on his bicycle and lit the lamp. He often changed the mantle and in some cases the glass, which we had broken on occasion, either by a football or shear vandalism. This wasn't really my thing or most of the lads I ran about with either, who actually frowned upon it. He would always remark about the dangers of turning the lamp off as it may have blown up from the leaking gas. He probably was exaggerating a little, but it was his way of trying to stop us doing stupid things. In hindsight he was right the streets needed lighted up for the elderly people to see where they were going.

Our house was situated next door to the Hawks gateway and I was born in my granny Biddy's across the street as previously stated where my Ma went for her few hours of labour. After a days rest, she was back to what she did best, looking after us kids, my Da and half the street as well. My Ma was back making diners, cleaning scrubbing and throwing the floor cloth at me when I was throwing a tantrum or just not doing what I was told.

A day after having our Marian I remember my ma scrubbing the floor on her knees and duly making her half moon mark outside our front door not unlike the mark windscreen wipers leave on a car windscreen. One sweep of the floor cloth back and forward as she knelt in the hall making the traditional half moon water mark which no one walked on till it had dried even though it was in the street on our footpath. I don't know if it represented our boundary but ninety-per cent of families had the same trademark and no one walked on it when it was wet no matter whose house it was outside. Having just had a baby it was like water of a ducks back, after all she had already had Brigit, Lily, Oliver, Paddy, Robert, me, and Geraldine, whom all had arrived before Marian and one or two that died in between.

One morning about a year or two after Marion was born I was up early and ready to run to Moss's shop for the bread, which consisted of baps, Paris buns and a coconut scone. I had to go over to my grannies to get the money or the treasured tick book from my Ma and I knew there would probably be a new baby as that's the only time my Ma slept in Biddy's. Running up the stairs and into the front room I saw my Ma lying in bed but there was no baby much to my surprise. I asked where the new baby was and she told me to take a look in a large wardrobe drawer sitting on a big table. As I eagerly looked in not knowing what I'd see I was amazed. There was a wee baby wrapped in a small white blanket, but it was dead. It was the first time I saw a dead baby and it was my brother or sister and I don't remember which. I don't know if I even asked what the baby's sex was. It just seemed normal to me . My Ma was a very tough and resilient woman but I remember a tinge of sadness on her face at the loss of her precious baby but in all honesty it meant very little to me and I didn't show any grief, remorse or empathy. I didn't understand life or death at that very young age. Later on that day, my Da got a friend of the family, Fra Adams, to drive him and a small box containing the body to the gravy yard (sic) to bury the baby.

My Ma always had her babies in my grannies, as our house was full of dampness as the photograph shows. Try as she and my Da might nothing seemed to make it go away and this caused countless bouts of sickness and in some cases a lifetime of bad health resulting in death. The landlords had a legal obligation to keep their properties wind and waterproof and that's all they done, most times reluctantly. She also needed the privacy of my grannies for her labour, as it wouldn't have been good to go into labour with a house full of kids and them all wondering what all the fuss was all about. They'd be running about shouting and crying and arguing. Everyone in our house shouted at least all the males did. I suppose we had to be heard, but if my da shouted everything stopped and everyone listened.

Chapter 6

We had four bedrooms

Our family and the people of Belfast as a whole were very resilient and used all the methods at their disposal to overcome the cold weather and beds had additional bedfellows, pun intended. Over coats, patchwork quilts and any thing that kept you warm along side the blankets that covered the beds. In reality in our house it was body heat that kept us warm, huddled together four or five to a bed with a hot water bottle or even a lemonade bottle filled with hot water at your feet. This gave great comfort and made it a bit more inviting to go to bed on a harsh winters night. Having said that I was and still am to this day, a night owl. I hated going to bed and hated getting out of it in the morning except on school holidays when I was up like a lark.

In our case we were quite lucky in some ways. We had a four bedroomed house, something unheard of in our district, even in later years. Yet some of our neighbouring families the Moore's and the Jordan's who had ten, twelve, or thirteen children and in some cases more lived comfortably in there two up and two down. In some homes they also had the grandfather and grandmother living with them and maybe a waif who may or may not have been officially adopted. It was all about survival as families lived under one roof in these conditions but we met hardship head on and that's what makes us the person or persons we are today. In our house there were five double beds, two wardrobes and a dressing table.

My Da's room had a bunk, a large box like wooden frame, which was actually the rise of the stairs beside his bed. This is where his ashtray and some literature sat along side his beloved woodbine. All set out in orderly fashion and all the used matches broken in the middle a habit that he had. The walls were adorned with holy pictures and maybe a farmyard scene or the cover of a chocolate box framed to look like a photograph. A small fireplace sat idle and was only lit when there was extreme cold. Coal was costly and you had to have the fire burning for hours to warm the room and it gave off very little heat. One day my Da sent me up to Joe Hughes yard at the top of the street for a handful of grass or hay which Joe fed his horses with. But my Da wanted it for another reason. That day one of the girls had painted and decorated his room and the fumes where literally killing him and he found it hard to breathe. So after getting the bundle of grass he then asked me to get a bucket of water put the grass in it and brings it up to his room as he lay in bed finding it impossible to breathe. He said it helped him to breathe a little better and I suppose it's a bit like putting a glass of water beside an electric fire, which we also did in later years. It's a similar theory.

The first room I slept in when I was young had no electric light in it and I was happy when I graduated to sleeping over the gateway and into the back room along with my late brother Paddy. Robert and Oliver shared the bed opposite and with the light on you could read a pair of comics until you fell asleep. One night I was reading a pair of superman comics and my Da shouted up the stairs to turn the lights out as the electric bill was sky high the last quarter. He blamed me for leaving the light on all night and then falling asleep. So he came up the stairs and checked to see that I had done what I was told but as soon as he went down stairs I got my flashlight out under the blanket and continued to read superman as he rescued some female from a burning skyscraper. I then I fell into a deep sleep and dreamt of Hop Along Cassidy, Roy Rodgers and Trigger and other cowboys. Roy's beloved palomino Trigger who I dreamed of seeing one day, as I was horse mad and it did become a reality. I eventually did see Trigger in Thompson's yard situated facing the Plaza where he stayed when Roy visited Belfast. The next morning my batteries were flat in my flashy and I was desperate, as I had no money for new ones. So I placed the batteries beside the fire for a day to try and breathe some life into them but it only shone for about five minutes after the fireside charge and that was the end of the flashlight until some money came around. The same went for my self; I had no energy, as I must have read about superman's exploits until the early hours of the morning the night before.

My sisters Brigit, Geraldine, and Marian all lived at home and along came Bernadette and they shared the other two rooms. My sister Lily was farmed out to Biddy's across the street. In later years my younger baby brother Gerard arrived and occupied a large cot set in the middle of my parents room. The house was now full but in all honesty it was freezing. As the night went on and the hot water bottle started to go cold it was miserable and I hated the cold.

I remember one night going down stairs for a drink of water in the middle of the night and it was dark, and miserable. The water tap, our only source of water was behind the front hall door. In all honesty it scared the shite out of me as I crept down the stairs for a drink, tiptoeing so as not to awaken the others especially my Da. I opened the living room door and stood in the dark hall and I was so scared I ran back up to bed without the drink and fell asleep after convincing myself there were no ghosts in our house and it was all in my mind.

Some months later we had the water tap moved to our back yard and eventually in later years to the scullery, or kitchen as its now called, where my Ma worked her magic cooking for a total of ten kids on a very tight budget. No hot water, an outside toilet, and the windowsill in our back yard doubling as a fridge. A large mangle, used for wringing out clothes stood alone like a work of art. It was designed in **art nouveau** form. It stood in the corner framed like a picture with the background of white washed walls with a black tar border. It really was a work of art and it must have cost a few quid as it was made of cast aluminium, which I couldn't wait to scrap when my ma got a washing machine. Aluminium was worth a few shillings and I knew I'd get a few bob out of it. My Ma would turn that big handle as I fed in my jeans and some other clothes in between two large rollers making sure I didn't catch my fingers. I usually scrubbed my jeans in the back yard with the yard brush to give them what's now called the stonewashed look. Why go to all that bother? Simple, jeans showed you off, but if you had the right ones, with the right look, you had arrived.

One day a man from the gas board arrived and fitted a Mini Main, a cheaper version of a geezer. It was a long gas lighted machine that heated the water instantly. In early days you only had to put a penny in the meter, which was a simple task. We now had the luxury of a hot water bottle at any time but it came at a price. The meter now needed a single shilling to provide the manna from heaven, hot water. Maybe that brings to mind the present day where all forms of heating have just went through the roof as costs soar. A twelve hundred per cent rise in cost at the stroke of a pen. How they arrived at that I shall never know and better still how they got away with such an enormous rise from a penny to a shilling in one act. But it was the best thing since sliced bread as far as I was concerned. No more using the water from a boiled egg in the morning, just to break the cold of the water that I washed myself in. I was a cold rife or *cauldrife* and the joy of hot water was amazing as you could now wash your neck, which my mother inspected every day before I went to school. I'm stopping for a minute to cast my mind back to this era then look around and realise how well off we all are now. I now try and appreciate how times have changed for the better, or maybe not it's all down to your mind-set.

Going to the lavatory or toilet on a cold dark night could be a very big dilemma. You would get a bit of a candle and light it, or set a piece of paper alight in the toilet, just for a bit of light comfort. Then use a piece of the Irish News to wipe your arse as you shivered in the freezing cold then hurried back into the house to see if your seat beside the fire was still available. In most cases one of my siblings would have stolen it and I would ask my ma to tell them it was my seat. As I pulled and hauled at whom ever stole my seat the arguments then ensued.

"That's my seat! I was there first! Ma, tell him to get up of my seat!" To which the reply was, " I don't see your name on it." My Ma never sat much as she was always cooking, washing, cleaning or ironing, changing nappies or breast-feeding one of my younger siblings or baking bannocks or soda farls or crumpets better known as pancakes to feed ten hungry children.

Chapter 7

Take your pick

Sunday night was a special night and I would go to my Uncle Sam Walsh's house in Osman Street where he and wife and sister in laws would play a card game called sevens. If you got a seat you were lucky and you kept very quite and gazed in amazement at the seriousness of the game. Every now and then young Francey Walsh and Jimmy Dimpers Prenter and me would be messing about and Big Sam would warn us, as would Clare his sister in law who shot from the hip. We were told in no uncertain terms to be quite. Sadie Prenter, Clare O'Hanlon, and Mary Walsh, Sam's wife, all sisters living in same street, whom all loved playing the game of sevens. The only noise allowed was the sound of the radio crackling as big Sam occasionally stopped to tune the radio and look at the clock. Then came the big moment, eight o'clock and the sound that everyone had been waiting for. "This is Michael Miles and take your pick", then the room fell silent and if you opened your mouth now, there was no second chance, you had to leave. So we all sat and listened to see if the contestant took the money or opened the box. The tea flowed for the adult card players as they took a break and enthused for the contestant to open the box or take the money. An hour or so later the cards resumed and some light banter ensued as everyone had a different opinion on whether the contestant was right to have taken the money or open the box, but all in all every one was happy as the card game concluded about eleven o'clock. The house then became busy as Sam's sons starting coming in from a night out and it was time for me to run around to my own house and get my arse up against the fire before it went out. When I ran into the living room, kitchen, and my da would ask where I'd been. I told him I was round in my Uncle Sam's and he just nodded and my Ma indicated that it was time for bed.

The next month saw me making my first communion and as the photograph shows I'm stepping out of line as usual. The other picture shows me posing with the Mc Donnell family including Joseph who later died on hunger strike. Making your first holy communion was a big thing on our road and as soon as the ceremony was over I went home and got my breakfast but not before I had a smoke at some corner, making my head spin like a perrie. I had fasted for twelve hours, as was the rule in the Catholic Church before receiving Holy Communion and the first smoke made your head spin like a perri. As soon as I got my breakfast it was time to do the rounds and visit all my uncles, aunts and granny and hopefully get a few quid out of this first communion thing.

As soon as I got my first dollar or five shillings I went to the shop and bought ten fags, as if they were the most important things in the world. In some ways, at the time they were to me. I had launched my first addiction, which in time would lead to more as I developed an addictive personality. When I went back to our house my Ma had a wee party organised and had invited some of my friends round. Next it was off with the suit and back into my glad rags, my old strides and my beloved water boots. After Sam's wife Mary died I used to go around and sit in his house and watch him prepare the dinner for his sons, Jim, Mickey Robert, Anthony, and John. Paddens had now married wee Rosy Brown and was living in Biddy's house as housing was at a premium. Our Paddy used to light the fire for them and run to the shop as well but I loved watching Sam peel the potatoes with his dagger like the one we yearned to have with the bone handle. He always wore his white skite, a silk scarf usually associated with a dinner suit. It was fascinating to watch this man smoke, peel potatoes and fry the meat for his family all in the one act. All I can say is he had his work cut out for him as his sons were all big hungry men especially Jim who came in some nights with a chip and then he'd butter about half a loaf and ate it all. It was all a picture to watch. The Walsh's actually shared our house in Servia Street long before I was born. They all mad a bit impression on me especially Anthony who I stayed with in Southampton.

Chapter 8

Radio Luxemburg v Ulster Television

I was always staying up late at night and I often wondered how I kept my eyes opened at school. Slate Street was now a new state the art school and the day I went to its opening I was amazed to find that the playground was on the roof. This was all new to me and everyone else. To our surprise it would play right into our hands and it turned out to be a great way of getting away for a smoke. We played beanbag throwing and some other stupid games, like five-aside football and believe it or not some Gaelic football, on an open roof. Take your point over the railings and that was were our wee gang came in. When the ball went over the wall so to speak or over the roof in reality someone had to go and retrieve it and it was usually, Buster Crossin or Terry Hanna and me or all three of us together. We were asked to go, as we were never interested in the games. We had other things in mind, money and how to get it. We were always scheming. I some times wonder why three had to go and get the ball but it was always like "Sir can I go along with him" so it turned into an expedition. It took us ten minutes to get down the stairs another ten walking to Grosvenor place and as long as it took to find the ball, which had invariably, landed in Garvey's painting contractors yard. In some cases we never found the ball at all. So when we got back usually about twenty-five minutes past three it was time to go home, so we enjoyed the games paradoxically.

I hated going to bed and was the proverbial night owl and would do anything to stay up late and listen to radio Luxemburg along with my brother Paddy who had a great influence on me, especially regarding music. One day he told me to listen to Buddy Holly as he sang **Oh Boy**. I was amazed with the sound but I was already into Elvis Presley. "I'm all shook up" along with Bill Haley and the comets "Rock around the clock" these were the only songs that rocked me then. But here was a little guy with black horn rim glasses who was now in my eyes the greatest thing since the mini- main or sliced bread. From that day music became a large part of my life and gave me some form of escapism and enjoyment unparalleled to this day. It was terrible listening to Luxemburg when a great song came on air only for the signal to fade. Some times the signal was strong then weak and in most cases you only heard half a song but that were the only station you listened to if you loved rock and roll. Then along came Eddy Cochrane, Gene Vincent, Billy Fury, Adam Faith and rock and roll was here to stay.

One day my ma brought me over to Gulping's. It was a large shop situated on the front of the mainly unionist strong hold, Sandy Row, where she purchased our first record player. It was a Dinette that played 33s, 45s and the now near defunct 78. It sat with pride of place on a table in our living room and was played at every opportunity, night and day. It was a joy to use, as you piled on four or five singles and watched as they played and the arm lifted to let the next record fall and it ran like magic. A wonderful piece of engineering of its time and it served our family well until the radiogram came along. My Ma again got into debt when she purchased our radiogram that sat in the corner beside my Das chair. It had two sliding doors and had inlaid boxed stringing that gave it an air of distinction above the ordinary radiogram. This was apiece of **art deco** without doubt and also a fine piece of furniture and we were the only family in the street to have one like it. But I was surprised one day to see the exact same model in my mate Liam Boyle's house about a year later. They must have copied ours I thought as Liam's Ma ushered us out of the house as she arrived home from work for her lunch.

One day, my brother Robert who was fond of kicking things when he lost the head, not unlike my self, he threw a natural. As he tried to kick something his boot went through the radio dial on our favourite piece of furniture. My ma went mad and some story was invented for my Da as he would have went even madder. Our Paddy or Oliver who were paying some of the weekly payments would have probably given him a slap but it was all covered up. In all my life I don't remember a physical row in our house. I think the doors were kept closed for a while and then when my Da saw the damage it was history. The time lapse also avoided a possible row. He said that it was the last radiogram that would be in the house, if we couldn't look after the one we had that was it.

One side of the radiogram housed a now fast growing collection of records mostly belonging to our Paddy who had a great eclectic choice of music and it became a life's love for him. His collection of 45s and LPs became legendary. A new radiogram or record player would soon be in the offing but television was now becoming the focal point of the house and records became secondary. That was for a while anyway, but not with Paddy, music was forever. He just loved music. My other brother Oliver bought the occasional record and I remember him leaving six shillings and eight pence for me to go to the premiere record shop to get a record by Dinah Washington, called September in the Rain. I had to make sure I didn't get a similar record by Sarah Vaughan. As if I could make a mistake like that. I now looked upon myself as an aficionado of music after being tutored by the expert, our Paddy. In fairness he was way ahead of the posse as regards music. He introduced me to Hank Locklin, Hank Snow, and Brooke Benton and before I ever heard anyone talk about him, Bob Dylan. I was now a real music fan and we had a copy of, "The Free Wheeling Bob Dylan". The title in its self conjures up some magic potion and I have to say I think it's the best album he ever recorded. When it was first played on a Saturday morning after Paddy carefully unwrapped it from its package, my Da asked, "Whom the hell is that trying to sing?" It was bought from Kay's catalogue and was delivered to your door not unlike Amazon today and in a way we always return to the old ways.

But like every thing else time marched on and it was moving fast as we all awaited anxiously for the advent of Ulster Television, the first commercial station in Ireland. It was nineteen fifty-nine. It was to be launched on Halloween and we waited and waited until its arrival like the coming of the messiah. Halloween was a great time, as my Ma was a great baker and made apple cakes, wee buns, and rhubarb cakes. But she was renowned for her dumplings. A week before Halloween all the stale bread if there was any left would have been saved up for the dumpling. Then I would run up to Mattie Mc Crory's shop and get a pound of raisins, a box of spices and some currants and immediately Mattie would ask, "Is your mother making a dumpling"?

Then I'd run back down the street and hand my Ma the ingredients for her famous dumpling and watch as she mashed all the bread up in hot water adding the currants and then the raisins. The smell of the spices as she sprinkled them over the mixture felt like I was in the Caribbean. It was like something that Long John Silver would have eaten or mentioned in *Treasure Island*. That's what came to mind for me as the spices came from afar, from a world that seemed so beyond my reaches as I whiffed the strange exotic scent into my nostrils. The next thing was for me was to hold open a flour bag that my Da brought home from his work in Andrews flourmill. Still bearing the company logo it would hold the mixture and soon double as a pillowcase. For now it was full of the mixture and recipe of my mothers dumpling. She then placed it into a large pot as I asked,

"How long will it be Ma"? To which she replied, "You will be fast asleep by the time its ready." The smell of the dumpling steaming was beautiful and filled our house with a sense of well being, after all she only made them twice a year and everyone in our family and other families loved them. A few hours later she took the flour bag out of the pot and poured the contents out onto the table. A large round white unsightly piece of dough with spots of currants here and there but I knew it was near ready and my eyes lit up like the proverbial Christmas tree. The last process of the operation was about to take place. My ma got a large baking tray, and then grabbed the dumpling quickly, placing it in the middle of a large tray. She then placed it into the preheated oven, set at mark four where it baked until it became golden brown all over. It then dried or baked into a work of art. The smell became more intense as the dumpling baked in the oven and my Ma gave me a single shilling to pump into the meter so the gas wouldn't run out and spoil the process.

My mum then used a very unusual saying when she was telling me to get to bed.

"Off you pop to Donaghcloney" which needed no explanation. It simply meant get up to your bed and it didn't matter how much I begged her to let me stay up, she had her mind made up. I never ever found out what that saying meant I just knew that was that. No arguing or pleading it was time for bed. Anyway I reconciled that the next day was a very important day in the calendar, it was Halloween and the birth of Ulster Television, a new television channel I had, along with a lot of others, been waiting on for months. I had tuned and tuned our television, as did other lads to watch the test card having no patience. I couldn't wait until the channel actually started. It was nineteen fifty-nine now and this was the birth of television accompanied with advertisements. This would be a life-changing day, not just for me but also for everyone else. After all we would get items brought into our living room that we could only dream off.

Next day I got up early as it was a school holiday and I always got up early on days off school. I ran straight to the oven, opened the door and there was the dumpling. It had now turned a dark brown with a dry skin not unlike that of a rhino hide. The first thing I asked my Ma. "Can I have a bit for my breakfast ma?" to which she replied " No you can wait till tonight" and that was that. The back room table was now covered with dishes of nuts, fruit and apple cakes and it looked like a feast or banquet fit for a king. I then went and got a seat beside the television and turned on UTV and watched and watched and waited and waited for what seemed an eternity until it appeared. A funny looking wee test card with lines running into wee balls, Ulster Television had arrived. Everyone including other members of the family and some others from the street all sat still and watched in awe as the long awaited arrival of this new invention took place. There was quietness and a feeling of anticipation for what was now to come.

The first program was Sir Lawrence Oliver talking in a monologue tone followed by the program we had acted out a million times as we shot bows and arrows at each other in Mc Kansas Glen or Shaw's Bridge. Robin of Sherwood better known as Robin Hood came in the shape of Richard Greene and his Merry Men. They arrived with the sound of an arrow swishing past with speed and accuracy. There in front of my eyes was Robin. He had come into our living room, as the sound of an arrow swished by again and again. It was amazing. Champion the wonder horse was demoted and was now a forgotten friend, for the time being at least. As I sat and watched every minute of Robin Hood without leaving my seat it was like the world had changed and in some respect it had. We were now going to be inundated and bombarded with things we could not afford and could only dream about, at fifteen-minute intervals. Lots of these things were unfortunately beyond our reach, or the reach of my family, friends and neighbours. But one could always dream.

Our home was a happy place and we had our needs but maybe not our wants. The adverts now on television were great to let your mind wonder and ask if only we could afford such and such. If my Da had been born on the Malone Road, the affluent part of Belfast. If only my Ma had been a rich farmer, or some big shots daughter. Not a mill workers daughter, originally from Castlewellan. To be precise, the town lands of Aughlisnafin, abbreviated, in colloquial terms, to The Finn not far from were my own children were reared. Set at the foot of the Mourne Mountains, one of the most beautiful places in Ireland and probably the world. A very under sold tourist attraction set idyllically in the Mourne Mountains that sweep down to the sea. If only, but then she wouldn't have been my Ma and look what I would have missed.

Chapter 9

The leather jacket

My mum was a big beautiful robust black haired woman who was the mother of mothers, to our family and half the street and beyond. My Da on the other hand was very thin and was for most of his last years in bad health. But he made sure of one thing. We would all get educated. He believed education was the answer to all our problems and in many ways he was right. He was mostly self-educated but knew the worth of going to a good school.

One day a big pile of books arrived at our house. It was twelve copies of Encyclopaedia Britannica and one large thumb edged dictionary, the size of a plain loaf of bread. That was the knowledge he provided for us and the rest was up to the individual. Once the parcel was opened a whole new world opened up for me. The Seven Wonders of the World appeared in front of our eyes, Sidney Bridge, the Queen Mary and her sister ship the Queen Elizabeth. The pages were covered with pictures of the other great marvels of the world in all their splendour and beauty that this world beholds.

So started a quest for information that haunts me to this day. One by one I read the books, all twelve of them. If I saw a word I didn't understand I had the dictionary at my side to find the meaning and it became a way of life for me. The quest for knowledge became insatiable. My Da always said the books were for reading not to be set-aside on some cabinet for show and I suppose it was his greatest investment in our family. In some ways it paid dividends, alas not for him. He never worked again and died at an early age.

One day after months of torturing my Ma about a leather jacket I wanted, my Da told me he was bringing me to Speckmans. It was a large drapers shop down by High Street and I was going to get the jacket the next day. I hardly slept that night thinking of what would be then the biggest day of my life. I was getting a real leather jacket not a plastic replica. As the photograph shows, it was a real leather jacket from **Speckmans**. What a statement I was going to make to my mates. I would be the all American kid or so I thought. The next day my Da and me walked down town to Speckmans and as I tried the jacket on in the shop, I realised that this was the first time I had ever been in a man's shop like this. Except when running through it or standing in the hall taking cover from the rain. It was a wonderful feeling as I ran the brass zipper up and down, then stuck my hands in the side pockets or as the yanks call them hand warmers. I looked in the mirror and I thought I have really arrived. Mickey Rooney, who I loved as an actor and whom I thought I looked like was looking back at me from the mirror. All I could think of was here I come. I was as pleased as punch. No one else in the district would have one; well at least that's how I saw it. Anyway it was a brown leather jacket and everyone else wore black ones.

The man who sold my Da the jacket also handed me an unusual triangular shaped pencil with these words printed on it, "When I was a lad I went with my dad and always got clad at Speckmans, now I am a dad and I have my own lad who also gets clad at Speckmans". I stuck the pencil in my pocket, as it held no reverence to me. I had only one thing on my mind getting home to wear my new leather jacket.

As me and my Da walked up High Street with me skipping along to keep up with him it wasn't long before we reached Albert Street. My Da told me to run on down to the house as he headed into John Taylor's public house for a well-deserved pint or two. After all he had just bought me a leather jacket costing six guineas. As I ran into the house and showed my Ma the jacket and explained to her that my Da had gone into the pub, I asked her, "Can I wear it now ma?" and she answered. "I didn't buy it for you to look at it in the wardrobe." I then slid the jacket on and felt the soft leather. It looked well and I was feeling great. It was lined with a warm fleece type material and I couldn't wait to get out and head up to the corner to pose with my new jacket. As I walked up to the corner I met Frankie Short. The first thing he did was to feel the jacket and confirm it was real leather. As if I needed anyone else to tell me. I had just come out of Speckmans where the man had assured me it was real leather.

Later as me and the rest of my mates ran about the streets of terraced houses broken up every now and then by a public house, the background theme of the **Falls Road**. As we dodged in and out of gateways that lead into large yards which contained piles of scrap metal, rags, or housed snooker or gambling clubs like the Adelaide or the Hawks club which I slept over. My bedroom was over the entrance to the club. I felt like a young American gangster and felt on top of the world, just like Jimmy Cagney. The rest of the gang were the Bowery Boys. The next thing on my mind was a pair of wrangler jeans as everything in my mind had to be American, as far as I was concerned. It was were they made every thing that was the greatest and best or so I thought. Then we went back up to the corner after teatime and listened to the big guys telling stories of events that happened as they sailed on the boats in the merchant navy. The exotic places they visited. My mind wondered to the encyclopaedias and the pictures of those big ships and I swore I would join the merchant navy by hook or by crook.

Chapter 10

Merchant seamen

The Wards, McQuaid, Clarkes, McInerneys, Dempsey's and the Mitchells from Varna Street were by now experienced merchant navy men as was a big guy called Tony Murray, a mate of John Walsh who could really tell a yarn. They told their stories to us and anyone else that wanted to listen to them. *The Rena Del Mar* a ship belonging to the Union Castle shipping company was mentioned in status usually reserved for royalty but in our case that meant men like Silver Mc Kee and Skewbald O'Hare, Barney Wilson Snr, legends in their own lifetime. Here was a cruise ship being talked about in the same breath. Charlie Duffy, Jazz Cunningham all seasoned sailors, Hughie, Gerry Spit and Tony Vam Clarke and others held us in awe as they told stories of New York and the Medi. That was their pet name for the Mediterranean were they cruised on ships they believed they owned instead of just having worked on them. The boys would stand at the corners in some cases, their sea book stuck in their back pocket for all to see. After all it was a status symbol, it meant that they had travelled the whole world. Bobby "Fargo" McFarlane, Chips older brother was a great guy for the sea books in the back pockets for all to see and was a great singer to boot. They all were looking every bit as if they where born and bred in Brooklyn or some other borough of New York. Some of them even talked like they were from there and one term was uttered that I'm sure was of American origin "Wise up". As they stood in their scrubbed out wranglers and blue or green bomber jackets and talked about the *Lizy* and the *Mary,* two of Cunard's great ocean going liners: *The Queen Mary* and *Elizabeth*. My mind wandered to my world of Superman, Marvel Man, Cadillac's, and Roy Rodgers and the greatest thing in my life at the time, Champion the wonder horse.

When my mates, Buster Crossin, Frankie Short, Joe Mc Donnell, Liam Boyle, Terry Hanna, Baldo and Liam Hinds and me plundered through the small yards in our world looking for something to sell to earn a shilling or two, as we adopted the persona of one or two of the fore mentioned stars. These places were our ocean going liners, our fields of dreams, our Texas ranch and our means of scraping up a couple of bob. On one occasion one of the yard owners told me and a mate to get out of his yard as he put it, "Get you two wee gets out of my yard. You've got eyes like magnets."

One hot summers day I think it was a Sunday as the Hawkes was closed and I was on my own in our backyard feeding our chickens. Suddenly I had the urge to climb over our back wall into the club for a nosy. I climbed up and over our yard wall and dropped into the yard below. I got up shook my now sore legs, as it was a big drop. I then wandered about the yard opening cars, getting into them and imagined being a racing driver as I pulled the starter and listened and hoped the engine would come to life and start. I plundered through the yard and I opened one of the stores and it smelt like hell. This was the only description I can think of were I experienced a smell of such proportions. There, hanging from the ceiling were rabbits skins, fox furs and other skins hung from nails hammered into the rafters. It was an eerie site and the smell was so bad I nearly vomited up my dinner and I thought, how does anyone work in here, it was stinking. A family called McMenamy from Cullingtree Road who later immigrated to America hired this part of the yard, which was under a room used by people learning to speak Irish. If you spent any time near this smell you could speak any language after a while I'm sure just to get away from the smell. I wondered how they sat up there with the stench but my mind returned to why I was here and I realised there was no plunder. The Hawks club that my Da was a member of, was named after hawkers, which describes someone who sells his or her wares on the public highways and I became a scrap dealer later on in life. Some may have sold flowers or the like but would probably have been a general dealer who sold and hawked anything he saw a profit in.

Gathering rags, scrap metal, skins, or waste paper, or anything that was recyclable. There was about thirty members but only a few where actually hawkers, the others came from families that had previously dealt in some sort of business including contraband in the shape of Free State fags and Free State butter. As you can see they are all turned out in their best and could be young lawyers or businessmen of the day or Philadelphia Lawyers the opposite to the seamen.

Chapter 11

Entrepreneurs and shopkeepers

Stinker Greenwoods shop sold every thing, literally, from a needle to an anchor and was owned by the Mc Keown brothers, Frank and Jack. You could buy a pound of nails, a yard of string, a tin mug in raw tin or an enamelled one. Fags, sweets, tape and just about anything you care to mention. Later Frank was shot dead by the British army at the height of the war, a completely innocent man going about his days work. Another tragic event lost in the annals of our history that then became a statistic. But not to the people who remember him, his family and friends and me.

One day my Da asked me to run around the corner to a house in McDonnell Street to get him a single woodbine or single fag. I rapped and opened Lizy Brady's door and walked in and said, "Givus a Woodbine," and Lizy replied, "Is it for you?" I told her it was for my Da who she knew very well but I know she didn't believe me as we got our single fag there most mornings before we went to school. Hers were different woodbine as they were thicker and they came from the Free State as it was called. So they were called, "free state woodbine' and everyone said they were full of salt petre. Anyway I ran back to the house with the fag and my Da lit it up using a long piece of paper from the top of the Irish News. As he smoked it you knew it was from the south of Ireland and had more salt petre because they burned differently from the local fags. But they where a penny cheaper than the real fag sold in Lizy Straney's wee house shop across the street from our house. My Da may have nicked that fag about four our five times depending on how long he thought he may have to wait until my Ma came back with the family allowance money or he got his chance to get a hold of the tick book. I also waited in vain for my Da to leave the butt so I could get a few quick draws.

Lizy Straney was a small grey haired woman who lived next door to my granny, owned a wee house shop that sold dulce or dulse, as it was more commonly known. She also sold broken rock, penny drinks, fags, candy, honeycomb, penny chews and caramels. She also made her own lucky bags and ran a Christmas club. All the business was conducted in her living room. You just walked in of the street and asked for a penny worth of caramels or two halfpenny chicks. One summers day about seven of us touched for a couple of bob we went in for penny drinks. Her son Francey or Banicker as he was called lined us all up and took our hard earned pennies and then filled wee shot glasses with Divis Attaboy, Sarsaparilla, or Orange crush depending on your choice. The problem was there was only two glasses, so you drank yours and then your mate drank his and so on. The glasses where only washed at the end of the day, but who cared, it was lovely. Sometimes we would pretend to be cowboys in the saloon as we gulped the drink down in one go. We then galloped up the street beating our arses as we rode; Trigger, Champion the Wonder horse or Fury, as we trotted off into the sunset.

One other day I was going into Lizy's to join her Christmas club with a penny, a whole penny. It was usually a three-dee bit at least to join but we were neighbours so she accepted the penny. She then produced a wee pink card and put my name on it and asked me what I wanted to buy at Christmas. The only thing on my mind was a three-coloured flash lamp and two batteries, as I knew my ma would buy me something bigger like a cowboy suit or something. Lizy informed me that it would be three shilling and nine pence and I looked at my we card and thought only forty four more pennies to go, a lot of money to save. Would I make it or would I only be able to afford to buy a selection box. My mind wondered. My ma would probably get me a stocking or a selection box, but I needed to get this flashy and I would have the only three ways flashy in the district, or as usual, I thought so. Come Christmas every body got one and the new thing was a flashlight that took three batteries and had a beam that shone into infinity. Christmas eve in Lizy's shop was like walking into a big toy shop, as parents arrived to get last minute presents for their kids and she just had about everything from Christmas paper to Christmas trees and toys piled high in the corner like an Aladdin's cave. Drunken men arrived pushing into the small living room looking for last minute presents for their kids. Christmas decorations hung from every inch of the room and they would ask her what they had ordered and arguments ensued as the men didn't really remember whether they ordered a doll, a dolls house, a cowboy suit or a set of six guns. So some kids maybe got the wrong thing.

But our street on Christmas Day was a happy place I'm sure for all its residents and if it wasn't they put on a good show. Another house shop that sold toys was Sloan's on Albert Street and it was a good place for something my Ma may have forgotten. You would probably have gotten it there, a doll, a cowboy suit, or six guns. But it sold toys all the year round and everyone bought something in it at one time or another. I remember buying a monkey on a stick - a great wee toy that gave great enjoyment.

Lizy Straney was one of many female entrepreneurs in our district along with Kitty Mc Crory, Sarah Moss and Lizy Brady who would be followed in later years by some others. But for me Andy Fennel was head and shoulders above the rest, men or women and one of the Falls Roads greatest entrepreneurs. He tried everything at least once. He hired part of the Hawks club and turned it into a snooker club that filled a void as Andy saw it. His club wasn't a structured club that was in a billiards league like the Adelaide snooker and billiards club in Osman Street that was known all over Ireland. Andy's was a place to play cards and enjoy a game of snooker and mess about and get a bit of heat on a cold winter nights. He only catered for young folk or those that where barred in the Adelaide or the Jemmy Hopes another organised billiards club in Devonshire Street. Andy had an eye for all things monetary and once had a great business in swapping comics, which he ran from his house in Varna Street.

One night my brother Paddy sent me round to swap a pair of comics and Andy just opened and closed them and said, "There's a page missing out of them". His son Joe who was Paddy's mate asked were they for Paddy and I said yes, so he got his Da to exchange them at the normal cost of a penny. Joe said Paddy would send the page around the next day or he would get it from him after school and so the exchange was concluded.

Andy also sold haystacks made out of Kellogg's cornflakes, candy apples, which he made daily and anything else that young people liked. He also hired out bicycles and was the first to make candy apples with coconut on them or maybe that was the Farrell's from Balkan street. We will call that a photo -finish. He also tried his hand as a bookmaker but the great Arkle put him out of trade but Andy was not one to lay down, pun intended. He just moved on and set up another enterprise selling socks and I think that was his most successful enterprise.

One event that happened in later years was farcical but at the same time very funny. Andy opened a pet shop, come amusement arcade and any other thing you could think off. I remember selling him a wee machine; called a duck shoot and the kids loved it. One day big Danny Rocky Ratcliffe knowing Andy wasn't in the pet shop, walked in and there was one of Andy's son in-laws minding the shop. Rocky asked. "You wouldn't have a sabre tooth tiger for sale, would you?" The young man replied, "You will have call back when Andy's in, I don't know where he keeps the big pets". Rocky got some laughs telling and retelling that joke in the local pubs and clubs.

Another summer's night a crowd of us hired bikes out of Andy's and headed to Shaw's bridge. I was on a wee two-wheeler and the rest where on bigger bikes. The chain kept coming of my wee bike so I only got as far as the Grosvenor Road and turned back. I then just cycled about the district on the wee scraper and then returned it to Andy and complained to no avail that the chain kept coming off. Andy had a great temperament and didn't take me under his notice and just parked the bike along side others in Varna Street entry. He then got on with his business as if I wasn't there. He was a good man with a great attitude to life and a great entrepreneur of our times who didn't get rich but provided for his family and also gave entertainment and joy to us all with his comics, bicycles and snooker hall. But that's before he became a stocking millionaire. Andy had one more try and bought thousands and thousands of odd nylon stockings. It took a long time sorting them into pairs, some with a longer leg than the other, hence the nickname. "The stocking millionaire".

On another summer's night a crowd of us went to hire bikes in Ramsey's in Coates Street who you could call Andy's opposition. The family sold sticks from a donkey and cart and developed skills and were quite adept on how to make a few bob. Coates Street was better known as the home of *The Jig*, a small dance hall frequented by all the lads from around our district. This was mostly unknown to their parents or schoolteachers who frowned upon it, wrongly, as being a den of iniquity, or a bad place to go. The Ramsey's traded from that wee street as well. Lots of my older friends and my brother Paddy met their wives there and in reality it was rock and roll that was frowned upon. Not **The Jig**, which produced some of the greatest dancers in Belfast. When we arrived at Da Ramsey's he asked us our names as some lads had hired bikes and stolen them or failed to return them. After a little reassurance he gave us the bikes, at six pence and hour. He then told us not to go too far on them. That was like waving a red flag to a bull and as soon as we got around the corner into Townsend Street we had a different view on things. Digus Mc Cusker, who was the oldest one among us, also the temporary leader of the gang. He assured Mister Ramsey we wouldn't leave the immediate district and what a laugh we had as we pedalled up the Springfield road. It was miles away in our minds as we headed for the flush, a large river gorge that ran under the Springfield Road and into the Springfield Dam.

The water was green as the mills and factories pumped effluent into the river as it flowed furiously causing foam to fly in the summer's air. It was banked between two large mounds or ravines as we called them where we played cowboys and Indians. In reality they were heaps of rubbish that had accumulated there over the years from people fly tipping. What an unhealthy place to play. To us it was one of our favourite places to go and we enjoyed every minute of it. This was our Rocky Mountains and our white river rafting that we saw in films. Except we threw pieces of old furniture or lollypop sticks in to see how far they travelled before succumbing to the raging river.

Digus was always up for a laugh and when we arrived at the flush, we parked our bikes and climbed over some railings. I ripped the arse out of my trousers in the process and then we all crept slowly and quietly into the Springfield Dam. This was a large area of green water and all we came for was to see were two majestic swans that had just hatched six little cygnets. As we where admiring the swans and the wee cygnets paddling in the pond, we started to play skimmers with stones. This was a bit of a competition to see how many times you could hit the water and bounce of it and how far you could skim the stone. Josie Riley was ok at it and so was

Sam Walsh as was I. If there was no money involved, it didn't grab my attention. Unknown to us Digus sneaked away as we lay in the thick lush grass that awaited Joe Mc Calls famous skewbald mare that grazed there. But Digus had other ideas. He had unscrewed a wheel of each of our bikes and as we where climbing over the railings, Sam Walsh, Josie, and Francey Riley and me watched as Digus pedalled down the Springfield road roaring at the top of his voice with two of our front wheels on each handle bar. Eventually after screwing one wheel back on we met Digus later on as we pushed our now one-wheeled bikes down the Springfield road. As we pushed our bikes with only one wheel we looked so stupid, and everyone laughed at us. One fellow remarked. "Do they make them bikes in two wheelers, and another said, "Did you steal them bikes out of the circus"? After a lot of arguing and offers of a fair go from all of the gang to Digus, he screwed the wheels back on our bikes but by then it was time to bring them back to Ramsey's as our time had ran out. But we had a good laugh and it was the talk of the corner that night, about how we saw the first cygnets born on the Springfield Dam, or so we thought. But it was more about how Digus made idiots out of us all.

One day I had been working in Twinbrook dairy farm now the home of countless Belfast people when I was riding a horse down a short cut from Dunmurry lane to the farm when I saw something I had never seen before. I stopped in amazement and there in the field was the nicest thing I had ever seen in my life. Twin foals! In my young life I had seen thousands of horses having worked for the biggest horse dealer in the whole of Ireland and make no mistake about it, that man was Henry Kane. A big man who wore a brown suit and a brown paddy hat to match. He had been a friend of my fathers in the old days and in fact my father was his best man. So in a way maybe he was trying to steer me in the right direction in life and gave me a part time schoolboy job helping with the horses. As soon as I had seen the foals I knew that I had seen something even the older ex jockeys as they were called hadn't seen. I couldn't wait to get down to the corner to brag about it. I had seen horses with bags over their eyes that were blown up to make them look younger, bled from the neck to help alleviate laminitis, a horse casting it's hoof and a stallion serving mares. So had all the other guys but this was unique this was different. So when I got home it was too late to tell anyone about the two roan foals but the next day was Saturday and I was standing at the corner when big Fra Ward came over. We chatted for a while. I then told him about the twin foals and he didn't believe me. So me being me, I told him that he could see the foals in the cruelty woman's backfield if he drove up. He bet me a fiver and wanted me to prove it. He may as well bet me a million because a fiver was much the same to me. He thought I was telling lies. By this time all the usual suspects had crowded around the corner and I was the brunt of a lot of innuendo. To settle the argument Fra decided to go and get his beloved Borgward Isabella and a few of us piled into it and made our way to the field. I prayed that the foals wouldn't have been given back to their rightful owners and were still in the field. I was explaining this to Fra and the rest of the boys that the cruelty woman only kept the horses temporarily until their owners were deemed fit and responsible to look after them again. I bit my nails the whole way up until we stopped at the field and there it was, empty, no mare and no foals.

After a lot of haranguing and arguing and me being told I was a liar, some even said there was no such thing as twin foals as the mare usually aborts one foetus. I felt like shite. Just at that a wee man came upon us. A craggy old man with a walking stick and a pipe burning and blowing smoke from it that smelt like old boots. He asked us what we were doing on his private land. I started to explain my end of the story as the others apologised and blamed me on lying and bringing them on a fool's errand. The wee man just laughed. He then started to shout and call and we thought he was calling for the police and we decided to get offside when he said, "Hold on a minute, just wait for a minute." He then called out again and again in a way that one does when they are calling horses to be fed. There low and behold the mare and foals appeared from another field to my instant delight. It was time to stick the chest out, as all the gang stood mesmerised and I knew none of them had ever seen twin foals before and one-upmanship set in. I was as pleased as punch. A first for a McCartney and a personal first for me and I loved it, every minute of it. The gang of ex jockeys had thought they had seen it all and in fairness it was a lifetime later before I ever witnessed twin foals again and some people have never seen them at all.

Chapter 12

Break a leg

Some time later I was passing Varna street entry when I spied a wee blue three-wheeler Raleigh bike. It was brand spanking new, a luxury at the time that was beyond our family and most of the families around our district. I knew it was my cousin Hugh Daly's as he was the only one in the district to own a blue one with a white carry tray on the front and a white box on the back. His Da Geordie had bought it for him for the previous Christmas much to the envy of the kids in his street and me as well. I saw my chance and sneaked up the entry and climbed on the bike and pedalled away like mad, as my older cousin Rab Daly, the original "Docky" came running down the entry fixing his jeans. He had been up the entry having a slash and had parked the wee bike. As I turned into Osman Street I looked back to see that Daly was right behind me and I was pedalling like mad, then all of a sudden I went up in the air and came down again with a thump. The next thing I knew I was sitting in the children's hospital with a nurse wrapping big white wet bandages around my leg. I asked her what she was doing and she told me she was putting on a Plaster of Paris as I had broken my leg.

When she was finished and the plaster had dried I hobbled out into the ambulance with the help of Daly and my Ma. I was on my way back home with both of them reassuring me I'd be all right. The plaster was a very uncomfortable contraption, very heavy and it was right up to my inner thigh leaving very little room to have a pee or go to the toilet and it made walking about a somewhat daunting task for the first few days. The plaster of Paris also had a big rubber heel and a little space with opening for my toes to stick out like the five little piglets that went to market, the nursery rhyme that my father sang to all of us when we were kids. Later they became five dirty little piglets, as it was a job and a half to keep them clean. I never wore a cover over them, as I liked the wind and rain to fall on them and give a little respite from the continuous itching.

That summer's day when I arrived at our house in the ambulance the whole street was out gaping and looking at me as two paramedics helped me out of the ambulance. You'd have thought someone had died and as the ambulance pulled away all the kids ran after it and the adults stood outside our house. They had all turned out to see my new broken leg. I felt like someone special as if I was some sort of a freak with the full-length plaster on my wee skinny leg. It looked as if I was someone of importance that had just arrived in our street as neighbour after neighbour asked what happened to poor we Francey Gerard. For what its worth I broke my leg on a three wheeler bike owned by my cousin and I hadn't done some wonderful thing but as previously stated I heard them say a horse kicked him up in Joe's yard among other exploits. All it did was make me laugh and I saw how easily we were entertained in the good old days.

Next day I was sitting outside the door as all my mates admired my plaster and asked could they write their names on it. Joe Mc Donnell and his brother Popeye or to give him his real name Patsy were always up in their granny Lizy's wee shop were slagging the hell out of me. I was sorry I told everyone I fell off the wee trike. My brother Robert the second Docky had broken his leg about a year previously but he at least fell of the top of the shelters in the Dunville park a height of about eighteen feet. For his period in plaster he was called Stick McCartney. After a little badgering I agreed to let them write their names in ballpoint pen, then some of them drew wee cartoons as well on it. All in all it was a work of art after an hour or so. The worst part of the whole thing was being slagged about falling of the bike; after all it was a three -wheeler and nearly impossible to do. I did it and it made for a lot of stories over the next lot of weeks. That night as I lay in bed the itching started and my Ma's knitting needles came in handy as I scratched the ball of my leg and tried to reach my ankle to no avail. Up and down I pushed the needle as I tried in vain to get rid of the itch, which caused me many sleepless nights.

Our street in the summer was a mecca of kids mostly locals but we had invaders or someone new moved in and we looked upon them as strangers until they integrated into life in the Fall's Road. One such family was the Hunters who moved into Osman Street and they came all the way from

Armagh city, a million miles away in the country. One of them was a great drawer at school and his Da was a fantastic sign writer. One day I watched him as he marked out and painted Mattie Mc Crory's grocer shop and in all honesty I thought he was as good as Leonardo Da Vinci. He scrolled the brush freely with his hand moving like it was floating in thin air. They were one of the many transient families that came and went like ships in the night. Another lad who came to our school was called Melady and he lived in Marchioness Street and made his first holy communion with us and then went back to Australia that was definitely a million miles away. Lets put it like this; my father had never been out of Ireland in all his life so that's how far it was away. None of the Hunters drew on my plaster but it was full of names and cartoons anyway.

Twelve weeks later I attended the Royal Hospital for sick children to have my plaster of Paris removed. As I walked into a large room I jumped up on a couch and the nurse put a strip of brass down the plaster and cut into it using a little electric cutting wheel while I closed my eyes, as I feared she was going to cut my leg off. But she had done this job before and the plaster opened likes a fish's mouth to reveal a treasure trove. There was my Ma's number six knitting needle and a number eight that she had searched the house for in vain. There was also a three-dee bit, which I quickly put in my pocket for safety. There were some pieces of lollypop stick, a few small nails, some sweetie papers and a pile of dry skin. As the nurse removed the plaster gently, the wind from an open window blew into the room and my leg lifted and floated in the air as if it was being blown away. I placed my hand on my thigh to keep it in place as it was now very thin and white and I took one last look at my old friend of twelve weeks with all the names, drawing, scrapes, scratches and said good bye to it. The doctor told me that if the bone had split just one more half and inch I would have had a short leg for the rest of my life so I was lucky in some ways. As I hobbled out in the strong sunlight into the ambulance, this time unaided, I was relieved to have the plaster removed but felt very ill at ease. I would have to attend school again. But it was the last time I would be called *hop along* and *stick* and in a few days I was back to normal. I wasn't taking any chances with my leg, no fighting, no climbing yard walls, but back to dreaded school, something I hated but more was to happen in a matter of weeks.

A few weeks later I was standing outside Mattie Mc Crory's shop under the sign writing Mr Hunter had done. It was a beautiful sunny Saturday afternoon. Joe Curley who was a few years older than me was telling everybody how he could knock anyone out without a punch being thrown. All you had to do was take three deep breaths then he would hold your stomach and then you would collapse into his arms as he demonstrated with wee Joe Moore. Well that was the theory anyway. Every one was amazed as Joe continued knocking all the kids out one by one by this ingenious method. When he asked me I stalled to see if it had any side effects. Paddy Moore was asked but he refused as he was boxing at the time and knew a bit about breathing and things like that so the next to volunteer was Peter Woods, then Anthony Jordan, Sam Walsh, and it all went well. Everyone was amazed and then it was my turn. I was a bit reluctant but after a lot of cajoling I agreed as long as Joe gave his word he would catch me like all the others. Joe agreed and as I took three deep breaths he grabbed me around the waste and squeezed until I went dizzy and he let me go and I leant against the wall. Suddenly the big Alsatian called Sooty belonging to the tallest man on the road, Seamus Quinn as previously stated, started fighting with Rebel Clarke. The dogs were known by the family's name and that became the focus of all the boys' attention including Joe and as they all ran over to watch the fight I was left standing alone. As the two dogs fought like mad I felt my self-getting more dizzy as the sun shone in my eyes. Suddenly I fell flat on my face breaking my nose, front teeth and receiving two black eyes and a badly bruised forehead into the bargain. As someone lifted me the blood flowed from my nose and I didn't know where I was and was kicking out in fear. I was trying to protect myself from the unknown. I didn't know where I was as and everyone was asking what happened and Joe was saying how sorry he was. It was too late and from that day onwards I never placed my fate in any human beings hands again, not one, not ever.

A few weeks later I was as right as rain and life went on but I had a twist in my nose and badly chipped teeth and carried the scars of battle. I do believe in horse parlance that wee trick broke some of our winds and made us short of breath.

Time moved on and one day a friend of mine named Sean Dillon told me he had joined the altar boys in St Peter's Chapel and I looked at him funnily and with a little disdain but then he revealed the secret. He had served at a wedding ceremony the previous Saturday and the couple that had been married gave him and the other boys a ten bob note each. On another occasions he got a pound note but in most cases five bob. That was a lot of money and I would have to yoke some horses in and out to get that sort of money in Hughes yard. That's when my ears pricked up and I asked Sean to put my name down if they needed any more boys. About a week later Sean introduced me to Brian Mc Ilwee who was the head lad and I was told I would have to go to some meetings to learn the Latin and then become an altar boy. Sean wasn't like any of our gang, he was a quite reserved lad who loved football and in fairness was a very nice person who just happened to be a bit quiet. He didn't curse or smoke or pull moves and was as straight as a die. After a few weeks training I had to go and get a uniform for the altar to serve on my first mass and then the next bonus arrived. If you had to serve on mass during school hours you got off school and nothing beat that. Anyway after meeting Father O'Neil and showing him I could ring the bell, carry the wine and recite the Latin I was told my first mass was the next day. He informed me it would seven o'clock mass. I looked at him as my jaw dropped. That meant getting up about a quarter past six and I hated getting out of bed. Next morning I heard my Ma shouting to get up for the mass and I was freezing. As I rolled out of bed and pulled on my strides and ran down the stairs to warm my arse at the fire but to no avail, the fire hadn't been lit yet. I cursed poor Sean under my breath. Anyway half an hour later I was kneeling on the altar and reciting Latin like an expert but it was to be a month or so before I got my first wedding. The main reason I became an altar boy was the money and nothing else. It wasn't the Godliness-I wasn't like Sean I was always on the make.

The funny thing about my first wedding as an altar boy was I knew the girl who was getting married. It was my mate Josie Riley's sister and as he was a mate of mine I thought they wouldn't bung me, or so I thought again. But to my surprise the envelope was left with a fresh ten bob note in it and a new enterprise had opened for me. After about a year I got fed up with walking up our street with my wee attaché case which I always found an embarrassment and to this day rarely carry any form of case. It contained my sumac and slippers and I decided that I was going to jack it in after Christmas. So after receiving my Christmas box from the priest, a box of Malteeser's, I decided it was time to move on.

But it was a great experience having had the opportunity to ring the bells of the church "as the rope pulled me of my feet and I swung like a cheezer on the end of a piece of string." At times I also got to see parts of the chapel no other parishioners would ever see. To Sean I will be eternally grateful. Later on in life he would point me into another way of making money, in fact more money than any other person in the house was earning at the time. It was all-legit, working in the Woodbourne House Hotel as a lounge waiter.

The big winter came along in nineteen sixty-three and for most nights we made slides or lit wee fires on the far hill. We roasted potatoes stolen from the house or from some of the shops around the district. Baked jacket potatoes held in the cuff of your pullover covered with salt what a feed. Some of the gang had taken potatoes and some salt out of their houses and they tasted lovely. One night Geordie Adams threw some onions on the fire and no one wanted to eat them, but after a tentative taste we all ate them both me and my new mate Gerard Hughes. I begged my Ma to call my young brother after him and she duly obliged. Gerard wasn't a McCartney or Walsh name but he got christens it anyway. It was a new experience for me and they did taste great but I preferred the old potatoes as black as coal on the outside and as white as the surrounding snow on the inside.

Most of the elderly people didn't like the slides we made as it made it very difficult for them to walk as they may have slipped on them early in the mornings, as they made their way to the shop. So you had to sneak in to Joe Hughes yard or the house and smuggle out a milk bottle full of water then pour it in a straight line and wait for a few minutes until it froze then you had a Belfast ski run. My Ma was forever shouting at me for sliding as it put holes in the soles of your shoes and shoes weren't cheap. We all loved it and some specialised in it like a sport. Jimmy "Dimpers" Prenter was one of them who was quite agile and was good at getting down low and going the full length of the slide down Slate Street opening without falling. I always fell on my hoop and finished up with a sore arse the next day but it was so cold you hardly felt a thing on the night. The more times I fell the merrier. I felt great sliding up and down with my wee woollen gloves on, stolen from one of my sisters and my jacket zipped up and my paddy hat on. One night I was going to bed and I was freezing, so I jumped into bed rolled myself up in a ball, but it was so cold as I waited for my body to warm up I had only one thought, the dreaded school the next morning. I was fast asleep when I heard my Ma calling me but I was listening for the sticks cracking. A sound I loved to hear as it meant the fire was blazing. As I rolled over for another few minutes in bed and pulled my Das over coat over me my Ma shouted up, "Look out the windy Francey!" I wondered what she was on about and I prayed it may be snow and that there may be no school. As I looked out the window I never saw anything like it before or since. The snow was about six feet deep and was up to my grannies front window still (sic) and the street was as bright as a new shilling. I shouted down that I couldn't go to school with that amount of snow and ran down stairs to get my arse in front of the fire. My Da winked at me as I stood shivering with my arse to the fire and told me there would be no school today as the snow was four feet deep outside. I asked my Ma what was for the breakfast and she told me that the bakers wouldn't be out so she had put on a big pot of porridge. I looked at my Da despondingly as I hated porridge and he told me to go and get a round of bread and he would toast it for me at the fire. I ran into the scullery and got the heel of a big plain loaf and stuck a fork in it handed to my Da and watched as he sat in front of the fire toasting it. As he handed it to me I ran back into the scullery and lashed some butter on it and was happy I hadn't to eat porridge, which I detested. I thought porridge was only for scotch people and it reminded me of bruised oats that horses ate up in Joe Hughes's yard.

Our living room was like Royal Avenue that morning with ten kids all in some shape of undress, arguing over who was going to get washed first or who owned what seat. As I stated before only one person had his or her own seat in our house, "My Da". I was as happy as a pig in shit or snow, should I say? After drinking my tea it was on with, two pair of socks, my water boots, jacket, gloves and somebody's hat, as long as it kept me warm.

I grabbed our shovel and dug my way out into the street like an explorer and made my way down to Seany Woods's house. He lived a few doors away from and he was always good for old gear as his mum Lena was a black bag woman. They had always a good supply of second hand boots and clothes, which she sold at Belfast and Newry markets. Seany and his brother Peter always had great boots for this weather, suede zip up ladies ones, lined with fur that his ma bought from rich old ladies up the Malone Road. I went calling for him to see if I could get a pair, but to no avail. He and Peter had the only two pair on, so I was out of luck but he gave a big scarf to wear out of his Ma's black bag. When I was calling for someone I stood in the hall and called his or her name out until someone answered. This was a ritual that everyone used but most just walked into our house as if they lived there and it was never a problem. The next thing Seany, Peter and me got some shovels, as the oul dolls needed their front doors cleared of snow and that was a way of earning some pocket money. The first thing we did before that was to build a wall of snow and make a little compound for our gang. Then we built a snowman that just got bigger and bigger but didn't really resemble a man of any kind.

Then the bigger boys came on the scene and they built a wall of snow right down the middle of the street giving it the semblance of an Icelandic village, as we imagined it. We made snow bricks, blocks, snow houses, snowballs and anything else we could think off. There was so much snow we couldn't believe it. The snow wall resembled a photograph of an air raid shelter from the war years I had seen. It must have been what the older boys where trying to replicate. This all made for great fun and excitement. We had never had snow like this in our lives and we enjoyed it while it was there. This was heaven on earth, cold but beautiful and then it thawed. What a mess it left. Slush everywhere, slipping and sliding, it was very uncomfortable and difficult to stay dry during any activity and I had to change twice a day and sit and watch as my socks bellowed steam out of them as they dried by the fire, much to every ones annoyance in our house.

Chapter 13

Kane's yard

Gerard Hughes and myself got barred in Joe's yard even though he was Gerard's uncle and I decided to work my way into Henry Kane's yard I remember the first day I walked into his yard on Albert Street. It was a nice summer day and the school holidays had just begun. As I stood in the entrance of the gateway half way up, some kids from Jude Street, the Peoples, Jimmy McCauley and Crunchie Mc Ardle, came running in and where shouting or name calling a certain Hack Kerr who was to become one of my good friends. Suddenly a bald man came running from the top of the yard in a rage and I ran as fast as I could along with the other kids as he looked like he would kill you if he caught you. Suddenly a fireman's axe skimmed past my head and the boul Hack grabbed me by the scruff of the neck. I must admit I nearly peed myself. Who are you he asked? To which I timidly replied, Fra McCartney. He thought for a moment. Did you do a bit of jockeying for Big Henry up in Twinbrook farm and I replied in the affirmative. Are you Rabby's son, I nodded in the affirmative again. I could hardly speak he had scared the life out of me. Where do you live he asked? I replied, Servia Street. As I started to try and get loose and make my escape he said he knew my da. Come on down and you can run a few messages but don't be hanging around with that mob. I was in, I had arrived I had made the transition from Joe Hughes to the main yard in the district. My dreams had come true.

Why you may ask arrived where. The answer to that was Henry was the biggest horse dealer in Ireland and I loved anything to do with horses. I had just graduated from Joe Hughes yard so to speak and was following in a long line of people who loved horses who started out in Joes and moved to Kane's. Peter Clarke, Jim O'Riley, Go Go Riley, Fred "Plumbo" Martin who later married Henry's daughter Rosaline. Tony Vam Clarke, Chip Mc Farlane, Tube Mc Ilwaine, Junior Canavan, Roy Fenton, the Tohills and others who will pop up later in the story. My cousin Paddens Walsh had worked for Henry driving one of his fine liveried lorries painted in Red and brown and bearing his name Henry Kane scrap dealer Belfast. Dan Braniff was another driver who drove for Henry along with Bud Dorrian and Jacky Mc Burney. They were all part of this playground on Albert Street at one time or another. There was one man Maurice Mc Corry, a great wee man as strong as a bull but the strongest of them all I thought was Tony Dickey Wilson. Then there was the metal expert a man called Isaac Moreland from the Newtownards Road who worked along side Tommy Smyth from Ballymurphy. They all sort of worked here, work being on the funny side, in truth there wasn't a lot of work done. There was one constant in the yard and he was the famous Joints, the one and only Mickey Mullan: what a character! Having sort of introduced myself to the work force there was also his son Henry junior, aka Young Snick and his sister Rosaline and the man himself Big Snick, Henry Kane who had given me a wee job before in Twinbrook.

One day as usual everyone was doing very little. It was Friday payday, when Maurice McCorry asked Mickey to run up and get five herrings in a wee fish shop in Sultan Street. Maurice had got his wages early as his wife was calling for the house keeping money, so he handed Mickey a fiver and told him to gallop up to Sultan Street and get the herring. Mickey duly mounted his imaginary horse and of he went. Having been gone a long time I was asked to go and look for Mickey but as I was going down the yard he appeared with a big parcel in his arms. They only had three pounds worth of herring left Fra and I had to go around to his other shop to get some more. I could hardly conceal my laughter as Mickey headed up the yard. I followed him at a bit of a distance as Mickey handed him the five -dozen herring wrapped up in brown paper. Maurice, who by this time was furious and in a rage unlike anything I ever witnessed before, was ready for war. Mickey then handed him the change and told him that was all they had left. Maurice's wages were only a tenner a week and here was Mickey spending two pounds of it on herring. The yard was in an uproar and some were laughing and some were cursing and Mickey was trying to explain that he couldn't get anymore as that was all was left in the two shops. As word filtered down to Big Henry he made his way up the yard all the while having a good laugh to him self. Hack was jumping about like a herring on a hot griddle as Bud and Tube laughed their heads off. After some deliberation Henry decided he would reimburse Maurice and the herring where to be shared. As big Henry made his way down to his office the fun began. The herrings were been thrown at each other, put down peoples trousers and thrown on the brazier a coke fire that sat in the middle of the yard to heat certain precious metal, brass, copper, gun metal and so on, so it could be broken from the steel. Every one was calling out Herrings Alive! Herrings Alive! Alive Alive oh!

Poor Mickey couldn't understand what all the fuss was about. Mickey tried to explain to Maurice that he had asked him to go and get fivers worth of herring and he got all that the shops had. Maurice let a roar out of him. Five potted herrings I sent you for and you brought back every herring in the Irish Sea. There were herring every were that day and it was talked about for months after and poor Mickey was none the wiser and couldn't understand what all the fuss was about.

On very cold nights we would light wee fires at the corner. The first thing you needed was a match and some soft paper. So half the gang would run around the street lifting old lollypop papers and some old newspapers that had been discarded in the street and the other half would go into the shops and ask for old card board boxes. When you went into a shop to ask for old cardboard boxes you had to let on they for your Ma or Da as the shop keeper wouldn't give you them to light fires in the middle of the street. On one occasions I ran into the house and run through the living room with a big piece of cardboard with flames coming from it with my Ma shouting "Where you going with that" as I ran out into the street to light our fire. We couldn't get a match anywhere so everyone took his or her turn at doing this nightly and I done it like everyone else. Most of our activity was confined to our own streets at night but in the summer we went out hunting with a lurcher or just an ordinary dog from the street that couldn't catch the cold.

In Servia Street and surrounding streets, the dogs where as well known by the family's name that owned them, and were named just like an extra child. Here are some examples of their names: Rebel Clarke, Sheila Darling, Shamrock Ward, Rinty Fox and Marty Daly who we mentioned earlier.

Every one said he walked home and when did get home his paws where red raw but after some Vaseline being applied to them he was as right as rain in a few days. He was in awful pain at the time and had a real sad look about him. Then there was big Teddy McGlone, Sooty Quinn in later years all receiving their owner's surname.

When we went hunting we took our belts off and wrapped them around the poor dogs necks and walked them up to Tornaroy to look for rabbits and hares but these dogs couldn't run out of your way. They wouldn't even know what to do if they caught a rabbit.

One day I was up at a place that's now called Glengoland and Big Long John Kane gave Tony "Vam" Clarke and me a real lurcher, or he implied it was a lurcher. As we walked it down the road admiring our newly found fawn friend, we stopped at every corner so all our mates could admire it. They all asked when could they go out hunting with us and how soon. Anyway we reached Clarke's house and Tony's mother, Big May, wouldn't let him keep the dog as they already had their own dog Rebel. So I decided I'd take it into our house and would keep it in our back yard. But we had chickens at the time so that was going to be a big problem. As I walked into the kitchen as we called our living room and so did everyone else. My Da took one look at the lurcher and asked. "Who gave you that dog"? " Big John Kane gave me it," I replied and he said, "Give it to your Da and tell him I sent it down for him." My Da stared at the dog for a while and then looked inside its ears and looked at me. "Get you that greyhound back to where you got it as soon as possible. He explained that he was always told if you don't like a man give him a greyhound and make sure it's a good one". I argued that it was a lurcher then my Da opened its ear to reveal to me its identity number and that was that. " Put it out in the yard for the night but tomorrow get it back to where you got it and tell John Kane there's no luck with a greyhound." A few years later, I sort of came to one conclusion that there was a lot of truth to that saying, for me anyway.

After a lot of arguing and begging my Ma to let me keep the dog and getting her on my side I thought my Da would have relented but he just looked at me and said. "There will be no greyhounds in this house." And that was it. So off I trundled out into the back yard and locked the greyhound in the toilet to keep it away from the chickens that were now roosting on the yard wall in fear of their lives. Early next morning Tony Clarke and me headed for the green bus and the long journey back with the dog.

When we arrived at the farm big John put his head out of the barrel top gypsy wagon he was living in and shouted in a rage about the bringing the dog back. "Get that dog out of here!" he shouted and I shouted back what my Da had said and he changed his tune. He told us to tie the dog to the wheel of his brightly painted wagon. Once John gathered him self together he came out and told me to go and get some water for the tea and I took the Billycan, ran down to a wee river and filled the can and John placed it on the potbelly stove in the wagon. We couldn't wait to get away. After a cup of well-stewed tea Tony Clarke and me headed back for our Sunday dinner and left John in his palatial gypsy wagon.

In my later years I had a couple of dogs: Vodka, Whisky, Pernod and a great wee bitch that had twenty pups in one litter. She had a few names, I tried Gin and it didn't work so she was just called Tonic. So you can guess were my thoughts were. In later years I also had a few greyhounds and all I can say is I wish I'd listened to my Da. The best and fastest one of them was called Symbol of Hope; I think that described me to the tee.

Horses and everything associated with them was how I wanted to live my life and loved the company of travellers and the like. One Sunday Buster Crossin, Chip McFarlane and Liam Robinson and me where heading to Henry Kane's land to jockey the horses. Jockeying the horses was how we described riding the horses without the owner's permission and was common on our road. That day we had got a few quid and where actually hiding until the heat was of as Chip had just rifled a slot machine in Distillery football club where his granda worked as the grounds man. It had accidentally emptied itself with a little help from a screwdriver and us. We where playing about and emptied the machine of its contents about two hundred sixpences and headed for the hills, Poleglass Lane. Which is now simply called Poleglass, a large housing estate on the outskirts of Belfast. As we went on our merry way out to the country to change and spend the sixpences in some shops on our way where we weren't known.

Anyway after a days plundering and eating ice cream we came across a single gypsy camp on Poleglass Lane. A flat two-wheeler horse drawn van with a canvas hung over the shafts and some ground sheets. It was all built around the cart and a wee fire burned or rather smoked away with a teapot hanging over it. This was the home of Joe Mc Comiskey and his family and I knew him from Hughes yard. He invited us to join him for a cup of tea and a bit of craic. It was just like camping out to us but this was Joe and his family's home. It consisted of a bivouac no larger than the one we went camping in. But for him and his kids this was where they lived and called home. It suddenly started to rain very heavily and we where invited into the tent and it was amazing. As I looked around I wondered how they done it and then I thought they just camped out all the year round but what about the previous winter I asked Joe. He told me they holed up in a house in Ardoyne but were glad to be on the road again with the piebald horse and cart.

Once the rain stopped we were all a bit wet so we headed home to face the music and as we went down the road we all got our stories right in case there was some kind of comeback from Distillery football club. We all got our alibis worked out and headed home content but slightly worried as the money was gone and so was the short-lived confidence that money can provide. It was never mentioned again, much to our delight and was just another day in the life of our ever-changing gang.

Seasons were a thing that didn't come to mind but in hindsight every event or happening had a season and now it was spring and it was time to go looking for a plank of wood, two pram wheels, two ball bearings and a piece of cord or rope to steer the guider that was going to be the best in the district. Everyone had their own source for ball bearings and it was like a military operation so secret that you told no one of your source of the materials needed to build the machine. We always went collecting copper wire, our means of a getting a few bob. To make the copper wire more valuable we would light a wee fire on the Far Hill and burn the plastic of and wait till the cooper shone like a new penny and cooled down with the help of us either peeing on it or placing it in a puddle of water somewhere to cool off. We then we took it to Pasty Kane's scrap yard in Cyprus street were we got about three bob for it. I remember a friend of mine big Joe Connolly or Alfie as we called him after Joe Hughes telling me about Jamesy Kane walking into Patsy's, his brother's yard and throwing a yard of rope on the scale as a young Harry Kane looked questionably at his uncle and asked, "What's that? This is a scrap yard uncle Jamesy as you well know." "Tell your father I've a million mile of that" and turned on his heels and walked out to his house which was next door to Patsy's yard. If only we had known we wouldn't have had to look everywhere for a bit of rope to steer our guiders. Sure Jamesy Kane had a million mile of it. Dealers my self included always talked in multiples. A ton of scrap became ten ton and so on but this statement takes the proverbial biscuit but it sits well with me and most dealers as it is a true portrayal of a dealing man.

One day in the same street two well known brothers squared up to one another for a fair go when the youngest and fittest of the two proclaimed, "Your putting your spoon in the wrong stew brother," meaning he was making a big mistake. You could say it was a good metaphor for a fair fight with only one outcome but in them days people had their own pieces of wisdom for just about everything.

Big Joe Connolly's Da was one of the first owners of the most famous horse in our district Bell. She was a legend in her own right, a small brown mare with dapples rippling on her back and as round as an apple. After Joe's Da, also called Joe, sold the horse to Joe Hughes Bell became the focal point for kids as they made their way to Saint Peters school better known as Raglan Street or Saint Josephs School better known as Slate Street. She would call at people's houses and rap the door with her head and the householder would then come out and feed her some hard bread. The first house she called at was in Cyprus Street and belonged to the Robb family. Totally unaccompanied, she then made her way to Varna, Osman and then Servia Street and then back into Joe's yard. After a long drink of water she would make her way back to her stable. This was her daily ritual except on Sunday as no one hired a yoke on Sunday and the yard was closed most of the day.

One New Years Eve, Bud Dorrian, Jackie McBurney and Jim O'Reilly would uphold the age-old custom of walking Bell, or a donkey into our kitchen and most of our surrounding neighbours homes as well. One year Bud

63

walked Bell into our house as I sat anxiously waiting on their arrival. As usual my mother had some bread for her but no one was prepared for her making her manure in the middle of the living room. Bud was under the influence and was very apologetic but the custom also said that if that happened you had more luck. So my Da and Ma weren't that bothered as I got a shovel and cleaned up the mess. Bell belonged to everyone in the district and was the only horse that was never for sale in Hughes yard. She was great wee driving horse that knew Belfast and the Falls Road as well as most of its residents and could have driven herself around the town and the district.

A few days later Liam Boyle and me were building a guider and we couldn't get the ball bearing to stay on their make shift axle made from a brush pole. So off we went collecting lollypop sticks to jam into the space between the bearing and the pole. After using about forty lollypop sticks the bearings still came off and someone came up with the idea of hammering a nail through the pole at each end thus stopping the bearings coming off. Now all we needed was a wee bit of rope to steer it with and as I said previously we should have asked Jamesy Kane for a piece. Anyway we had to make do with some baling twine out of Joes where we also acquired the plank and we where off. All we needed was a pusher now, someone who would push you from your shoulders then let go as you skidded in a semi circle to bring the guider to a stop, in other words a hand brake roll. Seany Wood's aka The Big Strong Man was a great pusher, as was Joe Mc Donnell, but he was also a bit reckless. He would do any thing for a laugh. He scared the shite out of me as he pushed me down Slate Street opening into the busy Mc Donnell Street and I could only pray that there were no cars coming up the street as I held on like grim death. Big Seany also played the horse as we put a rope around his shoulders and yoked him into a pram and raced around the district like chariots that we had seen in the film Ben Hur or stagecoaches in the Wells Fargo serial on television. As spring came to an end and summer set in, a new fad would come in. It was camping time, a time to plan, get a tent, some ground sheets and head to Tornaroy the greatest place on God's earth and not only I thought that, most of our boys did as well. So the plan was set in motion. In the meantime it was a waiting game for the weather to break along with school.

Chapter 14

The Adelaide Billiards Club

The Adelaide club situated in Osman Street was home to one of the best billiards teams in Ireland. It had different owners from time to time and in later times, it was owned by Fra Ward. He used it for tinkering with his beloved cars, a Borgward Isabella and a Citroen Traction Avant. The first front wheel drive car in general production. Through trial and error he succeeded in rebuilding engines he bought out of scrap yards in between playing his biggest love, the game of billiards. What a life and it all took place in a billiards hall. It was a dark and dingy place with three billiard tables and a large potbelly stove. For Tash Mo the marker up it was his home, as he slept under one of the tables surrounded by his loving cats. One day Fra got the Citroen going but the timing was off and it kept cutting out. After getting her running, Molser Mc Holland sat on the front wing fiddling with the timing as Fra blasted her down Raglan Street as the two winged bonnet cover flew of and landed in the middle of the street. He was as game as a badger Molser and they did get the timing right and the big Citroen ran like clockwork after that.

On Saturday night in the Adelaide, you'd find Fra's Da, Jimmy The Guvnor Ward, a wiry wee man with grey hair and a paddy hat that he always wore. He very rarely wore a coat just a pullover and he was never without a cigarette in his hand. He had just fixed the picture on a wee television set he was working on all day and he was as pleased as punch. He asked me what I thought of it and I admired his handy work with a little tongue in cheek then we the retired to the card school, when in came Digus with a couple of drinks on him singing at the top of his voice. A few minutes later the television went on the blink and Digus shouted to the Guvnor, "The picture's gone in your TV Guvnor". The Guvnor came over and as all of his televisions were a work in progress the backs were was always off them. He gave a sharp look at all the pranksters, Frankie Short, Buster Crossin, myself. He gave us the entire suspicious eye as he hoked and poked about it in semi darkness. We were all of us peering over his shoulder secretly sniggering at each other and covering our mouths just in case we busted out laughing. Every now and then he would receive the odd electric shock and he cursed all and sundry. He then realised that some fly man had stolen the picture valve from the set and everyone bar him knew it was Digus but we all remained tight lipped. There were ructions as the Guv, as he was better known wanted everyone barred, everyone including me.

That wasn't the end of it. Two weeks later either Digus, Buster Crossin, or Frankie Short or all three consorted and poured a bucket of water into the back of another of the Guv's sets and again it was another night of people including me getting blamed on it and the threat of us all being barred for life if it happened again.

A few weeks later as I was walking up Osman Street the Guv called me into his house. I thought he wanted me to put a shovel of coal on the fire or to do a bet in the bookies for him, but to my amazement he showed me a large wardrobe like piece of furniture. It was like a work of art. It was not just a piece of furniture that took up most of the living room by its sheer size but it had that look of class. I was totally amazed or so I pretended to be to the Guv. "Look' he said to me" "I bet you never seen one of these before McCartney it's the first in Ireland" I asked what it was and he opened the front door to reveal a combination of radio and record player. I said cheekily "It's a bit big for a radiogram Guv " then he produced the piece de resistance. A television set was also included in the piece and I was really amazed; as the Guv smiled knowingly he had got one up on me. The big piece of impressive furniture had a wee ten-inch television built in to it and to say the least I was very impressed. After looking over the piece the Guv and me got into conversation and he boasted that his neighbour and adversary Geordie "Poncho McManus" (he was called after Poncho Villa the Mexican bandit), because he bore a little resemblance to him would never have one of these. I agreed with him just to please him and told him Geordie wouldn't even know how to turn the set on. Poncho lived next door to the Guv and like him he fixed radios and the odd television and both kept homing pigeons. They were in a silent competition with each other all their lives. As the Guv explained the complexities of the combination set I dropped a clanger when I told him that the previous week, Buster Crossin, Liam Boyle, Frankie Short and me had gone down to Radio Rentals in High street and saw the smallest television set in the world. They had a two square inch set on display in their front window. That was it; he couldn't get me out quick enough. He and I always had this one up-man-ship about who knew the most about radios, watches, and pigeons another very important social standing in our district. "Your too old fashioned for me McCartney" it was a nice way of telling me to eff off.

Big Josie Walsh was a cousin of mine, a big gentle giant with the mind of a child, whose teeth protruded and it was very off putting to some people. He liked nothing more than a cup of tea, but he liked it in every house he visited. He was called names in the street, like foggy night, Joe the lover, which some people thought normal and funny and caused some fights as his other cousins the Walsh's from Osman Street always stood up for him and took his part. A lot of stories surrounded him about how he came to finish up with the mind of a child and people speculated that he saw his father shot by the Black and Tans in 1922. His father was my granny Biddy's brother and he hadn't been shot in twenty-two so she dispelled the rumour. But his uncle Joseph, Biddy's other brother and his cousins were shot in Arnon Street in nineteen twenty-two. But Josie didn't see it happening. He hadn't become backward or remedial for that reason; it was just the way the big unfortunate man had been born.

One day the brits arrested him and there was pandemonium in Osman Street. Try to imagine a big tall young man who a blind man could observe wasn't normal being arrested by the Brits and bullied into the back of a Saracen armoured personnel carrier. Paddens Walsh came out of his house and after some arguments and trying to explain to the soldiers that Josie was retarded but it carried no weight. It was all to no avail and he had to get into the Saracen armoured car with Josie and Fra Adams and accompany him to the barracks. What he was arrested for? No one will ever know but it left such a mental scar on him that he never returned to the Falls again for the rest of his lifetime.

Josie had a lot of adversaries around the district, like Bunny Rice, Vinegar Bottle McNabb and Wee Terry. Bunny was a wee small man not unlike the

Japanese generals in the films we watched as kids who with out a drink would hardly talk to you. But when he had a few in him he gained a totally new persona, which his relatives said was the result of being shell shocked in the war. It was what now would be called post-traumatic stress disorder. Josie was actually afraid of him when Bunny drank and Josie would shout at him and vent his anger and threaten him but he never lifted his hand to anyone. Bunny on the other hand was a funny wee character that wandered the district unaware of all around him, smiling at everyone he met and scaring the living daylights out of kids that didn't know him. In fact Bunny Rice was a true war hero who never got the help he deserved after fighting in the war. Big Joe as he was also called like most characters from the Fall's road had their own territory, not unlike a paper seller, or door-to-door salesman. He tramped the same run daily. First call in Servia Street was Fra Adam's house where he received a large cup of tea and a bit of a bap or a round of bread. He then visited our house about ten doors away and went through the same ritual, a cup of tea and a Paris bun maybe. After sitting for a while he would take his money out of his stocking and count it before making his next stop. He then headed to May Clarke's who lived three doors away from us. Again the same ritual occurred. His next stop was Raymond O'Neil's the butcher where he got a pint milk bottle full of tea. Raymond would give him some loose change before his final stop, his uncles; Sam Walsh's house in Osman Street and the same event ensued.

That was all the house visits done and Joe Hughes yard was his next visit and after a half hour waiting until Joe gave him some change he took a long drink of water from the tap that continuously flowed into the horse water trough in the yard. Once Josie had enough money he headed for a *smokie* in Victors ice cream shop in Divis Street. A *smokie*, why it was called that no one ever explained, was made from, a scoop of ice cream, a Cadbury's flake and some pear flavoured juice. It gave Victor's ice cream shop in Divis Street world fame and no other shop could replicate the *smokie*. To my knowledge this was probably made by the best ice cream makers in the world, an Italian family who settled in Belfast called the Angelo's and the head of the family was Victor, hence the name of the shop. To say it was the best in the world may be a big statement but I would say it was the best in Ireland with out doubt or as they say in gambling terminology, theres no betting. The *smokie* was the most popular ice cream concoction of the day, or any day for that matter.

One day we were all in Victors when Josie met McNabb who only ate a slider as he suffered from a disease not unlike Parkinson's. It was like war without a punch being thrown. Josie was in his element in Victors and this was his territory and McNabb had invaded it. I tried to pacify him along with some of my mates but he was in a rage and after McNabb left Josie sat down to his favourite ice cream the humble smokie that he ate in seconds. Josie could eat three or four Smokies quicker than most people could eat one and this was his last call before he headed home around the corner to his mother Nelly's wee house in Pound Street in the Pound Loney.

The day the Brits arrested Josie as he went about his normal routine, Fra Adams, and Padden's Walsh, took him to his sister Brigit's house in Earl Street after he was released and he never really left the house much again and he died some time later. He never did get over that arrest and it had a profound effect on him right up until the time of his death. Another silent victim of the war, that beset the North of Ireland, another character gone.

Funky and Doggy May where brothers from Balkan Street and were two very different characters, in looks as well as actions. Both had tragic deaths. Funky was a small robust guy who was the head of a wee gang at the top of Osman Street. They where more into football and handball which they played in between the two gable walls at the top of the street, but all of us played cards outside the May's house usually on Saturday and Sunday. Doggy was a guy with red hair who could play football and was great at rushing in and out as we called it in a match, a wee rushy. He was a great laugh.

One week he was Rodney Harrington of Peyton Place fame, or Brando. Whoever took his fancy or who ever were popular at the time? One night we where playing cards outside Willie Darks shop at the corner of Sultan and Osman Street when the boul Doggy appeared wearing a small green fedora hat, a silk cravat and a white shirt. Big Ward as Fra Ward was better known and was probably one of the best looking guys in the district was standing singing a Mario Lanza song when doggy started coughing and trying to get some attention to no avail. Try as he might no one was taking him on and he used his favourite saying, "Wonder would youse all screw your bobbins, you're all nut cases." The screw your bobbin originated from the mill where most of our lads started working before venturing on in life. Doggy lasted one day in the mill and never worked again. When the card school ended and we started to listen to him, he explained to Big Ward that Rodney Harrington was better looking than him and that someone had told him he looked like Rodney Harrington. All of us burst out laughing as Doggy had red hair and was no more like Rodney Harrington than the man in the moon. So after a bit of craic he left, dandering up Osman Street with his two shoulders going a mile a minute as only Doggy could do. Doggy was murdered later in life in horrific circumstances and Funky his wee brother who was about five foot one inch tall and had balls of steel for his height died in a fire. Two great characters from the road that are greatly missed, thanks for the happy memories rest in peace both of you.

Another great character was Jimmy Ward jnr who got killed in a street fight in England and as a kid I thought he was God. He told stories that would make your hair curl that's if his brother Peezer didn't get you first with the curling tongs. One night Jimmy whose ma Lizy owned two shops at different corners of Osman Street asked me to come with him into his Mas shop and hold a candle for him. As we entered the shop it was pitch black and I remember Jimmy searching the pockets of old suits that were hung on a rail. His mother had pressed them for the coming variety market. Lizy was a black bag woman just like Lena Woods her sister. After a few minutes he came from around the counter and showed me what he had been searching for, a small revolver. I was amazed as he told me not to tell anyone as he was going to do an armed robbery. This was about nineteen sixty and I'd never seen a gun before. Next day I saw Jimmy standing over at his Mas other shop his white shirt opened to near the bottom of his rib cage and his navy blue surge coat on. Jimmy stood there the picture of health as rugged as a mule and in some ways not unlike a smaller version of Rocky Marciano. Not a word was said as he smiled at me and that was that. He had given me four bob the night before thus buying my silence.

On another occasion up Varna Street entry Jimmy and some old fellow were actually punching the wall with their bare knuckles to see who could hit it the hardest as I watched in bewilderment as they slugged it out. Big Fra was messing about with a pellet gun at the same time and shot a seagull straight out of the air and it landed at our feet in the grating in the entry. He then took some pot shots at people going by in the distance trying to hit them on the arse. In one incident he shot his cousin Lena in the leg by accident of course, but she didn't see it that way at the time nor did her Ma, Lena who was Fra's aunt. I think for years big Peezer got the blame for it as like most incidents in our district they were always attributed to others.

Around about the same time a wee man called Jimmy Mooney, not to be confused with Frog Mooney, was frequenting our district as his sister wee Maggie Loughran lived at the corner of Slate and Servia Street. It was the first time I ever saw anyone being taken away in a straight jacket as he was diving at the walls in Varna Street headfirst. He was a very small man about four foot eleven but what a job the cops and nurses had getting him into the straight jacket and into the back of the ambulance and he was whisked off to Purdysburn hospital. I don't remember ever seeing him again. Another character gone and forgotten. There was also another Jimmy Mooney who lived in our district and his nickname was Froggie. On one occasion he got lifted while doing a move along with some of his mates who all got away, but he got caught. As Jimmy lounged in gaol he couldn't get the money for his bail so he sent out a note which read, " The Frogs in the well and he cant get out, if the frog cant get out he's going to shout, shout, shout!" What a character, I owe him a great debt of gratitude to, as he introduced me to a way of life that changed my life, forever.

Mickey Boolavogue Walsh was the" King of the Fat" a card game not unlike whist whose origins have been debated and argued over for years. Some say it was invented in the Curragh camp during internment after the civil war but that's another story in its self. Mickey's origins, where never in doubt, he was an Osman Street man through and through. One day we where playing Fat and Mickey's partner in this whist type game, Gerico Boardman lost the most important card in the game, the big Don, which was the nine of trumps. Mickey threw his hand down in a rage as they only

71

needed four points to win and the guy had the ace of trump worth the four points needed in his hand. Gerico his partner had the ten, queen, king and ace trumps in his hand and was trying to be smart but forgot about the jack in trumps and the other team had it and they won. It was like the loss of the Titanic; Mickey had to then stand and wait maybe an hour or so as other guys took their place in the most talked about game of cards on the Fall's road, "The Fat". Mickey was one of the greatest and most prolific Fat players in Belfast and was synonymous with the game as he was with the song Boolavogue. His favourite saying when he got annoyed was "would you like a mouth full of dandruff" or when he was in good form it was " no goose gab". Card schools where on every other corner and their was apprentice schools where you tried to take the wee school to get enough money to get into the bigger school. One night I was playing in the apprentice game next to the big card school in Balkan Street outside Funky Mays house when his brother Doggy asked, "What are the initials of Vic Oliver?" Then someone replied VO, and that was it, pandemonium broke out as a free for all ensued. Harry Short, Funky, Doggy all dived into the middle of the big school as I scrambled up my money as we all tried to salvage as much of the money as we could as it spilled onto our wee card school. VO was an unwritten law that when someone shouted it a melee started and in some cases before a card school started the ground rules would be laid down that there be no VO'S except if Durango appeared. This was the name given to the motorcycle cop. He was named after the cowboy who dressed in black and appeared in the films and the chapters on Saturday afternoon in the Diamond picture house. If he was spotted, or Pig Mc Neely, the infamous RUC man who rode a push bike it was all right to call a VO. He would confiscate the cards and the money and if we where playing football the ball. A VO was ok as it accepted that it was better some of our lads getting the money rather than the cops.

Cheating or lumping the cards as it was called was another reason for a VO and many fights. One day Rab Mc Donnell the eldest brother of Joe was playing with a guy called The Dip who was known as a card sharp. He was from the Pound Loney district and he decided to try it on. It was all right to cheat, everyone tried it, myself included, but the idea was not to get caught. As the card school drew to a close the last hand was announced and The Dip, who was the banker dealt the cards around and Rab announced that if he had the ace of hearts in his hand he was going to do him. The Dip was an older fellow than Rab but Rab was super fit and he didn't see him as a danger so he dealt the cards out. Every one was waiting as the Dip turned over his cards and there was the ace of hearts and without a heart beat Rab clocked the poor Dip with out even getting of his hunkers knocking him sparkling. Needless to say he never played cards in our district again but went to England where he took up another trade associated with the gambling way of life and his nick- name.

Card schools attracted guys from other districts and when word got out about a big school people from all over Belfast would come to play as it was a status symbol if you took the school in another district. This was about the time I met John McConnell who I was introduced to by my mate Terry Bonanza Hanna. John loved to gamble as we all did and the cards became his introduction to bigger gambling, although he came from Granville Street I didn't know him that well at this time. But as time went on we became good friends and we often visited Celtic park the home of the now defunct Belfast Celtic football club. It was also a Mecca for gambling and the place for greyhound racing that produced a buzz like no other sport I have encountered. John was like every other gambler myself included, no matter where it happened it usually resulted in us getting skint. One night Davy Wilson and me and some other mates tried to pay in but the man on the turnstile wouldn't let us into Celtic Park. He said we were too young, but that didn't deter us. We then went around the corner to Willowbank Park, climbed the railings and crossed the Broadway River, over the back fence and into paradise, Celtic park. We then were part of the punters and we met John Mc Connell with his Da Stack. Next Terry Hanna appeared and it was like the whole gang was present, but the truth was John Mc Connell had been minding a few quid for Terry and had done it in. He was up at Celtic to try and win it back, but to no avail so poor Terry got nothing. Terry was really annoyed but let it pass, as he was a next day new day man. He was nobody's mug and had won numerous championships for boxing and his only Achilles heel was the great Mick Dowling from Dublin.

Then, in the all Ireland final you literally had to stop your opponent if you from the north to win a title. Again there were different gangs out for different things, Celtic park for gambling, football fanatics and horsey men like myself, but the bottom line was we were all out looking for a few bob. Big Seany Woods wouldn't go punting and neither would Frankie Short but most of the rest of our guys loved a bet. They wouldn't even go to watch the Whites play, (better known as Distillery football club) but as the days ended we all did mostly the same things but from different angles and finished standing at one or more of the corners on our streets.

One card school I used to take most Friday nights was outside Tommy Soldier Flynn's house in Sultan Street next door to Maggie Marley's rag store. Another of those yards that we plundered every now and then to try and get a few bob. It was a small card school, three dee bits and sprazies with the odd two bob bit and half a crown. This was all our Friday night pocket money and it all could disappear in minutes. If you took the school you then went looking for a bigger school, which was a bit more difficult to take.

The Shots Club was another gambling hotpot, so called after its owner Big Shot Clarke. This was a very different place to any other club on the Falls or any other part of Belfast for that matter. Situated behind a row of houses in Panton Street and about four Doors down from a pawnbrokers shop on the main Fall's road, it was for real heavy hitters, not apprentices like myself. I would have been definitely punching above my weight in there. Entry and exit was gained by walking down a narrow corridor, which became an obstacle course when someone took the school as they were hounded by other punters looking for a few shillings or a bung to get back to playing again. This alley lead to a large dingy smoke filled room with a snooker table and a room to the right where the biggest gambling card school in Belfast took place, *Faro*. It was reminiscent of the places one saw in films were American gangsters rolled the dice in crap games and was just as life threatening in some cases. It contained a bunch of tougher men than we watched in films; this was real hard-core gambling and not place for a tender foot like me. This game was fast and furious and one needed to be as fast as the dealer to follow your money before he tried to beat you

74

even when you won. If you didn't lift your winning or call off in time he kept drawing cards and maybe beat you even if he didn't want to double up. The case keeper who kept track of the school marked a slate with all the cards that had been played and made sure the game went on without arguments or fights which usually followed a game of Faro. Two of the case keepers I remember were Mickey "The Hard" Smith and Jim Clarke from Servia Street, big May's eldest son and the cousin of the owner Big Shot. Jim and Mickey the Hard were the main case keepers in the shots for many years. One night I decided it was time for me to make my debut into the shots as my mate Frankie Short had been talking about the excitement of watching men loose or win hundreds of pounds at this game, **Faro**. I had only read about this game in cowboy books or western comics. But I had to get a new suit to portray that I was a big fellow now as in real life. I was five foot four and looked about twelve when I was fifteen and there was no way I could into the shots. So Short and myself planned to go to Burtons tailors to buy ourselves suits but we had to do a reconnoitre of Burtons to see how it all worked.

Chapter 15

Going for a suit

A few day later we were walking down Royal Avenue the once most thriving street in Belfast. I looked around and saw no visible signs of that once bustling street. Where did the grand central hotel go, the general post office, the avenue cinema and much more. But no memory evoked more nostalgia than a large shop at the corner of Berry street; that shop was Montague Burtons, the bespoke tailors, a place of dreams for many a lad who stood at the corners of Osman street and other places in the city of Belfast and it brought back memories of the day Short and myself went for a suit.

As Short and myself walked into Burtons and looked in a man asked us what we wanted and we left in a hurry.

A few weeks later I was standing at the corner when I heard our Al talking to his mate Dip. "Where you going Dip?" asked Al. "I'm going down to try on my new suit. "Are youse coming down with me?" I belted over to shorts house, which was just across the street. After calling him and telling him about Al and Dip we decided to follow them but had to watch and wait and then follow.

"You've tried that suit on that many times it will be worn out by the time you get it!" cries big Neddy Donegan. "It probably won't fit you; you've put on so much weight." Dip laughs, "Look I can try it on as many times as I feel like it. They wont let me have it until I pay what I owe of it." Short and me are standing at the junior end of the corner taking this all in and Short says, "As soon as I leave school I'm getting a suit out of Burton." "So am I you know you only need the deposit then you can pay it off while its being made." Short asks how long does it take to make a suit? About a month according to our Al and he knows. You wanna see the one he got. Two buttons single breasted, hand-stitched lapels, six inch vents, cloth covered buttons; it's class." "Is it Italian dee cut?" asks Short." "I think so, but it looks class. Hey Frankie lets follow the big lads down to Burtons see what its like then we will know the score. We shall be leaving school in about three months, so we need to know what to do."

Wee Dip our Al, Big Ward and Neddy head off down town with us following at a discreet distance. My imagination ran wild about the suit of my dreams, a black mohair, hand stitched lapels, four inch vents, Italian dee cut, full back, no seam down the middle for me and the strides cut neat. Then the **Plaza** came to mind, the largest dance hall in all Ireland. I will walk in and none of the bouncers will stop me. I will be left school and looking the part, but I would have to get a paisley pattern hankie for the top pocket. As we walk down Castle Street we pass Frazer's where I bought my first pair of wranglers for forty-two and sixpence. A fortune but it was great to get them with the wee cowboy comic book in the back pocket, which was nearly as important as the jeans themselves. Then we pass the Hercules pub and as we pass we can smell the Guinness as it flows freely inside as does the humdrum of lots of men making merry ringing in my ears. The big lads turn and head down Chapel Lane past St Mary's chapel then turn right into Berry Street and this is where we have to stall back. Then the big lads walk into Burtons and we wait at the corner for what seemed an eternity until they came out. Now it was our turn to go in to the shop. The big lads head on up Royal Avenue as we make our presence known in Burtons.

"Mister!" I call out to an elderly man with a measuring tape around his neck, resting like a piece of his apparel that doesn't look out of place on his shoulders and hangs graciously. "Can you tell me what it would cost for a suit for my mate mister?"

"About twelve pounds." he replied. "For both of us, mister?" I asked. "Now, now, I'm busy you foolish boy, twelve pounds each." At that the tailor walks away and Short and me are left standing like two stewed prunes in this large oak panelled shop. I walked over to a table and there was, as I now know a pattern book, full of all the different cloths. I meekly plied through it, as I nodded to Short.

"Look that's the one I want. Black Mohair. Look at the shine. It's class." " I want a brown mohair. I want to be different from everybody else, who wants a black mohair." I looked at him with distain. After all I was going to get black mohair. Is he telling me I'll be like every other guy? He's talking bollocks. Who'd wear brown, that's for getting buried in. "Can I help youse lads?" A younger shop assistant says with a politeness we never heard before. "We're just looking. Anything wrong with that?" I said cheekily and then I caught my self on. This guy only works here and he's trying to be nice. Short twists his face up the way only he could do, like no one else could.

"If I wanted measured up for a suit, when is the best time to come in?" "Any day. Even now if you want, you'll need a ten per cent deposit and I'll do the rest."

Short pulls two pound notes out of his pocket and says, "Lets go then." The assistant looks at him a little surprised, but not half as surprised as me. "Where did you get that"? " I won it at the Farah last night," a name we used for the card game really called Faro. "I worked it up from two bob. O'Hara was putting it on for me. We Simmy Clarke would never let me in never mind have a bet, he always said I was two young." I thought you said you were skint, as we passed Victors and I said, I'd love a smokie." " I never said I was skint. I didn't open my mouth. You're always looking something for nothing, if it's not a jam piece, it's a drink of water or something else." " I'm away on. Frig you and your brown suit. I'm away to get the money for a black one by hook or by crook." Short twisted his face again and laughed.

The following week I was in Burtons with my two-pound deposit for my black mohair suit along with my mate Roy Smyth. A tall lanky sort of guy not unlike Long John Baldry approached me. "What can I do for you two likely lads?" My mate Roy was along side me and we both answered in unison, "We're looking to be measured up for a suit," the colloquial term for a bespoke suit. "Ok whose first'? I looked at this big guy with his fantastic cut suit with a paisley handkerchief, no not an Ian Paisley handkerchief but a silk one with numerous pattern colours. It flowed out of his top pocket like a river of colour. He removed his measuring tape from around his neck and flipped it like a cowboys bullwhip. I'll go first I said." Step right up," he muttered as I approached his personal space. I meekly walked forward and stood to attention as he measured my back, shoulders

78

and chest writing the correlations down as he went along. Then came the legs. "What side do you wear it?" he asked. "Oh single breasted mister." "Everybody calls me Ken so what's your name"? "Me! I'm Fra and this is my mate Roy but we all call him Lenny from The Gorbals in Glasgow." "Is he Scottish?" " No, it's his nickname." Big Ken scratches his head. "What side do you wear it Fra?" I looked at him in amazement as he whispered into my ear. I felt my face lighten up like the proverbial Christmas tree and cringed with embarrassment. I looked down, had a look at it, and replied, "The left". After he finished measuring me up, he then started to measure Roy. By this time my embarrassment had left me and I was starting to think of extras for my suit. "Hi Ken can I have one-inch vents on the trousers please, four-inch vents in coat, full back, hand stitched lapels and mother of pearl buttons. Roy blurted out "Same for me big lad!" Ken gave me a long hard look and smiled. "Fourteen inch bottoms?" "Yes," I replied "and the trousers cut neat". "You really have thought this out." "You better believe it!" Roy retorted. After paying or deposits we both went home to await the news that our suits were ready.

About a month later my long awaited letter arrived at our house informing me that my suit was ready for collection upon payment of eighteen pounds and ten shillings. I scratched my loaf and wondered and then I got my answer - Hire Purchase. But how would I get me Da to go downtown to sign the forms. I decided to call around for Lenny and see if we could come up with an idea between us. After some discussion I remembered our Al talk about how him and big Jim Haughey had went down and asked for the hire purchase forms to bring home to their respective parents to be signed and all they done was walk up the town and they both signed each others forms and brought them back to Burtons. After a bit of arguing Roy and myself decided it was our only option, so we headed for Burtons for a try on, the term we used to describe going to Burtons and trying on your suit on. Some people tried their suits on that many times they started to shine and they weren't even mohair. After trying our suits on we decided we must get our hire purchase forms signed by hook or by crook so after leaving the shop with our forms gripped firmly in our hands we set out to get someone to sign them. The first person we met was a friend of my Da's, none other than Silver McKee who wee Lenny admired, as did I. He was the man in Belfast, known all over the world, or so we thought anyway. "Mr McKee, you know my Da Robert McCartney. Well he's not well today and he said if I seen you to ask you to sign my form for me. But you have to write his name on it." Paddy Joe McKee looked at me. "Is your Da's oul chest playing up this weather?" "Yes," I replied "He's in bed all week". Silver takes the form and starts scribbling my Da's name on the form and as he finished Lenny jumped in and asks for the same favour. I suppose your Da Tommy is lying in bed as well young Smyth. No Silver he's at work. Silver does the business on both forms and after a lot of thank youse, coupled with a bit of patronizing we marched off to Burtons to get our suits. As we walked in a male worker steered us towards the office were we duly handed in our forms and awaited a reply. This will take about a week to come back so you will have to call back next Saturday in the mean time just look around and see if there's anything you fancy in our ready made department. I looked at Lenny. "As if we would wear anything out of the ready made department what an insult".

I had now got my suit and I prepared for my debut in the shots. I put on my black mohair suit, snap tab shirt and tie, polished my Chelsea boots and headed for the shots. I was a bout five feet nothing at the time and I walked meekly straight into the Faro room the reserve of hardened gamblers who played all through the night and into the next morning in some cases. I took my place among the elite. No sooner was I in when Simmy Clarke the brother of Big Shot and marker up as he was called, came in and ordered me out. Simmy always reminded me of Mugs Mahoney from the Bowery Boys films, but dressed to perfection, his black hair slicked back, with his light coloured suit and a story telling broad tie and shining shoes. His elder brother was Big Shot who owned the club hence the name The Shots. He told me I was too young to be in the club and I told him I was fifteen but he said I looked about twelve and I could go and sit and watch as the others played rummy at the apprentice table in the snooker room. I was now reminding myself about how well big Ken looked. Six foot tall broad shoulders and here was me five foot nothing and so thin I got a deduction for being under a thirty-two inch chest. My confidence just left me like a plane leaving Aldergrove and I thought what was that all about, the suit and all that nonsense.

As I walked up to the table I met a guy who just by doing one thing formed a friendship that remains to this day. His name was Joe Mc Cullagh and he informed me that you always kept the bottom button opened on a two-button suit and that's the way it is to this very day. He was along with Joe Hennessy another classy dresser and across the table were wee Yacho, Geordie Caddell, O'Hara, and Short. I looked at him and he smiled, " Wanna hand"? "How much is it?" I asked. "Two bob." "I'm in." I replied. This was the starter school where all the small punters were trying to get enough money to move into the main room to play the real game The Farah. I won a couple of hands and I could see Short eyeing me up. "You going to the Plaza tonight?" he asked. I replied, " Come on let's go. It's getting late." We then trotted off to the Plaza but first of all we had to look into the Farah room and there was all the faces.

Diamond Jim, Danny Conway, Big Peezer, Skeeball O'Hare, Fra Ward, Jim Clarke the case keeper, Eamon Heaney, Dan Lindsay, Anthony Bob, Dirty Eyes and Micky The Hard. Here you had a bunch of avid gamblers who just lived for the game. As we were leaving, we bumped into my next-door neighbour, none other than Patsy Nolan who ironically was called neighbour. That being his nickname and he was heading in to try his luck.

About half and hour we were walking around the Plaza posing in our new but very different mohair suits.

It wasn't long before I was going to the Shots for a hand at the rummy and I met Joe McCullough again. This time he redone the knot in my tie, making it a bit smaller and then he asked me would I go a message for him up to his girls house. He was going out with a girl called Margaret Montgomery at the time. She lived in Urney Street. I had to tell her Joe would meet here later out side the Jig in Coates Street. I was to do that for him for a while before he went to England and we didn't meet again for some years but when we did meet again we picked up on our old friendship and have remained friends since. The shots were full of characters, hard men and would be hard men. It was the survival of the fittest and shrewdest that survived. One character that comes to mind was Danny Bowen who had a saying "All the way to Frisco and back again." He had always some sort of an answer to everything, "in a wise man fashion". Danny was shot dead in downtown Belfast by unknown gunmen and remains another of the forgotten dead. The place was full of wise guys and in some cases gambling was the only way of life they knew, or wanted to know in some cases. There were also some so-called great card players, Brendan O'Hara who drew a second card as fast as Wyatt Earp drew his six-gun. Geordie Caddel who waited for a card like the headwaiter, a name given to a good jockey who could hold a horse up. But the longest waiter of them all was Dan Lindsay who may have had only one bet all night. Diamond Jim was another who they used to say lived beside one of the big mills but never heard the horn blast. This actually was a metaphor meaning he never worked in his life. Another character that comes to mind is Danny Conway who had an uncanny resemblance to James Garner the star of the television shows Maverick and later on the Rockford files. As there already was a guy called Maverick Mervyn on our road Danny became known as James Garner, Rockers, Jim Rockford and he loved it.

One day Danny in later years was standing trading from his fruit barrow outside Joe Kavanagh's world famous, **I Buy Anything** shop in Smithfield. Suddenly a soldier jeep flew around the corner on two wheels and screeched to a halt. Danny had moved back from his barrow to talk to someone at the shop window and was then approached by the brits that pulled up beside his barrow and they grabbed Danny. One big officer asked," How long have you been standing here sir", Danny replied, after a moments though and in all innocence, "About thirty years". The brit wasn't impressed and arrested Danny on the spot only to learn later that poor Danny had misinterpreted the question. He thought he meant how long he had been standing and trading in that spot.

Danny was a very witty guy and one day as he and big Joe Connolly and I stood at the corner or the Springfield road a big truck rolled by with the black smoke coming out of its upright exhaust and then the smoke turned grey as the driver changed gear and Danny as quick as lightening said. "They must have elected a new pope" and that for me was wit at its best, sharp, unprepared and clever.

Chapter 16

Boxers and Street Games

There were three very talented boxers in our class at school. Paddy Moore, Terry Bonanza Hanna and last but not least Frankie Short all member's of the Immaculata boxing club. At that time Paddy Moore was regarded as the best schoolboy boxer in the whole of Ireland and in most pundits view that hasn't changed. Boxing was a family thing and his two brothers followed in his footsteps. Sean was good and handy and his wee brother Joe was a good wee boxer as well. All fought for the same Club more commonly known as *The Mac*. Pat as I knew him used to get a day or two of school to go to fight in Dublin and when he was fighting for a local title he may have gotten out of school early. At that time he was the only boy boxer who fought like a professional and I never saw anything like him then, or since. Terry Hanna also came from a family of boxers who included Gerry, Anthony and another brother Pat gave it a go, making four brothers from one family who all boxed for the Mac. Frankie Short was also from a family who produced another great boxer as well, his brother Jimmy. These where times when most working class boys thought or in some cases came to realise, that to become a professional boxer could change their lives financially. If you succeeded as a professional the comforts that money could buy came in most cases but alas not in all. One such person was John Caldwell who won the world bantamweight title in nineteen sixty-one. He had set the bench mark for others to follow and as the photograph below depicts a group of my mates and me standing under a hastily painted gable wall saying, "your our champ" celebrating his achievement. But it's the night that he fought Freddie Gilroy at the Kings hall that brings back memories. This as far as Belfast people were concerned, the fight of the century and everyone wanted to see it. But it was out of the price range of most of the guys who stood at the corner of Osman Street and other corners of Belfast. So a few from around our street made our way over to the Kings hall. I was just following the bigger lads, I was only eleven at the time and really shouldn't have been over that end of town, but in those days it was nothing, it was a different world then. As we arrived a big crowd had gathered and most of them were plotting about how to get in to the tightly secured Kings Hall.

Everyone had a different idea and it lead to some hair brained plots and plans. Everyone was giving their opinion as to how they could get in to the packed to capacity hall. Spit Clarke came up with the idea that we go around the back and enter by the show jumping arena and hope that a back door could be forced open or one maybe have been carelessly left open. As we climbed over the back gates and wandered up the yard we came across a show jumping arena and some of the lads started acting the idiot jumping over the jumps and pretending to be horses. Dickey Mc Nerney was the oldest of us. His young brother Joe aka Jonah was with us as was Tony Vam Clarke and others who were all acting the idiot in the show jumping arena. Dickey told us to be quiet as he wanted to get in to the fight and the noise may attract the cops. We then started pulling at the back doors and they came loose a bit, but not far enough for even me to get in and I was very small. So they decided to climb in from the top of the doors and slip down, in theory it sounded great. Spit gave Dickey a scout's lift and he climbed up and squeezed in, he then dropped down and he was in. Next up was Spit and he got scouts lift from his younger brother Tony and Jonah and when he got up and was dropping down between the two big doors he got stuck. Try as we all might to burst the doors to free him it was to no avail and we all ran off as the bouncers opened the doors to release a now frantic Spit. All we could hear was Spit arguing with the bouncers as we headed of in different directions across the show jumping arena, hiding in the stables until the coast was clear.

As we made our way back around to the front of the hall the crowd was now treble the size as it was previously and we all waited in anticipation on the result. It was customary on fight bills that everyone was allowed in free of charge when the main event was over so everyone was waiting patiently. Just then a wee man ran out the front doors shouting, "its over, its over!" I think his name was White and there was a charge for the front doors and try as they might the bouncers could not control the invasion of fans. When I got in the referee was looking at Caldwell's eye but allowed the fight to continue on for another round. He then had one more look and the fight was over. Freddie Gilroy had won what was to be the most talked about local fight in boxing history.

There were lots of other good boxing families in Belfast. The Wilsons, Barney senior and his son Barney were both champions, the latter being the Irish heavyweight champion. He fought in Australia in the commonwealth games and his younger brother David also boxed then there was the Quinn brothers and Toby Shannon who beat John Caldwell as an amateur all resided in Lincoln Street. One wee street that had its fair share of boxers was Lincoln Street. Frankie Quinn also won a few titles, as did the fore mentioned Toby Shannon. Andrew Mc Cormac also won a few titles, and he lived in our street, Servia Street' and his dad Ned was the chief trainer in the Mac after Jack McCusker retired. But the king of them all was probably Jim McCourt from Leeson Street. I say probably, the greatest amateur boxer ever to grace the ring for Ireland and a gentleman into the bargain. I don't think Jim ever had a fight in the street in his life as he kept all his energies for the ring. Then there was Terry Milligan whom some may say was better than McCourt, but it's a science boxing, but not an exact one and I will leave it there. A couple of other families who had more than one champ in the family and fought for the Mac where the Brady's from the Whiterock a family of all round sportsmen in both boxing and soccer. There was also the Shaw's and another family called Hanna who were great exponents of the skill of boxing who came from the Loney and the man who won a Silver medal in the Olympics, John McNally winning Irelands first Olympic medal in boxing history. There was also Peter Laverty, Peter Sharpe and his brother, Jimmy Carson, Rinty Monaghan, Spike McCormack and lots of others. I wont mention the modern champions as they are numerous but that's for round two.

One story I have to tell is about Dave Boy McAuley whom I watched winning his world title in London. One day I was talking to his brother about Dave and saying how he would have been rated higher if he had been from Belfast, it's a Belfast thing; he just turned and said to me, "Would his mother do." I looked at him in disbelief; yes Dave Boy's mother was from Belfast. I also have to give a mention to Wayne McCullough from Highfield who won the world title by defeating Yasuei Yakushiji in Japan, a first for anyone from these islands. He also had an incredible amateur record to boot. I also have to mention the Young family who originated from McDonnell Street where the Hanna's came from and they had numerous boxers in their family, Young Gabriel and Gerry to name a couple but in all I think about six of them done a bit of boxing.

Another story comes to mind at this time and it was about the fellow who brought Pat Moore to The Mac. He was Danny McMahon and he wasn't a bad boxer himself. He used to take us all to Shaw's Bridge were we played in a big wrecked mansion were dreams where lived out in that imaginary world of children. Innocence at its best and at the time Danny was the leader of that particular gang. He had a Superman suit that he used to wear as we assumed new identities of the stars of television and the large screen picture houses. It was all great fun and more importantly, full of happiness unlike today. Mobile phones, tablets, no, it was outdoor entertainment, that doesn't argue well with the life style with the children of today. The kids of today don't know what they are missing. We lived our dreams out in real time and made them our reality. What great times we had and it was outdoors in all seasons and it was healthy.

In the summer nights people flocked to play housey and arrived early some with a cushion for their arse as they wanted get a good seat on the cribby for Francey and Paddy Straney's game. The picture portrays the scene as the people waited as he handed out cards then you waited patiently for the first house to begin. As Servia Street was a busy wee street there was always a lot of pranksters, myself included waiting to take the hand out of some of the players. People were running about shouting house or check and everyone stopped as they thought someone had won the house and people wiped their cards clean. That meant there had to be a recall of all the numbers previously called.

It was a great and a very inexpensive way to pass a good long day and summers night that doesn't exist today. These where the days when I couldn't get up quick enough and out of bed when there was no school and the summer holidays seemed to last for ever. As the housey continued people used to throw their cards about when the games were over and this caused the cards to break. They were made from thin hardboard and in some cases cardboard so they didn't take much abuse. Paddy Straney then came up with a great idea. I think at the time he was working in the shipyard, well he was getting paid anyway. He decided that it would be a good idea to have them made out of light steel. So from then on the cards were a bit heavier but were near indestructible and they didn't have to be renewed. This was a good a time when people lived literally out of each other's good or bad fortune and when someone won at housey now referred to as bingo they usually shared their winning with a neighbour or someone they were in the whack with. That was known as a joint enterprise. All pulled together and it was a joyful time matched only by the street parties and bonfires that were held on the fifteenth of August.

Street parties were organised by people from the surrounding streets and it was all very informal. Some lent chairs and some even loaned their dinning tables and it was a great show. There was an abundance of lemonade, buns, apple cakes and all the things that you only got on special days. There was always plenty to go around and in most cases they where orderly and no favouritism showed. All the young people where treated the same. After the parties it was bonfire time and I remember one time we had one in the middle of Osman Street and Sultan Street, which believe it or not had a thousand tyres on it.

After it was lit the flame's shot into the bright skies then the whole place seems to turn dark as if a dark cloud had descended just above our heads. We ran around acting the idiot as the fire burned brightly but the acrid smoke of the tyres filled the summer fresh air with black smoke that near killed half the district, my Da included. As the bonfire raged windows in Garlands house, the first door in Sultan Street were the first to crack followed by the windows in Eedie Fox's shop followed by John Murphy's, then the wine shop better known as the off license. Then the blame game started, but all to no avail as any single person was to blame.

The next day the place was like a war zone that had been bombed into submission. Black soot lay a foot deep and no matter how much people tried it was carried into every house in the district at some time or another and all we heard "that's the last of the bonfires". But the bonfire was all about status and I remember all of the lads, young and old out gathering tyres as far away as Dunmurry and then wheeling them home. It was hard work but also very funny at times. Life was full of laughter and friendship and not a care in the world, the greatest times of our lives. One day we went behind a wee garage that was situated at the Belfast limit pole on the Andersonstown Road and there was the biggest tyre we had ever seen. After a lot of second-guessing and conjecture it was assumed it was a bomber tyre from an old airplane that survived from the war. Then it changed to some other unbelievable use, as it was over six feet tall, but in reality it was from a very big bulldozer now common but not in those days. We now all felt no matter what, we now had everything. We had reached the thousand tyres mark and we also had the biggest tyre anyone had ever seen and we were going to burn it. That was Osman Street. We had to be the best at everything that really counted for bragging rights. Was it all worth it, of course I wouldn't change it for anyone else's world. We had our own world and we all lived it and loved it.

Chapter 17

Alphie Joe Hughes

Joe Hughes yard was different place from all the fore mentioned yards and gateways. It was a place of adventure but not for all; you had to be a horsey man. It would play a very important part in my life, while some of the other places mentioned played minor parts. These yards and clubs, were called by my parents and others, "places of a misspent youth" or words to that effect. I didn't think so; these places were the university of my life, the beginning of a great learning curve, which has continued right up until today. Joe's yard, was in Servia Street facing the Far Hill or The Water-Tank, funny how a piece of waste ground that never produced one blade of grass could be so important to have two names. Joe's contained twenty or so stables filled with our Arkle or Mill House or other famous race horses of the day. In reality they where carthorses, but they provided us with the same fun as any country lad may have had, but smack dead in the centre of the Falls. Tom Sawyer, Huck Finn and Mickey Rooney were my heroes and they would have been quite at home here with out the gardens, sunshine, or the picket fences of America. There were Chicken's, the odd duck, maybe a goat and horses where housed in the yard so all in all you had a country scene reminiscent of any farmyard, but set in the city.

There where two other yards like Joes; in the district, Milan Street and Joe Browns in Leeson Street but they where dedicated yards where people owned there own yoke and didn't hire them out on a daily basis. Joe's yard had a hayloft and a large manure pit with smoke rising from it reminiscent of an American Indian camp, with piebald horses walking about halter less in the campsite. The only thing missing from the scene were the Indians, as there were plenty of cowboys, my self-included, who where always up to something. There was nothing of a sinister nature, but some sort of moneymaking enterprise that may have got us a few quid. We called the manure dump, the dump-pit, and the place where the horse manure was piled until it rotted and sometimes went on fire with the intense heat it generated. The manure was then taken and spread on fields to help some sort of vegetation grow, like potatoes, barley or some other things farmers grew but mostly mushrooms, a thing I don't think I had ever tasted as they were foreign to me.

The yard was littered with carts, some with big wheels, small ones painted red and yellow, the paint often peeling of with time, bits of carts, shafts and wheels all in some state of repair or disrepair. Four wheelers, two wheelers, traps and the pride of place the hobby horses in need of some paint or fixing, as was the norm. The walls in the enclosed yard where of a grey cement finish resembling a prison building of Victorian times rather than stabling yard where paint seemed as scarce as money. It had its own ambience, especially in long summers days that lead into long summer nights as the sweet smell of freshly cut grass, which was piled at the top of the yard whiffed its way through the air. It was grown in one of the two gravy yards (sic) where most of our grand parents where buried, but it still smelt great and as I pondered my next move I usually had a blade of it sticking in my mouth just like my hero Huckleberry Finn.

The grass from the graveyards was cut by men using scythes in Milltown and the City cemeteries and was bought for five shillings a load. Then it was piled onto a flat van or four-wheeler cart with the expertise of an artist, every grape full of grass strategically placed so as to maximise the load. On some occasions after we got the cart loaded we sneaked out the back gate in the City cemetery and didn't pay for the grass so that was even better as we copped the five shillings that Joe gave you to pay for the load. If the grass had been cut by a lawn mower it wouldn't have been any good for the horses as they cant eat short cut grass as it choked them, or gave them colic. So the cemeteries provided work for the cutters and the summer diet for Joe's horses, another very cheap ways to beat the economic crisis that beset the horses along with its inhabitants that lived here.

One day I was wearing my first pair of brown boots the norm for a horsy man, "I had swapped them for a pair of black shoes to a fellow called Clem Fitzsimons who lived in Ardglass." As I jumped into the dump pit I stuck my chewing gum in under the heel. I saw some cowboy doing it in a film with his chewing tobacco. They say films are not impressionable? But more about films later. We all took turns to load the manure onto a big red and blue country box cart drawn by a large mule that would be heading for Hannahstown. When we where finished I took the chewing gum from under my heel and stuck it in my mouth and chewed away at it just like the cowboy with his chewing tobacco. The mule that was pulling the cart was going to have his work cut out today, as it was one of those warm humid summers day. The manure was been drawn to Hannahstown to a farm Joe had about ten miles away where nothing seemed to grow or if it did it grew very badly. It was an uphill journey, always on the collar with no respite, no time for a breather; a tough task laid a head for him but Paddy the mule was up for it. He was as hard as nails and showed his class as Joe mounted the cart in Cyprus Street and Paddy trotted off and headed to the farm a long tough journey. Joes yard made Servia Street and gave it that bit of importance that other streets couldn't match, after all twenty families or so got their living out of the yard as their fathers or sons hired a horse, or donkey and cart to go and earn their living. It was also a great place of entertainment and learning that lives with me to this day watching the smart and not so smart try to harness and yoke a horse and cart. Then they even tried to drive it and it looked easy, but it depended on the horse. Most of them knew Belfast better than the drivers.

One day Joe asked me to be in the yard early the next morning as he had sold a big black horse and cart that once belonged to an old milkman called Nesbit. It was one of the yokes that were kept in Joe Browne's yard in Leeson Street. As the owner was retiring Joe bought the entire yoke and sold it and took a quick profit as the horse may have been twenty years of age there was no time to wait. Browne's had two very successful butchers shops on the Grosvenor road. The great thing about Joe Browne's house was that although it was on the Grosvenor Road you could also enter the house by the back door on Leeson Street so he only walked out his back door and across the street to his yard. Anyway Joe told me a man would be coming next day. He told me to be there early so I could yoke the big horse up for the man who bought the turnout. I was about twelve at the time and I hated the early cold morning but I was up out of bed at seven O'clock and running up the street to the yard, as I wanted to keep in favour with Joe. As I got to the gate Crawford Hutchison had already opened it, the key holder who lived two doors down from the yard. As I ran up the yard the man was already there about five minutes before me. As I walked into the stable he was trying to put the blinkers on the horse's tail having mistaken it for the crupper. I took the bridle of him and put it on the horse while standing on a big box, as I couldn't reach the top of the horse's head. Joe had given the man a quick run through the night before and I suppose anyone could have made the mistake between bridle and crupper. I still remember that wee mans face as this wee buck about four foot nothing started showing him how to harness and yoke his horse and cart that he had bought for a fruit and vegetable run after winning a small prize on the Littlewoods pools. I often wonder did that wee man ever become rich and famous in business, I do remember he was keen for work unlike me. My Ma told me work was for horses and I believed her.

People came from far afield to Joe's. The Shankill, Sandy Row, the Bone, Ardoyne and even further to hire a horse or donkey and cart to go and gather rags, scrap, skins, refuse, waste paper, sell fruit and vegetables, or ply other wares on the streets of Belfast. Picture a grown man in the fifties in down town Belfast with a wee grey donkey and cart going about his daily routine with big red trolley buses that sometimes short circuited and threw big sparks into the road scaring the living daylights out of everyone. Some horses didn't like it and lots of them shied as trams and cars went whizzing by with the odd roar of a motorcycle rushing by added in. This caused some horses to bolt but after time most horses got used to it.

Some horse and cart drivers or carters as they where called may have looked out of place, but he was far better off than then the less fortunate who had to push a handcart or in some cases an old child's pram, or drive a donkey and cart, which proved less hard work for the hawker. Ten shillings got you the loan of a horse and cart for a day and some young lad would go out and help you for maybe a shilling a day, or in most cases nothing as they where glad to get a days outing on the horse and cart and beak school and learn more at being a young hawker. The same lad may have then sold the Belfast Telegraph or the Telly's as they where known at night to earn the money to go to the Diamond or Clonard picture house or the Arcadian.

A couple of names that come to mind that hired a yoke from Joe, Jackie Malone, Geordie Scott, Paddy Darling, Digger Daly, Geordie Healy who owned his own yoke, Sammy Jones, Bobby McManus, Walter Saymes, the Croft family who sold saw dust, Ernie Scott and Mo McGivern, Crutchy Armstrong, Davy Hamill, Jackie Gray, Fra Adams, Sam Walsh, Paddy Ward, Larry Sloan and his son Harry, who actually was in the same class as me at school. They all hired a horse and cart from Joe. One man comes to mind to me that invariably arrived on a bicycle in the mornings. I think his name was Docherty and he was the most decent hawker I ever met. I got three bob for joking him up and joking out when he finished his day's work. I think he was from north Belfast. That was a small fortune at the time to most others and me as well. Paddy "Gog" Ward also hired a joke on and off and he gathered waste paper, skins, rags, scrap and anything he could turn a shilling at. I worked with him and most of those people mentioned at one time or another. Paddy Gog Ward lived in the village area of Belfast, Benburb Street I think which was a bit unusual. He tried everything possible to earn a days pay when there was no brew or dole, a good old grafter he was known as.

One man who I fondly remember who really deserved anything he earned was Sandy McCabe who succumbed to alcohol. He was an old friend of my Das and he pushed a handcart five days a week, hail rain snow or blow. I never met anyone who worked harder in all weathers and how he got the energy to push the cart I'll never know. But he did and he deserved a medal, but I hope this memory of him is sufficed for a man who tried so hard to earn an honest living.

Handcarts could be hired from a family from Urney Street called Yates who after all their hard works have done very well in business today. The cost of hiring a handcart was the princely sum of two bob a day.

I also worked at the hobbyhorses as they were called when I was a kid. Geordie Scott plied the hobbyhorses long before Mick Marley became synonymous with them. He also collected light iron for the princely sum of ten shillings a ton in the winter. He was a great worker and as strong as an ox. Scott as he was called always turned the arm or handle that made the hobbyhorses go around alone. He had a good attitude for the job and didn't let any of the wee lads that helped him turn the handle. He did it all. The only thing wrong with working the hobbyhorses was it was only profitable in summer but useless in winter as nobody would get on them, with the rain belting down. So in a way it was a seasonal job. The hoppy horses held twelve kids, four in each in a car and one on each horse well that's the way it was supposed to be but sometimes I saw two kids to a horse and six to a car. At a penny per person, that amounted to a shilling a spin if all the seats where taken, multiply by twenty you had a pound. It was hard work so it took some time and energy to earn a fiver. The hobbies where very naïve, made from carved wood, the horse's heads didn't really look like right but they done the job. They had legs that resembled boomerangs and the cars with their wee steering wheel didn't really look like a car. But they lasted over seventy years and the man who made them Dan Kane gave thousands of children their dreams and memories that they would take to their graves. I'm sure if he had more time or machinery he could have made a lot of other things and maybe invented some others on his way. As for me the hobbies were an ingenious wee invention. A crown wheel and pinion, or cogwheel, were the only real working mechanism? Yes a couple of moving parts and they worked perfectly. After a long and tiresome day we'd get back to Joe's yard after we had lifted kid after kid on and off the hobbies. We would yoke the horse out and un-harness it, then give it a long drink of water. I would then feed it and then we counted the money. All those loose pennies looked like a million pounds when placed on a cart for the count. In reality they where piled up in dozens to make a shilling and looked more like little copper towers some glistening in the sun light and in some cases as black as coal. Another problem arose and it called for runners who Scott could trust to go and get the large amount of pennies changed into half crowns or two bob bits as no one had a bank account or even the cheek to walk into the bank to ask for them to be changed. It was not even in our thoughts. When Scott was finished counting his hard earned money he would send me to the shop to buy twelve stummy cakes. A round cake about two inches in circumference and about a quarter of an inch thick sometimes coated with icing sugar along with two bottles of orange juice and a bar of Cadburys milk tray out of Sarah Mosses grocers shop at the corner of Cyprus and Servia Street where my Ma worked. This was a ritual just the same as Joe bought one big bottle of lemon flavoured cream soda between about ten of us as we loaded manure out of the dump pit. You where lucky if you got a slug and even luckier if Joe let you keep the three dee deposit on the empty bottle. These were all rituals followed to the letter on most occasions. The Stummy cake and orange juice was a wee cause for celebration as a stummy cake and a bottle of orange juice made you feel like you wee attending the school party in July or Christmas time when every class had a party. We brought in a Paris bun and a bottle of orange juice or maybe a snowball, if you were lucky. A great day in the annals of school history as it meant the holidays where about to begin and when the hobbyhorse season ended you knew it was back to school.

I remember one day Seamus Kennedy who was in our class was telling the master that his granda owned Kennedy's milk dairy to give it its proper name. We called it the milk factory and the master causally asked him could he arrange for us to visit the dairy located on Tate's avenue. Everyone in the class thought Seamus was spoofing as he lived on Cullingtree Road, not somewhere that the grandson of a big business man would live, or so we all thought. A few days later Seamus told the teacher, Mister Kerr that his granda had agreed and all that was left to do was to make a date suitable to both parties, pun intended. So a few days later we were on our way to the dairy and when we got there, a big surprise awaited us. As we all sat in awe in the gallery and watched the milk being bottled, without one bottle being broken it was like magic. They moved around like soldiers on parade on a conveyer belt being filled with milk and an aluminium cap being put on top. I then spied out of the corner of my eye what looked like the makings of a party being set up. There were snowball buns galore, custards, biscuits and everything else for a hungry class of kids. "Was it for us? I asked myself. Five minutes later we were all sitting around tables laden with orange juice galore along with the entire fore mentioned tit bits. Its one of those days you can never forget and I for one never will.

We talked about that party for years and its one of my best memories of school. After that Seamus was the bees knees for a while and we learned that because someone lived somewhere it didn't mean a thing. Upon reflection it was a great day and at the time we only appreciated the party when you think of it. Then you ask yourself, how many other local businessmen, or women, could have provided such a day and didn't do it.

One day later in years I decided I was going to play catch up. I had a bit of a property find and my commission was to be fifteen hundred quid and I thought what am I going to do when I get it. It was a lot of money to earn for just finding a bit of property and negotiating its sale. I always drove up and down the Ormeau Road by this time on my way home and something came into my mind. I asked myself. Are there young people in any place that maybe never had a party like the one at Kennedy's Dairy? I passed it every day the place I had been thinking of. One day around Halloween, which seems to play a big part in my life, either consciously or sub consciously, I decided to call and was introduced to a wee nun.

After a bit of discussion I asked her was there going to be a party for the kids for Halloween. She replied there would be but nothing special. I handed her an envelope and told here that maybe it would help. It was one-third the money I had made on the deal. I have found out to this day, but I haven't always done it, you have to share it to keep it. That's thirty years ago and funnily enough as I think, maybe, just maybe, that's what Fishing Poles a short film I made recently was based on subconsciously. But then that's another story for another day.

Coming from a gambling background and how it started may have been my Da sending me to do a one-shilling doubles and a two bob treble in Brigit Mulligans bookies in Osman Street. Or was it the card schools that started that addiction. Being a gambler everyone had a scud or a bringer of bad luck and as I now know, theres no such thing. One such person was a wee man who was born with a clubfoot and he had the unlikely name of Crumpet and if it wasn't bad enough being born with a deformity he was then classed as the biggest scud in the district. Many threw their dockets away as he entered the bookies but they always watched where they threw them, just in case he wasn't a scud. Well now as I look back there is no such thing as a scud but an excuse for a bad looser and in more cases than one the people found someone else to be the scud after the unfortunate Crumpet died.

It wasn't along before another came along, then another and another. In some cases people wouldn't have a bet if they saw their favourite scud but it was all down to how your cards were dealt. One guy who I shall call Bouncer used to call upon me to go the odd message with him. I'd sit in his car as he went and done what he done but he never bunged me, I suppose I just went along for the ride in the big car. One day he called me and asked me to go with him to the social security office in downtown Belfast and as he drove me down in his big flashy car I wondered why he was going to the social, a place reserved for the less fortunate. As we walked in he demanded to see as he called him the senior manager and within an hour we were walking out of there and he had twenty-five pounds.

From there he headed straight into the car and up to Kelly and Mc Cartan's bookmakers' office on Leeson Street. He had a few bets then the strange thing happened. As I was asking him what he had bet he said that he bet a horse called Dove Monster and would I mind going out of the bookies as he didn't want to share the commentary of the race with me. Did he think I was his scud? As I looked at him and walked out to stand in the sun and try as I might I wasn't able to hear the commentary of the race. Suddenly he walked out and bid me farewell. Not even a cigarette did I get out of the twenty-five pounds so I said to myself never again?

Another day as I was observing him and I was skint as usual, I watched as he took his docket out of his pocket and covered one eye as he looked at the results. This made it difficult to see the results thus prolonging the whole operation and making it agonizing for him. But that's because he thought everyone was a scud when in actual fact he hadn't learnt the simple facts of life, punters by nature are losers, myself included.

Another punter who we will call the Singer used to narrow a race down to three or four horses. He then went through a process of writing each fancied horse on a little pieces of paper and rolling them up in a wee balls and putting them in his pocket. All the bits of paper carried the same betting instructions on them, but with different horses written on them. He then went up to the clerk and put his hand in his pocket and handed in one of the pieces of paper turned his back and the clerk wrote his docket he grabbed it and put it in his pocket thus not knowing which horse he was on. Then when the result came in, he always bet win and place, if one of the three or four he fancied where on the board the sweat began. One bit of paper was opened and if it was a loser then the sweat got greater and so on right up till the last piece of paper was opened. He was his own scud you could say. Even at some card schools some people wouldn't take a hand if a certain person were playing. So if you got the name of a scud you had a bit of a hard time getting people to play in the same card school as you, or even punting in the same bookies. Brigit Mulligans was full of scuds and the beauty of it all was that it was full of mug punters, again myself included.

Chapter 18

The green horse

Some of the funnier or not so funny things that happened in the yard were getting dunked in the water trough, the dyeing of a piebald horse and the tarring of the chickens. On summers days some of the older lads ganged up on us younger ones and grabbed us kicking and cursing and then ducked our heads under the water till you felt you were going to drown and your clothes were soaked as you kicked and screamed but eventually you settled down to let your clothes dry in the warm sun. It caused a few fights but was all done in good fun, but some took issue with it and brought their Ma or Da up to the yard to complain. Mostly it was their Ma's as the Da's knew it was all fun. All complaints would fall on deaf ears and everyone got on with the messing when Joe wasn't about.

The dyeing of the horse was funny but not for Joe who also earned some money shipping horses to England and Scotland and the piebald horse was ready for the boat and was looking very prim and proper. In some cases the horse age was hidden by some ingenious if not cruel preparations. On one occasion Joe had worked most of the day washing the lovely piebald horse doing his mane and tail and washing him all over and then I walked him in the sunlight until he dried and he looked like a different horse. Joe then changed the straw bedding in his stable and went on home to get his supper and returned like clockwork to water all the horses at ten o'clock at night. You could have set your watch as Joe meandered down the street and up to the yard opened the wicket gate, got a bucket of water and in some cases let the horses walk to the water trough to quench their thirst. Imagine his face when he saw his prized piebald ready for the Scottish market. Instead of a nice black and bright white horse it was now green and black. Some of the lads had climbed over the back yard wall and done the deed with a clothes dye they found or stole out of the house. A great joke at the time but Joe was enraged and swore he would find whoever done it and as usual I came under suspicion. But the culprit although known to everyone was never caught but was later barred for life from Joe's yard. The tarring of the chicken was blamed on Jonah but to this day he denies that he done it but that's the way things went. Someone again had got over the back walls and got a tin of tar and painted the chickens so from that day onwards Joe called Jonah Tar the chickens, whether he was guilty or not. It has been open to speculation to this day.

Some of the tricks used to make a horse look younger were ingenious. Blowing their eyes up, dyeing the grey hairs, pulling their mane and tails and then platting them to make them look like an entry in a beauty pageant. Stumpy Joe Hamill from Portadown was called upon when they had a few horses going to the boat to travel across the water. He was the master of disguising a horses age and most vets who inspected the horses before they went on the boat couldn't tell a horses age by viewing his teeth. So if it looked good it got on the boat for the twelve-hour journey to Glasgow it was allowed to travel. Bags under human's eyes are usually a good way of telling someone's age, but a horse has them above his eyes. They were more like hollows rather than bags so Stumpy's job was to blow these hollows up and give the poor horse a face-lift. There was no pain but plenty of gain and the horses didn't really feel a thing as stumpy stood on a large box, stuck a pin in the hollow followed by a neatly cut piece of hay which he then blew into filling the hollow with air and so making the old horse look years younger. This was followed by a colour made up from potash and applied with a homemade brush made of what else, only horsehair. He would dab the potash on the grey hairs on the horse forehead and if he had any marks on his legs he applied it to there also. A transformation had taken place and fooled all of the vets who worked at the Glasgow boat. The vet would ask you to trot the horse up and if the horse wasn't lame you walked him down a steep gangway depending on the tide of the day. In some cases it was so low you just let the horse walk on himself as he could have jumped on top of you, or straight into the hold of the boat. I often wonder if some of the dealers who in some cases bought horses sight unseen thought when after a week or so the horse's facelift collapsed. I'm sure they looked all right as the left the boat in the early hours of the next day and were loaded onto horseboxes on the Broomelaw. It was a bit like mutton dressed as lamb or horse beautified for commerce and great ingenuity used to fool all and sundry.

Imagine a cold Friday and Jacko Hughes and myself out selling Ardglass herring on a horse and cart. Jacko was shouting at the top of his voice, "Herring alive!" As the stock was sold there may have been a dozen or so left and that was my wages. To get rid of the last dozen for my wages I had to rap all the doors and I remember vividly trying to sell the last few in Drew Street. Wish I had met Mickey Mullan that day. I sold them for less than half price rather than bring them home to my Ma, as I wouldn't have got paid for them, after all I would have been eating them like everyone else in the house. My ma who would have said "Aren't you going to be eating them?" A box of herring cost about four pounds and you could triple your money on a Good Friday pun intended as most people ate fish on Fridays but more so on Good Friday. In all honesty there is nothing like a potted herring or a well fried one and a round of plain bread with plenty of butter on it.

Davy Hamill or Lord Davy Hamill as he later became known, Crutchy Armstrong, Ernie Scott and Mo Mc Givern all of the opposite persuasion hired horses and carts from Joe Hughes, but in a few years that would all change. The site of big Davy Hamill walking down Servia Street as if he owned it still plays in my minds eye today. A larger than life character, "well he did give himself the title Lord Hamill", and he bought a title as well, but a nice big guy. I may be prejudiced but I think that's what made Servia Street more important than other streets. It was a Mecca for people and was like a trading centre with horses and donkeys being sold openly in the street. The Market area had all this in abundance but it's a different district, they had their Silver Mc Kee, the Murdoch's and Barney Ross, the markets equivalent of Joe Hughes but there's only one Falls road and this is it. Joe sold a lot of horses on the street and it wasn't unusual to see one of his head lads giving a horse a show out and running it up and down the street to the sound of the crack of a Steele liner whip, or throwing his leg over the horse and galloping up and down the street. Joe would take me or some other kids and pass us through the horse's hind legs to show how quiet it was or get us to walk under its belly, all old tricks of the trade. That was Joe's yard where everyone met and dreamt of owning their own horse and cart when they grew up. Not a big aspiration but then it seemed beyond our wildest dreams but some did make it a reality in modern times. The car is the young persons dream now but as they saying go, "horses for courses", and it was a horse I always wanted and got one in later years along with the car.

Servia Street was one of the main streets with a lot of corners, for what else, corner boys who were not bad lads. But the name corner boy may have implied being a bad lad years ago. Osman Street ran of it, as did Slate St where I went to school with the late Joe mc Donnell, one of the ten hunger strikers who gave their lives for Irish freedom. Joe was born in number thirteen if my memory serves me well, two or three doors from the school. Cyprus Street, which became synonymous with the **Sticks** or to give them their proper title the Official IRA, had their shebeen in Joes Yard in later years. Marchioness Street, the home of Gerard Digus Mc Cusker probably the first victim of the Shankill butchers. We will mention Digus later in this book. My mind now wanders to just how tragic our wee district was. Bosnia, Balaclava, Albert, Romania, Raglan, Varna, Sultan, Plevna, Balkan, Mc Donnell, Ross and so on have all their own tragic story to tell. Every street had its own story and character but to me the main streets where Servia and Osman. Why one may ask? Well Servia Street ran the length of the district from Albert to Cyprus then Osman ran through Varna, Sultan, Plevna, Balkan and into Raglan as well as Slate St. So it had lots of corners for corner boys and in reality that's how these two streets became the heart of the Falls as I know it, remember, or perceive it. It also depended on who lived there and their social standing. In those days that meant, you could fight, drink, or in later years one or more of the family being connected. I have actually a good friend who shall remain anonymous who was born in the Markets district. As I don't want his crowd getting on to him or disowning him, but he told me and Hughie Clarke from Servia Street that he said he would have loved to have been born in the Falls. He feels he may have missed something in life by that misfortune and yes he did.

Chapter 19

Starting school

My first day at school I remember a neighbours daughter, Mary Gilroy bringing me by the hand to my first day at school. I was wearing short home made trousers and jacket and a pullover on a cold January day, "I was always cold rife," so I remember leaving a warm house to go out into the cold early morning world and what seemed the long walk to Slate Street school or St Josephs as it was also known. I was brought to the headmaster's office and he then directed me to a large classroom where I was shown to my seat and that was it. I was on my own in this big world and this was the start of a long and eventful life.

The people I made friends with in those early years would shape my life forever. Paddy Moore, Terry Hanna, Buster Crossin, Frankie Short, Liam Boyle, and Liam Robinson and others who I shall mention later in more detail. It was a long day but as my zest for information or knowledge or whatever one calls it 'trivia today' kept me happy for a wee bit of the time. I got into the swing of school very quick and longed for when I would be fourteen to leave but they put the leaving age up to fifteen years of age before I could leave.

After a while I learned to lay in bed until the last minute and listen for the sticks to crackle - this meant the fire would be blazing- before I got out of bed to go to the shop for the breakfast, which was baps and Paris buns or coconut fingers or a scone for one of my sisters. Most days you got a Paris bun and a bit of bap, a cup of hot tea and that was it. It was great with no airs or graces and we never starved a winter yet. My Da always had a blazing fire going as the sticks burned brightly and the coals tried their best to ignite. When they did and glowed there was heat, real heat that I warmed my arse at most mornings if I could get in front of the fire. Mary Gilroy the girl who took me to my first day at school was the daughter of good neighbours of our family Mary Anne and Eddy who sold the Belfast telegraph and the Irish News for a living. Hail rain snow or blow they duly delivered it on time. You could see Mrs's Gilroy's weather-beaten face with all the seasons of the year written on it. Winter, summer and spring all etched on her face like an a la carte menu with a bit of each season, a great woman. Next to them was the Jordan's. Their son Anthony was killed in tragic circumstances on the night of the first Provisional Irish Republican Army (PIRA) ceasefire a quiet family and great neighbours. Next to him lived the Darlings who at times sold candy apples and candy. Aggie Darling and Paddy who drove a horse and cart and was a hawker. They also had a son called Paddy who also drove a horse and cart and the best Donkey and cart yoke in Belfast. Dominic was another son who my ma called "Sudden." No sooner had he started a job than he jacked it in. So Sudden start sudden stop was an apt name for him. Their daughter Peggy was married to a great boxer from Pound Street in the Loney called Spike McCormack that some people reckon given half a chance he would have been world champion. Then there was Lizy Straney's shop where you could buy penny drinks out of a little shot glass that everyone used and it was maybe washed at the end of the day, sure who worried then. Lizy sold lucky bags, dulce, broken rock, caramels, halfpenny chicks and fags the daily diet on the little back streets of Belfast. Woodbine, Park Drive, or if you had a few bob Blues, Greens, or John Players while some others bought Senior Service a sign that you were better off than your counterpart.

These were all status symbols that mattered to us as we perhaps envied some better of neighbours. How you dressed, what you smoked, where you drank, and whom you drank with. My first recollection of school was a cousin of Paddy Moore's. Francis Braniff let off a banger in class and it caused uproar. The head master Hugh Murtagh came down and gave him a slap on the face. I never remember a reddened face like it in my life. And I suppose it set the tone, don't mess around, this is Slate Street school St Josephs. Francis was one of the lads from Ballymurphy who attended our school and it was in those days a long journey just to get to school. In the winter mornings some of them had to walk in rain and sometimes snow, as it was not always economical to take the bus. But they didn't have a school close by and most of their parents went to Slate Street so they probably thought it was a good investment in their children's life. I went through school on an adventure and hated school until my later days and upon reflection and hindsight it was great. Nearly every day after school, Frankie Short, Buster Crossin and me went on a mission to the rich hunting grounds of the Malone road or Cherry Valley. I have to mention some teachers that I remember, first there was Geordie Burns a great teacher who loved both the Irish and American civil wars and had a great laid back attitude to teaching. He didn't drive it down your throat but he let you absorb it at your own pace. He also worked in a big bookmakers shop on the Ormeau Road and in fairness it was a pleasure to have been taught by him in my last couple of years at Slate Street School. Then their was the famous Jimmy Magee from Hannahstown who was your typical teach who wanted everything done right. I was sort of persuaded to enter for the eleven plus and I no more wanted to pass it than the man in the moon. It would have meant that I would have to leave all my mates for some grammar school but in all honesty I had other things on my mind. There was a steward's inquiry when I failed or got the borderline but I wasn't for sitting it again. My Da was aghast and I got some talking to as I previously stated my Da was education first everything else second. I'm the only one of seven entrants in our house to fail the dreaded eleven plus, which has gladly been done away with.

Big Magee as we called him used to go and stand outside the jig in Coates Street at night and turn some of his pupils away because he like many others thought it was a den of iniquity. The jig was just another dance were lots of people met their spouses and remained happily married there after. One day he brought a dead badger in for all and sundry to look at as we drank our milk in the assembly hall. As if we wanted to know about badgers. Another good teacher was Tom Sniffy Gordon who was a very relaxed man who you got taught by before you went into Geordie Burns class. He was a more serious man and he was a good teacher. Tom O'Hara was another teacher who was hard to work out at times. He used to arrive on his Lambretta scooter and was I suppose a bit trendy for his period anyway. Later he acquired a Ford Anglia the first of its kind I had saw in Belfast and I was a car freak. The problem with the car was that it had two badges on its rear quarter panels, which young guys used to collect. So that was a bit of a headache, as he needed to replace them every other couple of weeks. I didn't really get on with him and he smacked me one day on the face, which I probably deserved, and it took a while to mend the fence but it came all right. He would teach music, Men of Harlech being his favourite song, followed by Faith of our Fathers. He also loved Irish history and the French Revolution. Vive La Republique. Another great teacher was Colm Kerr who organised our trip to Kennedy's dairy and learned us all about how chocolate and coffee were made and got us to enter wee competitions that if you won you got a free bar of chocolate. He was a nice guy and a brilliant teacher. I can't leave the subject without mentioning the one and only Peter Mulligan the fiddle player. He also taught music and walked us up to the Edel Quinn hall in Sultan Street were we went for one or more of our classes. Don't ask me why but it was a twice-weekly ritual. He used to use a wee tuning fork for the tone you sang in. He then would take out his fiddle and off playing some screeching tune. He then went intermittently and had a drink from a cough bottle he kept in his drawer. It must have been a magic potion. I only wished my Da had got the same mixture. Poor Peter never coughed much so it must have worked but it did make him a bit unsteady on his feet probably the side effects. Miss McCool was my first ever teacher in primary school and had a great way with herself and set the stage for future learning in what I have to say was a great place for anyone interested in a good education unfortunately I wasn't. All in all school was a great place in hindsight, but you know what they say about hindsight.

One of my best memories is a Saturday afternoon trip to Cherry Valley to rob an orchard we had came across that Wednesday. The apples were red and we weren't used to eating red apples but more the Kemp apple or wee green apples we bought by the penny worth. Anyway we climbed over the garden fence at the back of the house and climbed into the orchard and were plucking apples and lifting windfalls when I was grabbed by the scruff of the neck by a big cop, with a face as red as the apples we were robbing. After ascertaining where we come from he went on to lecture us that we should be at home getting bathed for mass on Sunday rather than robbing good peoples orchards in Cherry Valley. He and his colleges then gave us a couple of slaps and sent us on our way. I always wondered did he ever think what having a bath entailed in our house or any of my mates houses. On a lighter note a good friend came to own that house in Cherry Valley in later years.

Did the cop not know we got bathed in a large oval shaped bath, brought out in front of the fire, the kitchen, we always called our living room the kitchen. Then my Ma filling it with pots and kettles of warm water and a big bar of lifebuoy soap and in you got and you may not have been the first in and you may have been joined by another sibling. You got your hair washed followed by the fine-tooth comb run through your hair almost descaling the skin of your head and then you jumped out and stood in front of a blazing fire and dried your self off. In later years we got a long bath that two people could get into more comfortably. It was long; much like a rowing boat and you could splash about in it and actually lay down in it. The other alternative to this was a visit to Public Baths for a warm bath, a towel that bare in mind was like drying yourself with a cardboard box.

Going for a swim with the school was another great event. Once a week we walked up Slate Street across Servia and up Osman across Raglan up Frere then across Ross and up Alma Street that had a great big horse trough at the top and across the Falls and into the baths. All in orderly fashion I jest. The only thing about this was if you were on the hike or beaking or mitching school we preferred the term on the beak, you had to watch the master didn't see you our one of your mates without malice called out your name when he saw you in the street. In the baths you got a pair of swimming pants, which were a piece of red canvas cloth with a string, which opened at the side and wrapped around you. They were mostly of the one-size fits all and as far as I know they are now a collectors item. So it was in, clothes off then some boys ran up stairs and dived of the balcony I think they saw themselves as Tarzan or Burt Lancaster. There were some great swimmers, in our gang, Peter Dempsey and Joe Mc Donnell to name a couple. I remember Jimmy Dempsey diving in and doing a belly clapper and it must have been sore as his chest was a bright red with pain. The cooler was another place for swimming, an outdoor pool in the Falls Park and many a night we went up there and got through a bent railing and went for a midnight swim. One night a friend of mine Martin O'Hare was drowned in the cooler in later years. He came from Ballymurphy and drank with me and my mates in Conlon's pub in Francis Street where we had many a good singsong on Friday and Saturday nights.

As I said earlier school days were great adventures for Buster Crossin, Frankie Short and me, as soon as we got out of school we headed for the land of plenty, the Malone Road where most of the legal profession lived in those days. A different place today as it is inhabited by lots of people from the west. Buster and me looked upon ourselves as mud-larks, Short was a bit more conservative than that but the three of us had some great adventures.

Our first visit was to Belfast Museum a palace like place, with big rooms filled with treasure of titanic proportion. But the one thing we loved was the mummy and we always went to see if her fingernails had grown any. Then we looked at some oil paintings like art critics and imagined places we could only dream of visiting or owning, things far beyond our comprehension. There was the Chambers car built in Belfast, suits of armour and artefacts the real antiques of their day until now when anything is collectable and the real antique is valued as something that has to be one hundred years old. After leaving the museum, we usually got thrown out for messing or if it was being closed we headed for the leafy streets of Malone.

I was always interested in cars and we judged houses by their size and if a nice car was parked in the drive. The three of us would stop pick a house and argue who would go and rap the door and ask for a piece. Short was as game a guy you could ever meet and saved my bacon on a few occasions but he wasn't up for rapping a door so it was up to Buster and me. So usually Buster and me went to door and knocked lightly, put on a wee sad face and when hopefully the woman came out we asked for a piece. If she was a good woman she gave both of us a piece with blackcurrant or strawberry jam on it then we meekly told her our mate was down the street and could we have one for him. We sometimes got a glass of lemonade if the woman felt a pity on us but if she gave us a piece of ordinary bread and butter we usually walked away, sulked and threw the bread away after a bite or two and off to the next house. Some times we got marmalade but it wasn't as nice and it met the same fate as the buttered piece. Sometimes the woman of the house may have given us a bit of cake or a bun then it was a real good day and the we sorry face turned to a smile and it even got better if she gave us a shilling or two but this lead to arguments over the division of the rewards. It was always the journey home that caused the arguments and maybe it was the fact we were coming back into reality. Buster would say I'm going across the railway lines down by the village. I wanted to go by Great Victoria Street and up by the GNR railway station and Short may have wanted to go the easy way over Sandy Row so some days we parted company and went our separate ways.

The GNR railways station was another place, which was a big draw for us with its vending machines. There was the chocolate machine, the name printer and the most modern one was for making your own record. We were always trying to get something for free as we had no money, so it was somewhere we went were there was some money and you had a chance. In our district everyone was looking for something so we travelled to other districts. That was our logic of course, but then it was just about having an edge. We never got anything grand but we had some great days that allowed us to be Tom Sawyer, Huck Finn or in my case Mickey Rooney.

One night we went to the Clonard Picture House to watch a film called **The Young Savages**. It had some effect on us as we walked down Leeson Street we actually walked over some guy's car as it was in our way and you can guess we had to do a runner as cars were few and far between then and a very prized possession. This film had a different impression on us as a western may have had. Then you slapped your arse the whole way home as if you were on a horse and galloped off into the night. Do films have an impression on us well there's your answer?

This brings to mind going to the pictures and talking about whom is **the fella in the big picture**? This referred to the good guy or the protagonist and when his back was turned we used to shout, "look out" at the screen as if he could hear us but we didn't care. When a catholic religious symbol came up we cheered and sometimes blessed ourselves. One night we were doing a stupid trick, (don't try this at home). You poured a wee drop of petrol or lighter fuel on your hand, lit it and then quickly put it out. Unfortunately the Clonard had got stuffed horse hair seats and as I tried to put my hand out by beating on the seats I set the them on fire but these were normal things then. Normal? It was also normal to throw the odd apple doot or a water balloon at the crowd and then sit as quiet as a mouse until the attendant threw someone else out to their total dismay. Their protests of innocence could be heard as they argued and fought and tried to explain that they had the wrong person.

Going to the Windsor Picture House was even worse. You bought a half drooper of Drawbridge wine in Wards Off License in Roden Street, down the entry, lashed it into you. Even the thought it, it was terrible and then stuck your chest out and you dandered like a hard man with your shoulders going, as we headed up to the picture house. It got so bad one night that they put up a caption asking, "Would those that don't want to watch the film please leave the cinema." You can guess how many walked out. None. Who wanted to leave, it was our gang who crossed the great divide to attend the Windsor picture house in that other territory just like in our territory we didn't like outsiders and neither did they. So we got barred many times and many a night had to fight our way home until we reached the safety of our end of Roden Street. Then we chased them back up to their own territory, which was at Dan's bar. This was our imaginary border -line at the Black Pad or Blacky River.

Bunking in to the picture house was another exploit of shear cheek or being a dare devil The Ritz or ABC was a great cinema but a bit out of our league at times as the cost outstripped our pocket money. So it was a case of the one with the balls paid in after we tapped the money and it was his job to open the fire exit doors. We then either took a run for it or crept like warriors on our bellies to the nearest seats, I have to say it was usually Davy Wilson that opened the doors. Lots of the time the attendant never noticed until our gang became very loud and starting shouting and messing about. Then it was a fast exit as the attendants raced towards us with their flash lamps pointing in our direction. It was a great sensation getting in, it was like you just broke into a bank or the equivalent and it was all about beating the system.

The Odeon across from the Ritz was another place but a little more difficult but the easiest cinema was the Grand Opera House but the only thing was you had to climb about a hundred stairs to get in but it was free and it was worth it. Yes the opera house did show films and the one that sticks in my head was Madame X and about ten of us got in that day. I think we were the only ones there. Everyone was yawning to hide the tears that we stopped coming as we watched the film, a story of love, desertion, and in some ways redemption. The ice cream woman never got much from us, only abuse in the cinema except of course on Christmas day in the News and Cartoons when we had a few bob.

It was as if it was yesterday, buying a wee tin of Tom Thumb cigars in Brigit's Mulligans shop on the Grosvenor Road. I also bought my first Rizla fag-rolling machine there for nine pence. Buster Crossin and me always went to the News and Cartoons together at Christmas and it was kings for a day for us. Fags, cigars, sweets, ice cream, what more would a fifties child want or need for that matter. We both smoked since we started school at the early age of four, a terrible habit, which I have now kicked thank God.

Christmas, now what a strange time, the birth of Jesus has long become secondary and I find that bad. We need some semblance of and I suppose when we celebrate anything it has to have some meaning. Lets say a birthday and it's no ones actual birthday wouldn't mean much or a reason to have a celebration. Anyway Christmas in our house it was a time for new clothes toys and chapel and a time of happiness. I haven't really enjoyed a Christmas in years so I may practice what I preach and get back to the meaning of it all. "The birth of Christ". After that little bit of preaching, I don't know where it came from. Maybe it's the inspiration I need to write this book.

Anyway I remember getting a horse racing game for Christmas. It was green shiny material that fitted to each end of the table and you turned a small handle and the little lead horses and jockeys galloped towards the finishing line. A simple but great toy, that provided great entertainment. I always wondered did my Da buy it for the both of us, as he was a punter as was I. Most guys around our district were horse racing mad and the majority of us had never been to a racecourse. The great thing about Christmas was also the selection box and the stocking. When I was young you put up your own sock and got a couple of oranges and apples but it progressed to a Cadburys selection box and stocking as time moved on.

I have, believe it or not, a love of batteries, yes-flash light batteries, as they were the things you needed at Christmas. A flashy and two spare batteries which you never got so you had to heat the flat batteries at the fire and hoped they would last for ever but that wasn't the way where designed. They lasted a few hours and then caput. The three-battery flash lamp was in my time the greatest invention since sliced bread. What a beam it could hit the stars we imagined and it was all about who had the longest beam, how things have changed.

It's now big cars, big houses and the rest but they have to be big. In hindsight I think the simplest things gave more enjoyment and gave longer lasting pleasure and I'm even getting pleasure writing about it some fifty years later. My Mobo horse was another great toy. I only found out in recent years that my cousin John Walsh owned it before me, but I didn't care. I could be Roy Rodgers or Gene Autry when I was aboard my white steed pushing down on its stirrups to make it go all the faster. John who was also in the Merchant Navy once brought cowboy guns and holsters for his nephews Sam and Eamon Walsh and maybe their late father Paddens who loved drawing with a gun and holster with his wee mate Paddy **Pudding** Brady. Where did the guns come from? Where else but New York, where as far as I was concerned they made everything and made the best of everything. I was a bit old for a gun and holster but in away I envied them, what great toys didn't come from America. They looked just like the real thing and again I bought some lately to live that dream in my life. I also bought a Mobo horse and I will probably do the same thing over and over again. But that's life, your life, my life and everyone that loves Belfast and nostalgia of the great city. That's what makes dreams and sometimes its better to keep it a dream; reality in adulthood is never as good as the dream and just doesn't really do it, so keep the fantasy.

One other night my cousin Hughie Daly fell into our Christmas tree and knocked his two front teeth out. Hughie was always jumping about and went smack bang into the middle of the tree. Most of us were more interested in my Mas collection of Christmas balls, little robins and her chocolate Father Christmases. What a time! Imagine a dark evening, all the lights other than the lights on the tree are off, a glow from a twelve-inch television, ten or twelve kids all hyped up on Christmas Eve with more adrenalin than a premiere football team could muster up. Crash in went Hughie right into the middle of the tree. After we pulled him out and washed his mouth he was as right as rain. It didn't cause him a second thought. In fact it had no lasting effect on him. A nice guy who luckily for him, it was his first teeth so he grew new ones very quickly.

Easter was another time for some sort of revelry and I remember getting a bucket and spade. No, not a work-mans bucket and spade, but a little brightly painted bucket with Mickey Mouse, or Donald Duck on it. It was filled with straw and a large Easter egg surrounded by smaller ones and two little yellow chickens set around it. It doesn't sound a lot in comparison with things today but again something I would buy if I ever saw an original one, what memories. What was a kid like me to do with a bucket and spade, the seaside and its sand were a million miles away. In my mind it was all a dream. Fortunately I had an uncle Geordie Daly, Hughie's Da, who had a Standard Vanguard. A big car copied along American lines, with a long bonnet and a big back, which he drove every other summer Sunday to Dundrum or Ardglass or beaches in South Down. It was a car like we would see in the movies, but the wait to see if you got picked to go on the trip was agonising.

A trip in a car was something else, again beyond my wildest dreams. So he would pile us all in and off we'd go to collect his favourite food, cockles and muscles in Dundrum bay or wilicks or winkles to give them their proper name in Ballyhornan. The car was amazing, far greater than any other family had, at least that's what I thought. He also used to bring us to Mc Kansas Glen to look at his greyhounds and then collect watercress, another of his favourite delicacies.

Then came along his new car although it was second-hand, it was a real dream. A black Zephyr Zodiac TZ4446 and it shone like ebony, with chrome subtly and strategically placed, that only added to its beauty and class. Robert his oldest son told us it was an Ex customs car that chased smugglers, so that added to the excitement as we imagined what it would have been like chasing smugglers up and down the back roads between Omeath and Dundalk. The things of dreams, films and our vivid imagination, that was better than the flicks. Rab Daly my cousin had a great mind and he told these stories and sometimes had you living in a world that in its time was like a real movie. Anyway for anyone that knows me I am called Docky two, as there is a Docky one, or big Docky and wee Docky, but in reality Rab Daly was the first Docky. As a kid cars fascinated me and I knew the Zodiac was special with its six cylinders and it was very fast. I knew it could fly, well metaphorically speaking anyway. What a great car and what great memories thanks to Geordie and his big cars and generosity.

All the boys

My dad with some friends outside the Bush Bar

Joe Comiskey with his wife

Away at sea

My wedding day

Mickey Marley's roundabout

The McDonnells and me

Future boxers

Micky Mullan,
Eamon Walsh,
me and Robert

My mum and the Walsh family

Up on the roof of school

The Walshes of Arnon Street and families

Housey, housey

The damp housing

Christmas Day at Nugget's house

Myself with Paddy

Brigit and me

122

Billy and
Martin Halligan

The leather jacket

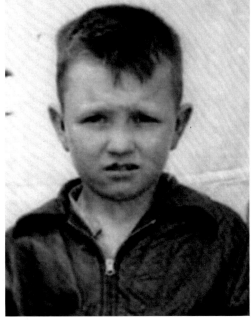

123

Chapter 20

Camping

Summer was a great time in my youth as it meant the long summer holidays and the biggest excitement in my life at the time. Going out camping. Well it was a rather impromptu affair, like who had or who could borrow a tent and a primmy stove (sic). Then it was all about supplies, a few tin of beans a loaf of bread, a bit of butter, a billycan or two and a few tin mugs and an old teapot. The primer stove to give it it's proper name was usually borrowed from someone or dug out of the coal hole and cleaned and prepared for the new season, the summer holidays. They never seemed to work proper and were very temperamental things and you had to then go to Stinker Greenwoods shop to get some paraffin oil and a prick. Yes a prick. A little piece of aluminium, knifelike with a needle on the end of it, that cleared the way for the paraffin to come up through a small hole which you lit and pumped to a certain level and you could cook on it like a stove. Anyway enough about pricks and primmy stoves, tents and the rest.

The next main thing was how to get the bus money or fare. When all our gear was packed into rucksacks we headed of to get the bus outside Rab Maguire's barbers, "the greatest barber of our time" who with his brother Paddy owned the shop facing the Falls bathes. We usually got the Catcairn or the Tornaroy or Hanahstown bus and walked a few hundred yards to our campsite beside the Rummy Hole in Tornaroy, the field of dreams.

This was like in my mind anyway, one of our American ranches, with fields as far as the eye could see. Buster, Short and the rest of the gang believed we owned it. It was if anyone interloped on our campsite we took great exception, but in reality it belonged to the farmer. But then so did our older brothers who camped on the same site, they thought it belonged to them. They also took exception to us being there but we where self contained and didn't need them and got on with our camping. Fact is they usually didn't go out camping when we went or vice versa but we sometimes we where camped within yards of each other.

One day we where in the Rummy Hole, literally a large pool with red clay sides and I was trying to swim. Suddenly I went under and came up shouting. Then I went under again and on the third and last time Fra Fox Mc Conville pulled me up by the hair and to this day I believe he saved my life. "Thanks Fra". Tornaroy was a strange place, were nothing seemed to grow, except rushes and grass that wasn't very good or picturesque in the winter. In fact I would say the land was near barren, as parts of it remain so to this day. Maybe that's why it was owned mostly by poor non-farming people, as it wasn't much good for anything like growing wheat or barley or anything one could eat. I never even saw a field of potatoes or cabbage in all my days in that part of the world, only the odd cow grazing and funnily enough no sheep.

All in all it provided some wonderful days for this dreamer or ranch hand. A cowboy, explorer, or any other idea, that was in my creative mind. In the tent at nights it was like a scene from the film Blazing Saddles, only difference was you could smell it. Heinz beans have a lot to answer for but theres nothing better than a plate of beans, a bit of bacon and a couple of rounds of a plain loaf and a big fire going. I'm sure we could all live with the smell and actually enjoy it.

On another occasion our Paddy my second eldest brother and Docky announced that they were going to Randalstown camping for a week. Now in my mind Randalstown was a million miles away but in reality it was only about thirty miles away. My Granda had a summerhouse there and that was the family connection. Anyway as soon as I heard about the trip I tortured my Ma to make Paddy and Docky bring me along. Older brothers didn't really bring their younger brothers with them; you know the big brother syndrome. After some talking by my Ma it was agreed I could go and that began my preparation in anticipation as if nothing of this importance ever happened in my life before. We started by getting tins of beans, peas and soup along with acquiring the money for the bus and some bacon and other victuals. We boarded the bus in Smithfield with our rucksacks and the most important thing the tent that had been bought out of Millets shop after months of saving.

Two others were going on this trip, Charlie Ward and a guy from our street called, Brian Pasha Mc Comish. The waterproof tent had a combined ground sheet, as it was a modern tent of its day. It had two vents on the side something we had not seen before. The bus Journey was uneventful except Docky telling me I better not be a nuisance when we got there. He was laying down the law, the big brother thing again, but our Paddy didn't behave like that. He was the easiest going guy in the world to get on with. I'm going to quote what and old friend of his said, a guy called Gerry Conway." I never heard Paddy McCartney say a bad word about anyone, better still I never heard anyone say a bad word about him," and that for me is the greatest accolade I ever heard about my late brother, or anyone else for that matter. On arrival at Randalstown we had to find out where the Blackrock Road was and find our way to the camp on Maggie Hutchison's land. When we arrived it was raining like no bodies business and we couldn't even get the tent opened so Maggie's brother Jimmy showed us into a small loose box with a brightly painted red door. The floor was covered in dry straw with some bales of hay piled in the corner. Our first order from Jimmy was no smoking in the stable. Most kids smoked in those days, as did Paddy, Docky and me, but Charlie Ward who was along with us never smoked, a lucky guy in that respect and neither did Pasha who actually got his nickname from a cigarette, in those days a common thing. I never forgot that red stable door in my minds eye and I did go back and visit thirty years later. The farm had a new house built on it but there was the little stable with its red door that provided us with a dry night's sleep. It was still intact, untarnished by modern times and memories flooded back. I suppose you could describe it like the five wise or not so wise men arriving from Belfast totally unprepared for the weather that lay ahead.

Two nights later we were lighting a fire at the back of the farm, more of a small bonfire, when Jimmy arrived shouting and bawling at the top of his voice to put the fire out. He was in some mood as he doused our fire and then went on to tell us we were burning a fairy ring. A clump of bushes that no one touches, not even developers would touch them today. I think he was for packing us off his land at that moment but after he settled down and explained that a fairy ring is never touched in anyway and what it meant to him and his family. He also scared the shite out of us. I think he realized we got the message. We did go an odd time to look for fairies but none where playing. I think they were all away acting in the film Darby O'Gill and the little people.

Our camping trip was mostly uneventful in Randalstown after that, except one day I followed a group of duckling and their mother into the duck pond which was made up of wet manure and chicken shit before I knew it I was up to my neck in it and both Ward and Docky threw me a rope made from hay cord to try and get me out. My water boots were filled with the stuff and I was covered in it from head to foot by now. Again it was Jimmy Hutchison who came along and pulled me to safety. Lectures ensued but you try telling five wise men or boys from Belfast whom thought they knew everything but in reality knew nothing. Big Gerard Kane whom I used to sell to in later years summed it up, "If your going to the country looking a mug you better bring one with you' a great lesson in life. We just didn't listen. We knew better. Paddy and Pasha were away walking in to town to get fags and some victuals at the time and when they returned they just laughed at the idea of it all, I can assure you I wasn't laughing I was stinking.

As we all got older the camping took on a new identity and was more like an evacuation of military proportions. Planning had to be put in place when maybe thirty or so went out on a weekend camping. On a few occasions I remember Tornaroy being like the corner of Servia and Osman Street. Jimmy Ward was out camping beside us along with his girl at the time Pat Denvir. Then Fra Ward arrived with his wife Marie but the biggest expedition was when the Dempsey's, Peter, Dipper, Scobie, Gerry Peezer Ward, Johnah, Vam Clarke, Patsy "Noaly" Nolan, his son Billy "Judas" Nolan, Sam Walsh, Josie Riley, Jim "The Other" O'Reilly, Charlie Ward the other Docky and Skee Skelly all arrived or invaded Glenavy for a weekend. One gang travelled in Peezer's LD van and the rest of us by bus to Glenavy and Crumlin and both villages didn't know what hit them that weekend. There were never so many wines and cider bottles brought to those wee villages in their history, but it was all done in the best possible way and the villages returned to normal, after we left. Camping was great in those days before the availability of cars and international travel but I have been in most countries in the world during a wee stint in the merchant navy but give me Tornaroy of the fifties anytime and I would be in my element. All in all that's what this writing is about a nostalgic trip down memory lane, not whose right whose wrong but memories of a bygone era that wont be returning no matter how hard we try to relive it. The smell of a log fire, cut grass drying in a field, getting ready to turn into hay, baked beans being boiled in a billycan, or simply a pot of tea stewing on the fire. That time of our lives is all gone now; our food is different as well. It may carry the same name but we shall never relive the taste buds and the joy of sitting around a campfire. The primus stove and billycans and tin mugs have gone and most of all the excitement of lying in bed the night before not being able to sleep with sheer thought of pitching a tent with no pegs, no ground sheets and stealing a blanket out of the house to keep you warm as you lived the outdoor life brought about with little or no planning and little money. Dreams to cherish and hold closely as we move along into a world that has no semblance to those days.

Chapter 21

Making money

To make money for the finer things in life, like going to the pictures, camping, swimming, or just getting a smokie in Victors ice cream shop or a chip in Fusco's sometimes took a bit of doing. Once Liam Boyle and me started going into town and collecting copper wire long before the skip became the dumping place of the nation. We always started at the back of Hogg's the fancy goods shop opposite the city hall. We searched through large wooden packing cases full of straw to find small broken ornaments that we could maybe sell to others and maybe take home to our own houses. Collecting copper wire was serious and was the most precious metal we ever came in contact with in those days. Red black and green wire cut-offs from electricians working on building sites and extensions was like mining for gold. Once we had collected what we thought would be about a stone of it we headed of to the Far Hill, Opening, or Water Tank. The entire one place with three different names was the place we lit a wee fire and burned the plastic to reveal the shining copper. The smoke was desperate and all the women in Mc Donnell Street used to come around some with basins of water and put our wee fires out. On reflection one couldn't blame them as the black smoke billowed over their back yard walls and meandered into their homes and ruining any washing they had on the line. A lot of the people, my Da included had a bad chest so they suffered really badly at times like that, or when smog or someone was painting a room.

So to get the money for the Clonard, Diamond, or the Broadway picture houses, you had to get it somewhere and this was one of the ways. Lead, copper, brass, were at a premium, as was going a message or an errand for someone who paid you well. One other great way of getting a few bob was selling Telly's or to give it its proper name the Belfast Telegraph. We sold the Telly at night and most sellers had their own territory or run as it was called. One of the bonuses in selling them was that you got on a bus for nothing and could travel a few stops for free, so it was a win, win situation.

Earn money and travel free. Some great Telly sellers were Wicky McGrath, who was also a great handball player and a character in his own way. He sang "Telly up! Telly up!" or his favourite song *The Rock Island Line* as he sold his newspapers. There were paperboys all over Belfast and some became very well off from the profits of selling papers. Another paper man and in my opinion the best player of street handball was Bitter Price and a very good street footballer to boot, pun intended. He was also as we would say a mad gambler who loved the cards and the horses. But everyone gave the Telly's a go at some stage of their early life as it was better than tapping, another great pastime of some of the lads from parts of Belfast.

Tapping involved asking people for money and in some cases some tappers tortured their victims into giving them a penny or even a halfpenny just to get rid of them. One guy that lived in the same street as me would start at the bathes and work his way down to Castle Street and back up again. He was one of the ones people used to reward just to get rid of him as he plied his run.

Another way of getting money was chopping and selling sticks. Some of the lads had their own runs just like selling the papers. They had their customers but that didn't deter others from venturing into their so-called territory. One family I used to run around with was the Hinds, Liam and Baldo. The Da Joe and the mother were a great wee team who would sit and chop sticks prepared by the Da Joe in pieces the right size, pre cut. He would get old packing cases and cut the wood into pieces ready for us with the hatchets or a knife and a hammer to chop them into sticks or as they were known or now firelighters. Then came a bit of ingenuity that people were very good at in the Falls . To wrap the sticks in bundles you had to tie them with cord, which was very laborious as the cord tended to loosen so we decided to put elastic bands around them. But elastic bands cost money and the reason for selling sticks in this family and many others was tough financial times. So some clever person thought of getting old bicycle tubes and sitting with a pair of scissors and cutting them into what else but elastic bands. This again was labour intensive. I'm laughing, buts let say it wasn't boring. Chopping the sticks was sore on the hands especially if you missed the wood and hit your hand with the hatchet. So no one really wanted to do that. When we got two- dozen bundles done, one of us held out our two arms and the bundles of sticks were built on to them. With your arms outstretched the person accompanying you would then go and knock the doors and ask, "Want any sticks Mrs.?" The one who was carrying the sticks got tired very quickly and arguments ensued as they swapped over tasks and one would say I'm not carrying them in case one of our mates see me. When we had them sold we got our cut, four dee a dozen, the sticks cost a shilling a dozen, so every dozen we sold we got our percentage. Mrs. Hinds, Kathleen was her name was always good for a Park-Drive and Joe for a Woodbine and you always got something to eat. A big round of toast or whatever was going and I have to say I enjoyed many a night sitting listening to the Da Joe telling stories smoking one of his fags and eating his food. They were a decent family who at times got it rough like their neighbours but just got on with it without complaining.

Again as I write I also remember another way people earned money in this ingenious district. Playing cards. Now one asks how would you earn money as this is gambling. Answer, hold the card school in your house and lift kitty. What was kitty? Every hand that was played, the owner of the house lifted an agreed amount out of the winning hand and in some cases if the card school went on all night there was only one winner, kitty, or the house. Some made tea for the card players and even the odd sandwich if it was a real good school as it meant the players would be back the following night to play again. Funny, we used to play every Sunday in Eileen Hinds house in Burnaby Street across the Grosvenor where lots of young married couples from the Falls Road started their new lives as married couples.

Burnaby Street backed onto Grosvenor Park the home of our local football team Distillery, better known as the Whites. The great Martin O'Neil started his professional career there along with the Meldrum's, Kennedy's, Martin Donnelly, and Carlo Fusco, Geordie O'Halloran all played for the whites. Grosvenor Park was the only ground I ever was at where a horse grazed on part of the hill where the spectators stood on a big day. Paddy McFarlane owned her and his Da was the grounds man at the park. Again why employ someone to cut the grass when you have nature, a horse to eat it down, but not the pitch, just the grass that grew on the banks around it. I always thought and I may be wrong that Paddy's Da was a shareholder in the whites as well as being the grounds-man. Some great times where spent at Grosvenor Park as the whites took on the blues or to give them their proper name Linfield. These matches were wars and spilled out onto the streets and running battles between them and us ensued. The biggest match I ever attended was to watch the Whites when they played Benfica who the great Eusebio played for. John Mc Connell, Terry Bonanza Hanna and myself walked to Windsor the home of the Blues to watch a great match and I never saw as much rain fall in my life just as the match ended. I'm sure the Benfica team where glad to get off the pitch, as I don't think it ever rained like that in Portugal.

On the football match thing the biggest match I was ever at was Celtic v Aberdeen in the Scottish cup final in nineteen sixty-seven, what a day. Celtic won two nil and 126,000 people watched it. When you compare it to the Distillery or more commonly known as the Whites, six or seven thousand in attendance and in the end hundreds. On one occasion the blues men as they where called attacked houses in Mc Donnell Street and broke windows and threw paint over windows displaying holy symbols, such as statues or holy pictures. But true to the boys from the area they sent the blues men packing and they never came back by that route again.

I have now left school, I'm fifteen and I feel as if the world out there is mine for the taking. I have just left Saint Peters in Britons Parade in the Whiterock area and I am so glad that that's the end of the hated school. Buster Crossin, Frankie Short and myself have decided it's a good reason to celebrate and decided to meet at seven o'clock that night. Geared up in suit collar and tie my thoughts wandered. All I could think of was going to the Plaza, the largest dance hall in the whole of Ireland. So at six o'clock I tapped a half a quid from my Ma got on my new black mohair suit and headed to meet my two mates and buy a bottle of three keys wine and enter into a new world and a fondness for drink.

As I was walking up Osman street to Short's house in Plevna street I met Buster and we decided to go to the wine shop more commonly known as the off license and get three big ten glass bottles of red wine of the Three Keys variety. That was the favourite tipple of the bigger guys from around our way so we were now big fellows or so we thought. One bottle for him, Short and me, I also got a bottle of Wee Willie brown ale to drench down the wine, as it was rotten. We then dandered over to Short's house and in the usual manner called for Frankie. We stood in the hall and called in unison. " Frankie are you coming out." After a few calls he came out into the hall and we flashed him the bottles of wine and the wee bottle of Wee Willie brown ale. Short got alarmed in case his Da Dan came out and caught us, as he would have broken the wine and maybe our faces along with it. Frankie told Buster and me to go to Raglan Street entry and he would follow us up in a minute or so. Off Buster and I went up to the entry like two seasoned drinkers and decided we would have a race to see who could drink the wine the fastest. I was a midget compared to Buster, a name reserved for fellows of a big stature with a belly to match. Both of us lashed it into us and before long we had emptied half of our bottles when Short arrived. "Could youse not have waited on me, where's mine" Buster slipped the big bottle out of his inside pocket and gave it to him but he really didn't like it. After a few slugs he caught up with us and we decided to drink the rest in one go. We all finished our wee race. Buster came first me second and Short third and that's the last I remember of the night except for making a total idiot of myself in the shelters at the Dunville park were we went to hide as we were all mad drunk. I was probably more drunk than the other two but it was like the Titanic, a night to remember, or in my case not to forget.

All I remember is my sister Brigit smuggling my wee black suit out to the dry cleaner man from the Monarch Laundry who called on Saturday to our house. If my Da seen the mess it was in I would have been in trouble, big trouble. I never found out, did my Da know, I came home drunk the night before but if he did he didn't say anything. I presume he didn't know, as I'm sure he would have punished me in some way. Something happened that night and it changed my life forever and drink then became and integral part of my life.

About twelve o'clock on Saturday morning it was lunchtime and I crawled out of bed and down for the Saturday fry. Dipped bread, one sausage and one rasher of bacon, an egg and a potato farl. As I looked at it I nearly threw my ring up but after sitting down and trying to wonder what happened the night before I heard my name being called. It was Buster and Short. As I ran out into the hall to hear the post-mortem of the night before and believe me what I heard I never lived it down or got the chance to. It was the topic of conversation for weeks on end and I always hated post-mortems as we called them, but it was now part of me. I decided to bring Short and Buster in as our house as I always did, everyone got brought in got a piece with sauce or sugar on it or on Saturday dipped, but I had to make sure what happened the night wasn't talked about. "What were youse talking about in the hall?" asked my Ma, "Nothing Ma we are going out on Monday to look for jobs." My ma replied jokingly that work was for horses and I took it literally as work was not one of my great fortes in my life, but obla dee obla da, life went on.

My first real job was for Briggs Lemonade Company as a van boy. It was great, as I was always sleeping in the wee lorry driven by Billy Hill and there was always a few bob to be made. We never delivered around our way until I was in the job a while and then we would have sold a few bottles to neighbours as most districts had their own brand of lemonade and delivery man. Divis Lemonade, well that's a no brainer, it covered the Falls Road and surrounding areas but didn't do house deliveries but all the shops sold it, especially their famous Attaboy. Ross's was down by the market, and so on. Anyway there was a wee move in every job and as usual I had my end of it and I enjoyed it jumping out of the wee lorry delivering bottles of lemonade sometimes by the dozen to houses but in our case at home we shared one bottle of Attaboy sometimes mixed with butter milk, or milk to stretch it and make it taste like ice cream. After a while in Briggs I left and went looking for another job.

My brother Paddy got me a job in DC products where he had already worked for eight years as a fitter. Anyway I started at eight o'clock one Monday and I hated every day of it. It was a cold factory with little consideration for the worker and little or no comforts. I was to be an apprentice welder and was sat in a wee seat and handed a welding gun. I was very au fait with the welding gun having knocked about Henry Kane's yard and he had burning equipment, which was similar if not the same but used with more burning power. I sat along side Harry Mc Garry and the only thing I liked about it was the heat from the lamp and I knew there and then this wasn't for me but I couldn't let our Paddy down as he worked for this company when it was in a hut in Wilson Street. I decided to give it a wee go and try as I might and Harry Mc Garry did try his best to teach me I just couldn't get the knack of it. To put it mildly I wasn't for staying for a fiver a week getting the balls freezed off me.

The foreman was a guy called Colum or Cheetah as we called him and he drove the car of my dreams, a chocolate and cream Vauxhall Cresta PA hydromatic. What a car, a take off of a fifty-seven Chevy but I swore I'd own one some day. Well Cheetah knew I wasn't interested in welding but what lay in store was ten times worse than learning to weld. DC products made exhausts for all makes of cars and some specialist cars had to have their silencer filled with fibreglass and I was sent to the pit to stuff silencers with this stuff. It became the bane of my life; to this day the very sight of it makes me want to take a shower. As I worked away with this terrible stuff a young guy called Gerard Scott joined me. It didn't cause him one bit of annoyance as he pushed the fibreglass into the exhaust boxes before they were welded, sealed and then fitted to some gentleman's Rolls Royce or other exotic car.

Eight weeks later I got my walking orders. I got a wee note in my wage pack and I celebrated the whole way down Shields Street and thanked God he had ended my tenure in DC products. In hindsight, some time later I thought how I must have embarrassed my big brother Paddy whom I idolized. But I was fifteen and I was out to take on the world.

Chapter 22

Day trip to London

One day Chip and me touched for a few quid and decided to go for a drink in our local the store bar in the town. It wasn't really our local but I got served in it but had to hide in the boxes or snug, as they were more commonly known. After a few pints of single we decided to head up the road again get something to eat as it was the weekend and we may head to the Plaza. Later on we got our diner in Chips house and we headed to the corner to see what if anything was happening. It was nineteen sixty-five and it was quiet and its seemed like any other night until we met a few of the lads at the corner of Leeson Street. After counting or tank it was decided we would go to Lynch's at the corner of Distillery Street for a drink, as it was somewhere different. As we arrived at lynch's, Chip, James Peter Morgan, Roy Lenny Smyth, Sean Walter Wilson and myself got a table and ordered ten bottles of stout. After about ten minutes we ordered the same again and the barman duly obliged. The craic was mighty and then JP Morgan aka Morgy started reliving his days in London.as the drink flowed we were all in awe as Morgy relived his days and how he knew the Kray twins and his mate John Donnelly was one of the hard men in London and knew everybody. Chip said he was talking bollocks, and some of us agreed but the stories sounded good. Walter and Morgy were good mates and he said that we should listen to Morgy, as he didn't tell lies. After a few more drinks it was wearing on and we were all thinking of were to go next. We then ordered another round and the barman told us that he thought we had had enough. Morgy continued and told us his mate had a flat in Cleveland Street in London and he would put us all up if we went over and we would meet all of the people he knew. The Kray twins, Spotter Murphy, the Gunning brothers and a few other Belfast hard men who knocked about the Edgeware Road. As the drink was getting low and the stories became more exciting chip said lets go. Lenny said were, to London with a bout a tenner between us. I chirped in and said, as I looked the youngest I could ask for five half fares to heysham and see what happens. As the conversation became louder and everyone arguing the barman came over to the table and asked us to leave. After a bit of slabbering to the barman he told us to leave or he was calling the peelers. So we drunk up and headed out and decide to go for a drink down town and we headed back to the store bar were I knew I would be served. As we entered the store bar which wasn't far from the Heysham boat Lenny said, " Fuck it Fra you go and try and get the tickets I'm game who else is coming". After a bit of arguing we all walked over to the Heysham boat and I duly walked into the big shed and meekly walked over to the ticket office and asked for five halves to Heysham. The man asked me my age and I told him I was fourteen and so where the rest of my travelling companions. I really didn't use those words but something like that to make it sound good.

After I got the tickets that cost in total two pounds ten shillings I walked back to the lads and said, " we only have to get on board' then I dished out the tickets." Whose going first asked Walter who was about the tallest then they all said as I bought the tickets I should hold them all and lead the way. With the dink in me I didn't care one way or the other whether we go on board or not as I had been to sea already. As we all walked up to the gangplank I handed the guy the five tickets and we walked on as nice as you like. We then wandered about the ship until we found the bar that didn't open until we sailed so we all sat down and talked about where in London we wanted to go. I said I wanted to go to Savill Row and Claridge's hotel and Lenny agreed. Chip wanted to see big ben and Walter wanted to get off the boat but it was too late. Morgy then started telling more stories and it seemed as if he had been in the big smoke all his life. The people he mentioned amazed the rest and me and we couldn't wait to get to the other side. The bar then opened and we ordered a few pints and borrowed a deck of cards for the long journey to Heysham. After a couple of hours we all found a soft seat to sleep on and before long I was fast asleep.

The next morning as we all awoke and gave ourselves a good shake and after a bit of a discussion we realised that we didn't have the money for the train fare to London. It was cold damp and we were all starving and some of us cursed Morgy for bringing us on this mad wild chase. Be assured us all would be all right as soon as we got the train to London. One by one we boarded the train bound for London and asked ourselves what will we tell the conductor if he asks for our tickets. A few minutes later and the train started and off we went we were on our way to the land of milk and honey. After about half and hour the announcements came over the public address system. Change at Crewe for all these different places. Walter decided he was getting of at Crewe and he was going home, after some persuasion without success it was decided that he could go and no one would hold it against him but we did call him Kleenex, but it never stuck and we went our separate ways at Crewe. But first we told Walter to tell our parents were we were after all we only went out for a drink and were heading for London. After us waving him off Walter was heading back to Belfast and we continued our Journey to London. On arrival at waterloo or Houston station we alighted from the train but we had now tickets but it was early morning and there were hundreds of people scurrying to work and we just blended in and ran through the ticket collection gate.

"What do we do now Morgy" I asked and all was quiet. I said fuck it we shall head to Shepherds Bush as I knew some people there and they can point us in the right direction then Lenny said if we have no luck there we can head to our Margaret's but she lives in Ealing. On e thing about Morgy he knew the tubes and how they operated so we headed for Mary Anne's in Woodstock Grove in the Bush, as it was colloquially known back in Belfast. After some messing about and a cup of tea we left the train station and headed for the tubes. Morgy lead the way as he new the score and as we got on they were packed to capacity with people heading to work or coming from work. As soon as we got to the Bush we all ran up the escalators and straight out onto the Street, as we hadn't paid any fares. We then headed for Woodstock Grove, or Richmond Way, as they were actually One Street that ran in to each other. I knew were I was having being there a couple of years previous. As we made our way to Mary Anne's we stooped at her house and knocked the hall door but no one opened it and we presumed she was out. Another Belfast family called Cupples lived up the street and we headed for there house and were invited in and they told us how to get to Lenny's Sisters house in Ealing. After we had a cup of tea we decided to go up town before we headed for Ealing. Lenny and myself wanted to go to

138

Savill Row were supposedly the best-bespoke suits in the world were made, a far cry from our wee twelve quid suits from Burtons.

On arrival in Savill row we gazed in the windows of the tailors and imagined what it would be like to have a suit made in one. Chip said he would rather have a new pair of jeans and Morgy agreed. We then stopped at tailors and there was a mannequin with a set of tails on that were made over seventy years ago and were still in great condition. Lenny and myself were in awe as we were into classy suits and shoes but the other two didn't give fiddlers. We then went to Claridge's hotel jooked in the main entrance and that was as far as we got. Lenny and me had worked in hotels and this was the crème de la crème of hotels at the time and we were amazed at the Rolls Royce's and Bentleys parked out side. I also noticed a lot of chauffer driven Daimlers. I think they were showing of their class, as it was the car of the want to be lords and ladies of the day. We then headed to Ealing Broadway to try and find Margaret Smyth's house.

On arrival in Ealing we started asking people how to find our way to the address written on the back of a Park Drive packet. Just then as we were looking in windows of shops Lenny shouted there our Margaret and she was on the cashiers desk at a supermarket. He then ran in and after a bit of a yarn she gave him the key to her house, which wasn't far and told us to go there and she would be around later when she finished work. After finding the house we made our way in tentatively and I found a good chair and fell asleep, I was knackered. Some time later we were sitting down to a good feed and then what iffs started? How do we get home? We were all sober and the thoughts of meeting the Kray Twins had all but evaporated. This was nineteen sixty-five and London was a very inviting place but not for us we couldn't wait to get back home to the Falls. After a lot of chat and another bite to eat Margaret rustled up a few quid for us and we were on our way home, our worldly visit to London was over. As we boarded the night boat to Belfast we talked about all the slagging we would get like, did youse se the time by big ben, or, I was longer on the toilet, is that a Cockney accent and so on. We all decided after a few drink to get our head down and within minutes we were all fast asleep.

The next morning we awakened by the sound of the boat tying up and the gangplank being set. We were back from our expedition and we now had to Face the music. As we walked down the gangplank on a typical cold damp Belfast morning there was Chip's Da, my Da and some others, the prodigal sons had arrived home and everyone was happy we were all safe and sound. It may have been the end of that trip but more were to follow.

Chapter 23

The Woodbourne house hotel

At this time a very good friend of mine who in fairness wasn't the same type of kid as me entered my life for the second time. Sean Dillon who had told me how altar boys got a few bob at weddings was now telling me he was working in a hotel up in Andytown and making a fortune. Sean was a great lad and was a nicer lad than me and was sort of more polished in attitude to life. He was a natural born worker, which unfortunately I wasn't. He loved football but I couldn't tell you offside from eff off, but here he was telling me he could get me a job in a big hotel and the tips where brilliant. So I tortured him very day I saw him until one day, true to his word he got me an interview for a job in The Woodbourne House Hotel as a lounge waiter.

The hotel had three managers, Jackie Calendar, a great man, Jack Watson who wasn't bad and Des Davison who knew what he wanted in life and I think he achieved it. I started work on the fourteenth of June nineteen sixty five as my references say and that was the start of another quest, to get a few quid. The hotel was a great place, continuous heat, and you got fed, but most of all I became the highest earner in our house at the age of fifteen as the tips where phenomenal and in fairness I was good at the job. I remember one night bunging my Da a ten bob note and he was over the moon but he didn't realize how much pleasure it gave his sister, my aunt Lilly and me. She always remembered me for being good to her brother, my Da. Money was no problem but I didn't save or anything and the next thing on my agenda was a pair of McManus's hand stitched Chelsea boots or as we called them *seven guinea boots* as that's what they cost, a small fortune in those days. One day on my day off I walked down to McManus's shop in Royal Avenue and tried on a pair of the boots. The boots that everyone in our district owned or wanted and handed over the princely sum of seven pounds seven shilling for them. I had arrived or so I thought.

The Woodbourne as we fondly called it was long hours and hard work but the rewards were good. My wages were a fiver a week and you had a day and a half off and it didn't open on Sunday. I started early one morning a week and finished at three o'clock in the afternoon. Then later I started at three in the afternoon and worked till two or three in the morning and then was taxied home by the company. What a life! It was like being at sea, which I always aspired to do, constant heat, no rainy days and a few quid and no real heavy work. Des Davison would never let you stand around. You could be busy for two hours and taking a breather when he would approach and tell you to polish tables, clean ashtrays and generally you learned not to stand about as Big Des ran a tight ship metaphorically. As a big scotch man called Joe Campbell who I later sailed with would say, "Keep moving" and I learned to do just that in The Woodbourne.

The days of weddings were great in the Woodbourne and you could earn your wages in tips or gratuities in one day depending on how many were in attendance at the wedding. The best weddings were the working class ones as they tipped after every drink and maybe it was their way of living as the other half lived but it didn't really matter they were generous to a man and woman. The weddings were a seasonal thing and started around St Patrick's Day half way through March until October and I think it was to do with the tax year. That's when the punters got their tax rebate. We sometimes called the hotel a factory as it produced that many weddings, sometimes three a day and on one occasion four and as it was our source of revenue we all said the more the merrier and it got your day in quickly.

One Thursday a sort of hush went around the hotel and lots of people were whispering and the hotel was unusually quite and I wondered what was wrong. After a few minutes I called Tom McCauley a barman and asked him what was happening and he said you will find out in about and hour. I asked another barman called John Lyttle and he gave me a glib answer so I waited and wondered. Later on that day there was a lot of activity and big Des and the rest of the management staff were running around like blue arsed flies and then it happened. A few taxies arrived at the front door and low and behold Mick Jagger alighted from one followed by the rest of the Rolling Stones and their entourage. Now if it had have been the Beatles I would have been star struck but to me The Stones were not in the same league as The Beatles but in fairness that's not quite true. It's how I saw it then. How do I remember it was Thursday? After a few hours Brian Jones with his blonde hair sitting without a hair out of place asked me where the television lounge was and I informed him that there wasn't one. He told me that he wanted to watch top of the pops hence Thursday night and I told him some of the live in staff had televisions in their rooms but there were no others, it was something to do with the licensing laws of the time. I then asked one of the barmaids a girl called Lena did she have a television in her room and she cheekily ask me why I wanted to know and I informed her that Brian Jones wanted to watch top of the pops. Her mood quickly changed and either her or big Des accommodated the late Brian Jones. Well one of them could say they watched top of the pops with one of the biggest acts ever to appear on it. I served most of the stones tea or a drink except Keith Richards who was always in the garden, I wonder why? Next day a wedding was taking place in the hotel and the Stones joined in and had their photographs taken with a very surprised bride and groom. The Stones then went out, got on a blue bus which stopped outside the hotel and went down a few stops followed by a camera a crew then ran all the way back to the hotel followed by screaming girls and boys from around the Horn Drive, Lenadoon area. I remember retelling this story to a few people and they didn't believe it and in fairness the Woodbourne was a Mickey Mouse hotel without all the luxury, which I'm sure the Stones later demanded and received. Rooms or suites with televisions in the rooms and all the other modern appliances would be on their rider demands. Anyway a film came out a few years ago and low and behold there is it the film of the Stones just doing what I described right to the letter.

One day while working in the main lounge of the Woodbourne, I was cheeky to a customer who had whistled at me, and I replied, "Do you think your calling your dog?" He reported me to the manager and I was brought before Jackie Calendar who gave me a nice little warning but someone told Des Davison and he brought me to his office. He pointed out the window to a car park and asked me did I ever see his car. I knew his car as it was and still is the car of my dreams, a gold coloured twelve cylinder E type Jaguar. I said it was a beautiful car and then he told me that the customer that had whistled at me was a contributor to the cost and upkeep of the car. I learned a valuable lesson that day and was sacked there and then.

Some time later my Da died and Jackie Calendar, again through Sean Dillon sent for me and reinstated me. He was a nice man. Two other friends of mine had joined us by then, a guy called Roy Smyth who had been in our class at school and Manny Curran and we all worked away contently. Sean Dillon played a substantial part in my early life. First by telling me that as an altar boy I could earn a few pounds attending weddings and the odd funeral masses. He also got me a job in the Woodbourne Hotel and placed me in a position of a newfound wealth. Some days after my fathers death Sean informed me that Jacky Calendar, one of the managers and a great wee man had went out on a limb and was going to give me my old job back. All I had to do was to attend and interview where he would read me the riot act and that would be it. True to his word a week later I was back at my old job with some of the characters I had worked with previously. I did get a bit of slagging as I at that time had been the only person ever to get their job back after been sacked. There was Liz, Lena, and John Little the bar staff in the bar who didn't look so pleased, but all the other gang Joe McGrath, Tom and Mickey McCauley, Patsy Fagan, and of course Roy Smyth were glad I was back.

After a few weeks I was getting restless for the call of the sea and one night wee Roy Smith told me that Gerry Fitt was having a victory parade after he had won the election the previous day or so. This was going to a big event so me and Roy decided that we were going to leave the Woodbourne in style. It was the first day of April. I had only been back in the job a few weeks and it was a busy weekend when Roy and me ripped of our white coats and ran out of the hotel as if we had escaped from prison, or was it we had seen a light of change that was about to come for the better as we thought, or worse depending on how you saw Belfast. As we ran out of the grounds we headed straight down the road and the victory parade that was literally attended by all the people of the road.

Chapter 24

You're too small

After a while running around the corner I sort of got used to not being out of work but the lure of the merchant navy or a job on the boats as we called it began to rekindle my thoughts again. So I set off down to the shipping federation more commonly known as "the pool" and asked some men who were leaning on a iron rest bar meekly how could I get a job on the boats. One told me to bend down and tip my toes and I though he's a clever cookie. I didn't under stand there and then but soon tippled that he was making a reference to the so-called large gay community in the merchant navy. After telling your man to fuck off, I walked over to the counter and spoke to a man in an officer's uniform with the gold braid rings on the cuffs. I later learned the gentleman was called Jackie Ross. He informed me I would have to go to sea school and duly gave me the application forms and told me to get one of my parents to fill it in and sign it. I was now sixteen at this time but I was very small in stature. I was along with my mate Chip Mc Farlane. I later got him on a boat in Belfast harbour a few months later called a pier head jump. I grabbed the papers and when I got home, asked my Da to fill in the forms, which he was very good at. The next day I landed back at the pool and handed the papers to a different guy called Harper who then informed me that I would have to see the doctor on Friday morning before twelve noon. That was even before I could be considered for sea school. I was fit enough but I knew I was rather small but I still thought it would be a formality; after all there were no height restrictions that I knew of in the merch.

Anyway I got a bath the previous night in the baths and the next morning put on my best York's and a white shirt and headed down to the pool with Chip and couple of other mates. I was leading the way to all of us to join the merchant navy or so I thought. I sat and waited like a nervous wreck. Then the doctor called me in and looked at me, done the usual medical routine then he got a tape measure out and measured my chest. Now as I said earlier I got twenty five per cent of my suits in Burton's the tailors as I was under a thirty-four chest and liked the idea that I got them cheaper than my mates. But I wasn't ready for the bombshell that was about to hit me. I wasn't too small in height, but in chest size, to small go to sea school. What was I going to tell my mates when I went outside, that I was a skinny wimp like the guy who had sand kicked in his face in the Charles Atlas advertisements? The doctor went on to explain that if I done a few exercises it would not be long until I made the tale of the tape. There was a funny thing about him, he had a cigarette dangling from his mouth as he spoke only removing it once to light another one. He was a chain smoker the first I ever saw but not the last. It was never removed from his mouth even when he spoke to you and I realised that was my problem. I smoked like a train and was under developed so I would stop smoking.

As I left the doctors surgery he called me back and said to me there's a way around all of this you know. I waited open-mouthed waiting on him to tell me he had another plan for me. I listened as he told me that if I had an uncle or someone I knew well that could put a word in for me I could get on the boats without going to sea school and there would be no difference. I would get a discharge book more commonly known as *a Sea Book* and that would be that. My brain went into over drive as I scanned my memory for people my Da knew or that I may have known who may get me on the boats. As I walked out from behind the desk in the pool, the doctor shouted at me to come back when I was seventeen as I was too young. The chest measurements were never mentioned again.

My Da was, from I could remember when I was a child, in bad health. He worked in the flourmill and smoked as much Woodbine as he could afford and that didn't auger for good health. But he worked until he physically couldn't work anymore. I don't know how many cough mixture bottles I went for to Joe Mc Aufields chemist shop for but I'm sure it would run into hundreds. Every winter my Da's health seemed to deteriorate and on some occasions he had to have a bucket of water with some fresh cut grass "from Joe's yard" placed in his bedroom so he could literally breathe. It was coming up to Christmas and my birthday. I was going to be sixteen and the sea beckoned me again. That Christmas was not like every other year were me and my Da went down to the markets for the turkey and met Silver Mc Kee or some other wide boy who would have purchased the turkey for my Da thus saving him some money. Then he could buy a few pints with the money saved.

As usual the tree went up and my Ma did her best for all of us. The three young ones Marian, Gerard and Bernadette got the usual toys. I had bought Gerard a scale electric. Sometimes I wonder did I buy it for myself but we both got a lot of fun from it. In fact every one enjoyed what was to be our last Christmas as a family intact. January came and it turned out be a very cold winter. I used to think the winter was October, November and December. I forgot that January and February were cold as well and in January my Da landed in Musgrave Park hospital. The ward was in a Nissan hut that I think had once been used during the war. Musgrave Park hospital was a military hospital as well as civilian and had all the feel of an army camp. One night Buster Crossin and me went up to visit him and as we sat talking to him I realised he was talking gibberish. It must have been the drugs they were pumping into him to relieve the pain or lack of oxygen through not being able to breathe. As we sat there I looked at him. A man with all the knowledge in the world a physical wreck brought about by Woodbine and working in a dusty Andrews's flourmill. Buster and me sat for about an hour and as we were not far from our old stomping ground the Malone Road we reminisced about rapping doors, asking for jam pieces and drinks of water as we watched my Da struggle to get a breath. After a while I decided it was time to go and Buster and I made our way down the Lisburn Road towards home. We looked at some of the streets where we had knocked on doors and asked for things we could now afford. Our world was changing. The memories came flooding back.

A few weeks later on the first of February I was lying in bed beside our Paddy, freezing and unable to sleep when my Ma walked in, turned on the light and announced that our Da was dead. Every one got up. Firstly Oliver who had recently returned home from working in England and Robert who slept in the other bed along side ours. Then the whole house got up out of bed and it became clear to us all that our Da was dead and memories came flooding back of childhood.

I don't know what I was thinking after the memories but I later on I went to bed and my brain started to race and after a long time I fell asleep exhausted. Three days later and it was the day of my father's funeral and I met for the first time a cousin of mine who was called after my grandfather. He stood out among the crowd as he carried a black umbrella usually or perceived by my mates and myself as being a thing only Protestants carried. We were right, my cousin was from the Shankill Road and as I recall he was the only person of the opposite persuasion present. I'm sure my Da had a few other cousins as his father came from Lorton Street and was called Robert Law McCartney. "Quite a name to carry". I was probably more interested in whether my boyhood idol was there, Henry Kane, the biggest horse dealer in Ireland. The number of horses he bought yearly was phenomenal and it was very important to me if he attended my Da's funeral. He was everything I ever wanted to be in life. A scrap and horse dealer and he generally dealt in anything to turn a profit. Some lads wanted to be firemen, doctors, politicians, but he was everything I wanted to be in my childhood. After my Da was buried life went on for me as normal but not for my Ma who had ten mouths to fill daily.

Knowing that I hadn't added two inches to my chest size, I decided I had to find another way of getting my foot into the navy. My cousin Annie Daly had married a big fellow called Gerry Doran and they lived in my granny Biddy's house across from us in Servia Street and he and I became good friends, even though he was older than me. He had given me pigeons, a couple of years ago along with the odd few bob; he was a big time pigeon fancier and more important he had a brother Hugo who had been in the *merch* for years. One day I asked Gerry could he ask his brother Hugo to try and get me on the boats. Gerry went on to tell me that Hugo was away on a tramp steamer and could be away for eighteen months or longer on one trip. He didn't know when to expect him back but he did have an uncle called Harry who lived in Lincoln Street across from my aunt Lily Daly and he said he would ask him to see what he could do.

Well true to his word he asked his uncle Harry and he arranged for me to go and meet Harry in his house. As I sat drinking a cup of tea with Harry I explained that I was literally too small to go to sea school, the normal method for joining the **merch**. Harry told me to get a reference out of some public house or hotel and he would arrange for me to go down to the shipping federation and take it from there. I asked myself where was I going to get a reference, as I didn't deserve one from the Woodbourne. Again Sean Dillon came to my rescue and he asked Jackie Calendar would he give me a reference and a week later the reference duly arrived. Big Harry Doran then brought me down and introduced me to Jacky Ross and after some private conversation I was on my way. I filled out some papers and showed my references to Jacky who looked at them and gave me some papers to go the board of trade to get my discharge book and then join the seaman's union. First I had to run around frantically and find a photo booth to get my photograph taken and then get three quid to join the union. As I was doing all this there was a bit of rumblings of a seaman's strike looming so I had to work fast before it all became immaterial if the strike started. After all if there were a strike there'd be no boats sailing. As I handed the photos to the man in the board of trade office he stuck them in my blue discharge book and then my red identity or ID book the equivalent of my passport. I grabbed them eagerly and done the thing I had seen everyone that I knew who went to sea before me. I stuck them in the back pocket of my Wrangler jeans to let everyone know I was now a merchant seaman. It probably was no big deal to some people, but where I came from, it was the top of the proverbial ladder. After a few minutes I thought I may bend them in my back pocket so I stuck them in my inside pocket as I felt that they'd be safer there. The next port of call was the seaman's union a small office not far from the big clock. As I walked in, Harry had prearranged everything so I knew it would be all right. I had to meet a man who would make me a member without any questions being asked. As the man handed me my union book after what seemed a lifetime talking and filling in forms I had the full house. The discharge book, ID book, union book. I had arrived. Now all I needed was a boat.

Next day I attended the pool as recommended to me by Jacky Ross and duly handed my book over but there was no jobs available. A week or so my mates and me trundled down and sat in the pool like hardened seamen as I awaited my first boat. One day Jacky nodded to me from behind the big counter and as I walked over he handed me a piece of paper and told me to report to the chief steward on board **The Royal Ulsterman** and I would get a job as a pantry or galley boy. I was full of nervous energy, but I was stunned. What does a pantry or galley boy do on board a big ship like the **Ulsterman**? It was ten o'clock and Jacky a kindly but wily man told me to run across and do it right there and then, as if I left it till later it could be too late.

I ran across to were the big boat was docked and asked a docker how I could get on board and he told me it was only crew and dockers were allowed on board and I stuck my little chest out, yes the small one and told him I was a crew member. I had been aboard the boat a few years earlier as I walked horses bound for Glasgow down a steep gangplank and into the hold for Henry Kane and Joe Hughes but had never seen the other parts of the ship. So away up this gangplank I went and was shown into the galley. I asked for the chief steward and someone introduced himself as the second steward and brought me through what seems miles of alleyways and into and office were I signed some papers.

I was now a crewmember of **The Royal Ulsterman**, owned by the Burns and Laird line. My wages were to be twenty-six pounds a month for a seventy-hour week, no Saturdays or Sunday over time, unless the ship was at sea. The second steward brought me back down to the galley and I was introduced to the other pantry boy who I later new as Billy Greer from east Belfast. I looked at him and thought he's a giant, compared to me, as he dried some plates as nice as you like. I was given a white *coat* and told to wear it when I was going through the public alleyways on the ship but for now I could help wash the dishes along with Billy. There was a lot of activity going on aboard the ship and a few of the crew welcomed me on board and tried the usual pranks like, go get a bucket of blue steam and so on. The next I knew Billy and me had to get a bundle of plates and carry them to the iron lung and I was quite hesitant but it was real. The iron lung was a room that housed the entire cutlery for the ship in reserve and we started filling up the racks with plates cups and saucers, knifes and forks that were put in large drawers. A few minutes later we went back up to the galley and Billy McKee from sailor town, Joe Campbell from Glasgow, Paddy Prenter "Jimmy Dimpers Da" who was married to my cousins the Walsh's aunt and was one of the ships cooks all appeared. Then Paddy Duffy appeared and he actually lived in Servia Street and I knew him well and then the bombshell dropped. The seaman's strike would officially start at twelve o'clock noon. It was ten minutes to twelve. I looked around me and didn't know whether to laugh or cry.

It was the sixteenth of May nineteen sixty-six and I had just joined the union, and there was going to be a strike. What was I supposed to do? At twelve o'clock noon everything stopped and the chief steward made some announcement to a mixed bunch. He told us to leave the ship as and how we found it. That's why we had been putting the entire cutlery in the iron lung, very prevalent and understandable. The ship wasn't going to move so everything was stowed away and my sea career had floundered on its first day. What away to start a new job, with a strike and a tour around the ship and all my anxieties seemed fruitless.

As we all left the ship we were told our jobs would be there for us depending on how long the strike lasted. The strike would end on the first of July nineteen sixty six. It lasted all in all six weeks and I was scundered as I was entitled to my union money every week like every other member but I had to do my duty and carry a placard for a few hours outside a pub called **The Dufferin Arms** at the entrance to the deep sea docks. I called in the help of my old mate Chip McFarlane who was as keen as mustard to carry the placard so I organised him to do a bit of my stint, well a bit more than I did. It was the summer and it was good craic and a lot of slagging went on and I met a few seamen who became friends in later years. Big Dan Mc Quade aka Dan Fenton was our unofficial leader and every weekday I done my stint and informed our union rep I had been there and that entitled my three quid a week. Much the same as I would have earned on the **Ulsterman give or take a couple of quid**. Once the strike ended I went down and re-joined the **Ulsterman** and became au fait with my job and life at sea. The cabin I slept in was like a large bedroom with bunk beds placed strategically against the bulkheads and housed six seamen with a wee locker for your clothes or valuables if you had any.

A few weeks later I had settled into my galley boy job well and had the odd week off. Chip Mc Farlane who was a very close friend by now was torturing me to get him away to sea. I decided we would go down the docks the next time I had some leave and see if he could get him a pier head jump which basically means joining a ship at the last minute because it couldn't get the crew member it needed.

One day as the sun was splitting the trees Chip and me decided to go down the docks where we had played as young kids. We knew most of its berths and where the ships tied up and I could get by the dock police better known as **bulkies** because I had my ID book and could tell them I was on a boat. We were never challenged as we made our way all around the deep sea docks about two miles from were my ship the **Ulsterman** was berthed. After boarding a few wee coasters, I did all the talking, for the simple reason I didn't care if I was refused I wouldn't be taking it personal. It was Chip who wanted a job. Then we came across a wee rust bucket and I jumped down on the deck and made my way to the galley and asked for the cook. The galley was about the size of the scullery in our house or even smaller and it hardly had room for the cook never mind a galley boy. After meeting the cook I asked him did he need a galley boy and he said that he did and he could start right away as he was fed up washing all the pots and pans that lay about on the galley deck. This was the twentieth boat we had tried and it was six o'clock at night, the pool was closed and they couldn't get a crewmember. So that was an opportunity for Chip he couldn't miss. I asked the cook would he have time to go up to the house and get a bit of gear and some money but the he said that they were sailing in ten minutes and as I looked at Chip he looked despondent.

After a bit of deliberation I decided that this was the best chance he had of getting on the boats and that I would tell his Ma and Da, Paddy and Kitty that he had joined the boat and was away at sea. After all it was only a wee coaster is wasn't going far. Chip had a brother Bobby aka Fargo who was away at sea at this time so his parents would understand, I hoped. Chip agreed, a bit reluctantly and came up on deck with me and I gave him four embassy cigarettes and two bob, all the money I had on me and watched as the wee rust bucket sailed away. Chip had now joined the merchant navy and I felt good, I had done for him what Harry Doran done for me. I'll never forgot what Harry Doran done for me he was a good man.

152

Later on that week my leave was up and I re-joined **The Royal Ulsterman** and it was the football season and that meant plenty of hard work. I had to go down into the hold of the ship where years earlier when I was a kid, I had walked Henry Kane's horses into. Now I had to sell ice cream to Celtic and Rangers fans on alternative weeks and hated it. I didn't hate the work I hated the embarrassment. There I was wearing a wee white coat and carrying a tray, just like the ice cream woman in the picture houses. I did get some slagging, as I knew lots of people from both sides who travelled to the matches. There was something about being a seaman of any description in Belfast so it didn't bother me a lot; all the slagging ran off me like snow of a ditch. In ways you were held in a bit of esteem but not me, I'd become and ice cream man. I should have got a job in Victors.

One Friday night I was down selling the ice cream in the hold, yes that's were the football supporters travelled. There I met a few mates and arranged to go to the match the next day with them. It was the cup final at Hampden Park between Celtic and Aberdeen and it was played on April nineteen sixty seven and the boat was jammed packed. I think there were twelve hundred Celtic supporters on board that night.

After selling all the ice cream we had on board, about six small boxes full, I went down to my cabin to polish my seven guinea boots I bought from McManus's shoe shop in Belfast. Roy Smith and I had bought a pair each at different times from the money earned from our previous benefactor the Woodbourne Hotel when money was no option. You have to realise that in nineteen sixty-six that was a lot of money for a pair of shoes or boots. As I sat on the side of my bunk polishing them, I looked at them as my pride and joy. After nearly rubbing a hole in them I set them in my locker knowing well they would be safe after all those in the hold were Celtic supporters like me and my belongings would be safe. That night as I lay sleeping there was a lot of noise in the gangway and I was awakened to the sound of our old tin lockers being bashed open and I jumped out of my bunk and ran to awaken a few of the older stewards. It was too late my boots were gone and I later found out it was one of my mates who unwittingly stole them not knowing they were mine, but should it have mattered who owned them. A few of the older and bigger stewards done a quick look around and

Chapter 25

Finland, my first foreign port

After a few trips after the strike on The ***Royal Ulsterman*** I jacked in and was out of work, as I now wanted to go deep sea. So I arrived down at the pool handed my book over and see if I could get another ship. I had heard of the Headline Shipping Company and when Jacky Ross told me there was a job on the ***Bengore Head*** I accepted it without hesitation. I was overjoyed as they all went up the great lakes to Canada, or so I thought. I was thinking of Canada and some of the stories some other seamen had mentioned. One in particular that Malcolm Brady told was about a pub called ***Joe Beefs*** and I wanted to relive his story. Anyway I went down to the docks and found the ***Bengore Head*** and went aboard and asked for the chief steward. After he inspected my book and looked at the note that I had received in the pool I was brought up and signed on as galley boy on an old ship. It wasn't one of the newer Head boats as they were called and I was then informed that it was sailing for Dublin that night. I had just enough time to nip up home and tell my Ma I was going away for three our four weeks. After grabbing a few things some of my mates dandered down with me and I walked aboard my first deep sea or middle trade, as it was called, ship.

I then found out our first port of call was Dublin, then Helsinki, no Canada for me. Anyway we set sail that night and the cook called Andy from Carrickfergus and me set about getting the galley ship shape. He was a nice guy and had only retuned to sea after some years absence and was finding the going tough. I don't really think he was a ships cook, more of a second cook and baker. Next day after cleaning the galley from top to bottom, every pot, pan, plate, cup and saucers I was totally knackered. I then went to my cabin just across the working alleyway from the galley and fell instantly asleep. Next morning I was a wakened by the second steward as we were pulling into Dublin. I was standing in the galley freezing as Andy tried unsuccessfully to light the big stove. Anyway after some anxious minutes the stove ignited and Andy prepared his first breakfast for the crew. There's one thing you don't do and that is not to have breakfast ready on time for the crew. If you cooked or made bad grub or it was late for the watches hey would then bully you, as some of them on deck were grumpy and had sailed too long and hadn't a laugh between them. After getting breakfast over and we had ours it was time for the daily routine, prepare lunch and scrub out the galley. The next think was to peel the spuds and they were up on deck in the spud locker. So I took a bucket of water up and peeled the potatoes on deck and brought them down to Andy. As Andy prepared the food I noticed that there were no niceties on this boat like the **Ulsterman**, so it was make do with what you had. The stores, meaning food, were of a basic nature but they were ok but there was plenty to go around. Andy was a bit under pressure as he was about to start baking bread for the first time on this trip when the stores from the Dublin side came aboard and there was ample amount of bread. I don't think Andy fancied baking anyway. After lunch was prepared it was dinner that had to be cooked and this became a routine, breakfast lunch and diner and some sandwiches for the night watch.

That night as the Dublin dockers unloaded what cargo we had left from a previous trip I went ashore with about six pounds in my pocket that I had subbed that day. I was sort of lost in the big city of Dublin and found an amusement arcade and met an English kid about the same age and height as me. We went for a pint and then went into the arcade and blew whatever money we had left, as we pursued the hope of winning some money. It was to become in later years another of my addictions that I had to deal with, gambling. After exchanging names and address as you did in those great days of meeting people and making friends we parted company as I walked back to the ship, skint, with the Belfast feeling that you had late at night, starving. I had encountered my first addiction gambling and I pumped all of my money into the machines that night and escaped into oblivion. When I arrived back on the ship I got a cup of tea and something to eat of the night watches plate as it was called and turned in and thought about what if and what if an and what if and fell asleep through shear mental exhaustion.

Next morning I was up and some of the able-bodied seamen or ABs as they are called, asked me to go and do a bet for them in the bookies shop before we sailed. Dublin would be our first port of call on the way back so if they won they could collect any winning due to them. I had got another sub and I asked the AB that sent me if could I join in but he was a grumpy fucker and said that boy ratings weren't allowed to gamble. Little did he know I was gambling most of my life, in some form or another? By this stage I probably knew more about backing horses than he did. Anyway I went and done their bet, a Yankee, paid the tax for them on the bet, as this was part of my job and returned with the docket.

About an hour or so later we let go from the berth in Dublin and sailed for Helsinki, somewhere I had only read about. After getting lunch over and diner prepared I went up on deck and watched as we slowly left the shores of Ireland behind us and I wondered again what if and what if, as we steamed out into the Irish Sea. That night the bond on the ship opened - the bond is the place where the duty free cigarettes and drink are kept. We formed a queue in orderly fashion to get our duty free allowance from the chief steward. Mine was two hundred Pall Mall the all American fag of my dreams that years before I had tapped off American sailors when they visited Belfast. Two cans of beer or Guinness and that was I, as happy as a lark. Just to be on the safe side I chose the Guinness but it was rotten. It was made for the South African market and it was like treacle and much sweeter than normal Guinness. So after that it was two cans of larger for me. I suppose they helped me get to sleep as I have pointed out, I had difficulty sleeping. I was what if, merchant, that can bring some strange thoughts to ones head for the uninitiated.

All in all I was happy except for the fact that someone got the results and the Deck Hands better known as Abs bet touched and it ran into about a hundred and twenty quid and I wasn't in on it. I cursed that AB and some forty years later he told someone I didn't talk to him because he didn't buy me a drink, the lying bastard. He never really could look me in the eye after that but I soon forgot about it as I had more on my mind for this big world.

After about six days at sea the trip became quite enjoyable, but imagine you're up on deck in the pitch black of night and you can't see nothing only a group of lights like little Christmas trees sparkling all over the place. It's an eerie feeling and as a kid it could be quite scary but all you had to do was go below decks and into the comfort of your bunk. About a day out of Helsinki I was up on deck in the afternoon and saw the biggest ship I had ever seen in my life sailing close to us. It was a sixty thousand ton tanker and it was heading straight for us about a hundred yards away. The next thing I remember is our captain on the loud hailer shouting the rules of the sea at the oncoming ship that would have cut us in half like a pound of butter if we collided. As the captain kept shouted orders through the public address system I was asking deck hands the weight and so on of the tanker and one said if it doesn't change course you will feel the weight of it. As it got closer we started to change course as our captain shouted frantically at what he called a stupid so and so who wasn't aware of the naval procedure for passing another ship. Suddenly the tanker pulled hard to starboard and we pulled hard to port. A collision was avoided and we sailed on our merry way to our next port of call in Finland. That afternoon we tied up in Helsinki but for some reason there was no shore leave. So all we could do was watch as the dockers unload first and then reload us with Formica the miracle wood of the day. I sat and watched two apprentice officers as they got the hatches undone and got the steam winches up and running on the boat. The dockers were mostly women who looked like men but in some cases were very attractive. I wanted to go ashore in Helsinki. After all the Olympic games had taken place there and it was somewhere I could say I was.

The next day we set sail for Kotka and a day later we tied up and were assured we could go ashore that night. After we wiped down the term at sea, for having finished work I had a shower and got on my whistle and flute and we all headed for the local nightspot.

Nightspots usually are big entertainment centres but this one was a bar type café so you can forget any grandeur. It was a large room with some music, a few locals and that was it? The second steward didn't come with us that night as he had been invited to a family's home for a sauna. I wondered what a sauna was and when I asked him what it was he told me it was a steam bath synonymous with Finland. I was confused. Here we were doing what seamen usually do, hitting the nearest hotspot and he was away for a bath.

Although Finland was a democratic country it still had the feel of a communist country, what with the female dockers and every thing else it seemed so far adrift from my world back in the Falls road in Belfast. Finland was cold just like the early mornings in the bad winters in Belfast, dark, very little light, and very uninspiring, but the people were nice and warm which was a sort of paradox. It was a nice country bordering on the Baltic Sea and that was it in reality, no flash and no dash to put it mildly. After a few days on the Finland coast we set sail for home.

Some time later we tied up in Belfast. I couldn't wait to get ashore and go home and tell the tale of my first deep-sea trip abroad. This was the only way guys from around our corner could see the world. I had started my journey, all be it, in one of the coldest places I had ever been, but it was a nice experience and I could now understand the second steward going for a sauna, as the people were very hospitable. After signing off and getting my pay off, or wages I went and made ready to leave the ship. I had hidden an extra four hundred cigarettes from the customs in the spud locker on the top deck and as soon as the customs left I packed them into my suitcase and headed for the dock gates to get a taxi home. I had a few pounds and a few wee presents for my Ma and some for my kid brother and sisters. I had seen a part of the world, not bad for a wee lad from the Fall's whose Da had never been out of Ireland. Back home after a few days leave things returned to normal and I have to say I was glad to get back to my Ma's cooking after all it was better than Andy's or should I say the Head Line rations. But then I always thought my Ma was a magician in the kitchen cooking for twelve of us with little or no money.

The next ship or boat I joined, we called it going on the boats and the Liverpool lads called it going on the ships and we all had all our own way of describing life at sea in our own parochial way. It was **The Orwell Fisher.** The captain of the Orwell would be murdered in later years as he drank ashore in a Belfast bar minding his own business. It was a nice new container ship and ran up the Manchester ship canal and delivered containers for the home trade. It was a nice crew and I was the galley boy cum captain's batman and that entailed making his bunk or bed up in the morning after having brought him his tea and toast on a tray all for the princely sum of five pound fourteen shillings a week, plus the a similar amount for over time.

By this time sleepless nights had become more frequent and drink had worked its way more into my life. It was the fourteenth of august, nineteen sixty-nine the night that was to change this country forever. Peter Patterson, who came from Derry and me were watching television in the saloon or mess room of the ship in Larne. We watched in amazement, just as I have watched hundreds of times since, the burning of Conway Street by loyalist mobs. I was shouting and effing them as if they could hear me on the television. One guy an ex army man, a crewmember who worked down below in the engine room said something derogatory to Peter and me. Peter who was a bit bigger than me told him to mind his own business and I called him an English bastard and he cowed down and Peter and me left him alone after the six o'clock news had ended. A few hours later Peter and me went for a drink and I wore the first pair of flared trousers I had ever worn and I thought I was the bee's knee that night.

As we dandered up the town in Larne for a drink I was still thinking of Belfast as we walked past the police barracks and headed to a pub called Robinsons. After a few drinks I noticed a guy originally from Varna Street. His family were one of the first sea faring families from our district. His name was Jooker Mitchell and I had remembered him from when I was a kid running in and out of his house going messages for his Ma who was a lady. After a few drinks just as I was going to approach Jooker a fellow crew member advised us that we may be in the wrong pub and after a quiet deliberation we left and sought out some where else for a drink. As we passed the police barracks a few hours latter things had changed since we passed earlier, we noticed the B specials. They now had built a sand bag emplacement and had a bren gun mounted and I wondered was this normal for Larne at the weekends. As we walked by the picture house about ten o'clock the pubs were now closed but someone informed us we would get a drink in the hall not far away and there was a dance going on as well. What more would one want, a dance, a late night drink, so we made haste and made or way slightly intoxicated to the hall that turned out to be the local Orange Hall. Well, there was no drink and very few women and after a cup of tea and no drink available we decided it was time to go back to ship and get a drink. After hitting the sack I woke up the next morning in Belfast tied up in our usual berth but things were different. I signed off the **Orwell Fisher,** as I couldn't forget the scenes I saw on television the night before. As I made my way to the Fall's Road I couldn't get a bus or taxi so I made my way up Castle Street, along Durham Street and entered into a completely different place I had left some weeks previous.

Albert Street was like a war zone and the first person I encountered was one of the big Gillen twins who looked at me with my wee suitcase. I asked him what the score was and he told me that the whole district was barricaded in and to watch myself as I made my way home. Belfast would never be the same, for me, or for anyone else for that matter. The war or troubles had started and there was no turning back. After dumping my wee suit case in the house and asking what happened I made my way to Osman Street, the hub of our district as it bordered on most of what I perceived as the more important streets, as far as we were concerned anyway. When I went around the corner there was a certain amount of trepidation, as I didn't really know the score and what had happened. But like everything else I shoe horned my self into the new way of life which unknown to me, or others, was going to last a very long time. I was back and quickly joined the siege mentality. In fact, this was a reality we were going to live under a siege mentality for a while.

Being Osman Street and thinking we were the best at most things, we also had the best barricade hut. A round aluminium watchman's hut spirited away from The Belfast Corporation yard in Willow Street. It was one similar to the hut a watchman and I had sat in years ago and passed the night listening to stories that he told and warming myself at his coke fire, as we both coughed and spluttered from the fumes arising from it. After finding out from the lads all that I had missed, I settled into the hut and joined the gang. Scobie Dempsey, Josey Riley, Sam Walsh, Francey Riley, we were the young gang, and the older gang better known as the awkward squad consisted of the unofficial leader Gerry Peezer Ward, Jim The Other O'Riley,

162

Liam Willie Dark McMahon, Joe Johnah Mc Nerny, Robert Docky McCartney my elder brother, Charley Noggin Ward, John Chang Mc Manus, Paul McCorry, Andy Fennel jnr and a few others.

Our hut was situated outside Willie Darks Ma's shop at the corner of Sultan and Osman Street and was the hub of activity, mostly of it the wrong kind. We had the transistor radio to listen to. Free Belfast radio which was being broadcast from the shoe makers shop in Cyprus street next to the back door to the Long bar which ran from Leeson Street to Cyprus street. The long bar was owned by Paddy Leneghan who was the father of president Mary Mc Aleese and was a hive of activity. It was also a great short cut when being pursued by anyone. You could enter by Leeson Street and exit by Cyprus Street, thus saving a long walk thus evading anyone who was in hot pursuit. Belfast Free Radio was situated next door to the long bar in Cyprus street and you could get requests played. You just walked around and shouted in your request. Time and time again our requests went unanswered as we always asked for the same song. *Little Old Wine Drinker Me* by Dean Martin that was synonymous with our district as most of us drank cheap wine at one time or another. Being the type of guys we were meant we didn't jell much with the Leeson Street crowd. Except those who may have went to school with us or maybe sailed with us. The Leeson Street crowd looked upon us as renegades, which in time would lead to friction between our two areas that were only a hundred yards apart. So every time they played *Little Old Wine Drinker Me* in between Irish songs, we felt that it was our signature tune. We all joined in and sang as loud as we could thus make a general racket. One night we were all sitting in our hut talking and slabbering about what was happening when a bearded Che Guevara look-a-like walked in with a Thompson sub machine gun slung over his shoulder.

He asked for a guy by name and told us the same guy had twenty-four hours to leave all republican areas or he would be shot on sight. He went on to warn us of our behaviour and general rowdiness and warned us we would be in big trouble if it continued. He also made reference to the wine that was drunk in around our hut, or on the barricades. Who was he kidding? That was like cutting a lifeline of to our lads. Then Scobie Dempsey asked Big Peezer what he had in his inside pocket just to get a mix going. He kept hitting Peezer on the chest just were Peezer had secreted his half bottle of three keys wine, snuggling in his inside pocket. Peezer exclaimed that it was a book and without further ado the Che look-a-like left. The strange thing was that the guy who they had threatened later became a leading member of the stickies or the official IRA after having fled for about two weeks.

One night around by Leeson Street, Jim Lord Leeson as we called him or Solo as his people called him announced from the back of a lorry, "When on duty on the barricades everyone must be on their guard and question all persons, on foot or in a car, that encroached into the district. No matter who they were, they were to be stopped and questioned." Little did he know we would hold him to his word, right to the last letter of it.

A couple of nights later Scobie arrived at the barricade with a pickaxe handle with a load of nails hammered into the head of it. A real cruel looking weapon that said what it was for without explanation. We sat in the hut talking and singing among ourselves after we had lay in bed all day. We were all night owls. Suddenly we spotted two men walking along Sultan Street towards us. Scobie and me and some of the boys jumped out and asked the two men to identify themselves and give us the password. It was Jim Sullivan wearing a wig but we knew rightly and told him to get up against the wall. We gave him and his friend a quick once over. He protested loudly but we told him we were only carrying out his explicit instructions and he was no different from anyone else. After some deliberation we let them go and retired to the hut and had a good laugh but within ten minutes a car pulled up in the middle of Sultan and Osman Street and a man about fifty who we later found out was from Lady street called us over. As we poked our head in the car he pointed a Luger at us and told us not be so smart in the future. He also advised us that we would be as well to evacuate our barricade. We ran up to a big Citroen DS car parked outside Charley Wards house were Peezer was sleeping behind the wheel. As we knocked on the window he wound it down and sheepishly asked what was wrong. We then accused him of being asleep and he made one of the greatest statements of the troubles." How could I be sleeping while there's a war going on, I was only resting my eyes."? After recounting what had happened

Peezer got out of the car and became very busy and headed down to the hut to await any further developments.

Around breakfast time Willie Darks Ma opened the shop and as usual gave us some tea and crumpets and Paris buns. As we drank our tea and discussed what happened we headed home for bed as our night shift on the barricade was over. Later to our surprise when we came back to the corner that night our hut was gone. Confiscated by Jim Sullivan's IRA men. That didn't thwart us and we continued to stand at the same point and make the same racket as before, minus one watchman's hut. That night Scobie and me were playing hurling with a big bone and some hurls when I hit it and it went right through Virginia Ward's bedroom window. That was more trouble as Virginia explained that the large bone just missed one of her kids as they slept in their bed. After we told some lies they accepted that it wasn't us who threw the bone through her window. The trouble had now begun to settle as each district in Belfast developed a territorial mindset. Life returned temporarily to something like normality and I then got itchy feet and decided it was time for me to set sail again.

Chapter 26

Joining the Southern Cross

It was the Whitsun holiday when Desi Rogan and me arrived in the **Hamp** as we called it, expecting to see all the older lads from our district who had been shipping out for years from the there. It was a public holiday unknown to us and there was no one around. After a nights kip in a friends house, we went to the pool the next morning and lined up to get a job among the unemployed seamen. I'd never seen as many seamen in the one place in my life. After queuing for about an hour Desi and me finished up getting a job on the **Alonia**, a Cunard container ship. When we boarded the boat to sign on we were met by two guys from the union office I was then informed that I should be shipping out as a rating not a boy rating. After some discussion it was agreed that I do one trip to France on the **Alonia** along with my mate and it would be all sorted out when we came back. After signing on I thought, I'm near twenty by now and still hadn't got my rating but the union man called Hilary Paddmore assured me that he would have a job for me as a rating when we came back off the **Alonia**. So I signed on for a seven-day trip. The day we signed on her we met one of the most charismatic seamen I had ever met. Terry, "Cockney Terry" Downs was his name and I never forgot him. He knew everyone in Belfast although he was from London. He had visited Belfast many times and had been to the jig, one of the best-known dance halls in town. He told us stories about his time in Belfast and you'd have thought he was born there. He was a good friend of Boko Brown and a lot of other well-known Belfast seamen. Terry was about fifty-five, but he dressed like the all American boy of the fifties. The bomber jacket and Levi jeans accompanied by a pair of baseball boots or sneakers and full of wise cracks.

That night we sailed for Calais and I got drunk in a nice little pig aboard the ship. I was wearing a sweatshirt and scrubbed out wranglers and I was smoking a Pall Mall. What else? I was a real seaman now, or so I thought. Then I flaked out drunk and was awakened abruptly. My sweatshirt was on fire. The cloth was so dry that the cigarette had fallen on it and it went up in flames. Luckily I awoke and put it out. My chest suffered just a little scorching but it was very small, my chest that is, so I wasn't seriously hurt.

A week later we were back in the **Hamp** and true to his word Hilary had got both of us our rating and a job in the plate house on **The Southern Cross**, a passenger liner belonging to the Shaw Savill Line shipping company. Getting your rating meant you were now getting adult wages and treated as one. A few hours later we went aboard **The Southern Cross** and learned quickly of its unlikely nickname of "The Suffering Cross." When I joined **The Royal Ulsterman,** a few years earlier I thought what a big ship it was and it took me about a week to find my way around it. But the colloquial or euphemistically titled "The Cross" was ten or twenty times larger than the **Ulsterman**. When we went to sign on I had never witnessed anything like this in my life. Desi and me queued up in the first class saloon behind a hundred or so guys to sign on and get our advance note. **The Bengore Head** seemed like a barge in my mind now, compared to the "The Cross" with its working alleyways some hundred feet long. It's public rooms and dining rooms the like I had never seen before. There were hundreds of people walking about, painters, carpet layers, plumbers, electricians, and every other tradesman one could imagine. After about fifteen minutes we found our way to the dining room or the saloon as it was called and signed ships articles as others signed off. This was to be the longest trip to sea I would ever undertake. The trip was to last three months and as I signed on I thought, three months away from home and on a strange ship as big as a town that sailed the oceans of the world.

As we made our way to our cabins I met some of the old crew as they made their way ashore after doing the same trip that we were embarking on. The ship carried immigrants, better known as **ten-pound poms** among other things to Australia and New Zealand. Some of the old crew were friends of mine, Charley and Noel McKiernan and they quickly told us the score and who to watch out for and so on. They also told to me that I was joining a mad ship and to watch myself and to make my mark right away and not to get bullied. I wasn't really that worried as Desi and me were mates and we would look after each other, not like hard men, but we were streetwise. As

Charley and his brother Noel made there way ashore we took over their old cabin and wondered what happens next. This was a new world to Desi and myself. We had never been on a ship of this magnitude but had heard many stories about it, as we stood at the corners in Belfast. As we waited with bated breath for instructions from one of the bosses we decided to have a look around the ship. Six bunks to a cabin; showers were across the alleyway and it all seemed sound. As other crewmembers joined us for a pow wow we all picked our bunks and we held on to the same bunk for the whole of the trip. Some had been on the ship before and told us what we needed to know, well all that they thought we needed to know.

A boss arrived and we were told we had to turn too the next morning at seven thirty for breakfast. We could now go and change our advance note or sub to get some gear before we sailed. As we lined up to get the sub among what seemed hundreds of men I wondered what was this going to be like when it was all up and running and sailing around the world. So many men and women crewmembers, how would it all gel? After getting an advance note for a fiver we went ashore to find someone to get it changed and there were no shortage of people willing to give some kindly advice. I had been staying with my cousin Anthony Walsh and he told me to go across the road to the supply shop and he may give me four quid for the advance note instead of having to buy work clothes as all I needed in the plate house was jeans and tee shirts and the ship had its own laundry.

The mind boggled, the ship had its own laundry and he went on to list the things it had. A cinema, a couple of swimming pools and there would be plenty of plates to wash. Well I had washed the plates on the Ulsterman in the big deep sink so I was ok for that or so I thought. I maybe washed along with Billy Greer about a hundred plates per passenger sitting but this was going to be different. I thought it would be a synch as they had a dish washing machine on *The Cross*. Was I in for a shock? After changing the advance note we had a cup of tea and a rock cake in the Criterion café then we made our way to the Bunch Of Grapes pub for a session. The first drink I ever had in England was with my cousin Anthony Walsh and it was called a boilermaker that was sweet and easy to get down. Little did I know that you got evicted at two o'clock in the afternoon from the pubs in England

168

and that was to be one of the main reasons I never stayed there very long? Unknowing to me the pubs closed in the afternoon and this meant that you had to go home sleep it off or find a shebeen or some other place for a drink. Any way Desi and me wanted to meet and see some of the people and places we had heard of at Osman Street corner as we were growing up. One place was Gaddies, a pub in Southampton high street that we had heard so much about. So we decided to go and have something to eat then go back to the ship and get dressed for Gaddies.

Our first stop that night was the Stewards Arms, a great pub where I watched in fascination as Walsh as he was affectionately known played a football machine. He was like Pele. I had never seen one of these machines in my life and as the jukebox blasted out my favourite songs I felt like I was in heaven. There was only one pub in Belfast that had a jukebox when I was a kid and it was the infamous Dubarry's and it was where you went when looking for a lady of the night and I hadn't reached that stage. I literally fell in love with the pubs in the Hamp with their music, women and beer. What more could a man ask for.

Our next stop was the Horse and Groom another infamous pub were I met my first real lesbian who dressed as man and looked at me as if to say, "Who the fuck are you looking at?" This was all new to me and I suppose part of growing up and anyway I had Walsh as my protector with me. He told me what to drink and how much, well for a couple of days anyway as I found my sea legs so to speak. Some time later Desi and I made our way to Gaddies as Walsh had declined but told me to be in before twelve, as he felt obliged to look after me. After all he was my big cousin. I reminded him I was now sleeping on board the *Cross*-as we left him drinking his pint. As Desi and me walked into Gaddies pub I thought, what a pub. There was nothing like it in Belfast, not even in the same ballpark. This was what Belfast was missing. As the music blared out I felt right at home. This was all I ever dreamt about, wine, woman and song. At this time Belfast men really ran this town, you could even say they owned it. There propping up the bar was Pasha who I had went camping with a few years previously. Anthony McGreevy and some other Cunard yanks as we called them stood there posing and looking at themselves in the bar mirrors just in case their hair may have moved out of place, even though it was well oiled with brylcreem. There was no chance of their hair getting wrecked as it rested lightly on the collar of their High Boy Rolls, the shirt that made the Belfast man look like an American.

After introducing ourselves to Pasha who I really thought should have remembered me, after all he had slept in the same bed as me in Servia Street when he ran about with my older brother Paddy. He had literally lived in our house when he was young. I became somewhat annoyed that he didn't remember me or was he being economical with the truth. After all, he had only been away a few years at this time, not a lifetime like Idler Kelly, a Belfast man I came to know and much like in Southampton. He had been there for a lifetime. After a few drinks Desi and I left and headed back to the ship, which was now going to be our new home for the next twelve weeks.

The next morning we were awakened by a guy, who was called a glory hole steward, don't ask me why but that was his title. In Belfast he would have been called a rapper upper. As he awakened us we got ready and made our way to the mess room and after about fifteen minutes running about we couldn't find the place. As we stopped and asked guys where the stewards mess was we got sent one way then another until we found it quite by accident. In side there was plenty of cereals and jugs of milk and I thought, are they feeding an army here or what. After finishing our breakfast of some cereal, bacon and eggs, and fruit juice I pondered and thought, "this is the fucking life." A little later Desi and I made our way to the galley to find where we would be working and what we had to do. A boss met us and showed us how to work the plate machine and it wasn't really meant to wash anything else and I thought this would be a breeze and then he told us that there was a fore and aft plate house and Desi should go to one and me to the other. After an hour or so messing about with the machine, a guy called Raymond Black appeared and told me he would be working along side me in the aft plate house. He was a typical Carrickhill man, small and robust. Carrickhill was the district my father had been born in and I knew it quite well and had heard stories about it and how about how my Da's uncle and child had been murdered in their bed in nineteen twenty

170

two. After a little interrogation I learned that Raymond who we came to affectionately call Dinky was a cousin of Kevin Davies one of the celebrity type guys we had heard so many stories about. Kevin was a Tony Curtis look alike, as we say a ringer for him. I had met him a few days earlier in the seaman's mission as I watched him playing snooker. He really was a fine looking guy who had the women drooling over him like lots of other Belfast guys in the Hamp. So Dinky was okay and as we set about learning the workings of the plate house and washed some cutlery we both thought this was going to be one long cruise. As the day went on I became accustomed to the machine. I decided that I would load the plate machine and Dinky would empty it, after all I was there first. Every thing went well and we went our separate ways after lunch and I went ashore and Dinky went to see his uncle Kevin.

That afternoon I met Walsh and he and I went into the laundry come dry cleaners at the corner of Latimer Street to collect my suit. Behind the counter was a real good-looking girl called Carmel and she smiled at me and then at Walsh. After a bit of a slagging match between her and him as I looked on, I wondered what was happening. Being young I looked at Carmel and thought "wouldn't I just", as Walsh asked me the question I had been thinking and I replied in an Americanised statement, "You better believe it." After collecting my laundry and my now dry cleaned suit we walked towards the pub and Walsh asked me what I thought of Carmel. I replied in no uncertain terms " she's great". Walsh told me to leave my laundry in the pub and to follow him over to the laundry again. I duly obliged and we walked back towards the laundry again and as we entered Walsh said something funny but derogatory to Carmel and everything changed and my world came tumbling down. She or as I knew now, was a he. Carmel answered in a deep voice and told Anthony and me where to go. In two days I had learned two important things. One, some one that dresses like a man may not be one and because someone looks like a woman don't take it for granted. What you see is not what you get. I think Walsh had put me on a learning curve in life, as the merchant navy held some surprises and I think he knew I needed to be aware of such things.

Chapter 27

We are sailing

The next day our sister ship the Northern Star was tied up along side of us and I went aboard and met my neighbour and friend Hughie Clarke who had come back to sea after a few years sabbatical and we had a cup of tea in his mess room and he told me all about my trip that lay ahead. He had done the same trip all be it on different ships, but he new the score. The next thing Joe Scobie Dempsey, and Billy Judas Nolan appeared like lost children on the horizon and as we greeted them Hughie got them something to eat immediately. They had come over to get a boat but hadn't any luck and were a bit on the down side. After eating and yarning I said I would try and get them a job on *The Cross* and I told Judas who was younger than me that I may get him a job in the laundry as a new found friend of mine was laundry manager. He looked at me and asked do they have a laundry on the ship? What do they have a few washing machines and I assured him it was a full working laundry just like the Globe or Franklin laundry back home.

In my few days on board *The Cross* I had become friendly with the laundry manager, a scouse guy called Billy Kilcourse and his mate Mick Browne, but we were sailing the next day so I had to work fast and we left immediately for the ship. I went and talked to Billy and Mick and they told me they would keep the job open till the last minute and Judas would get a pier head jump literally. After a lot of running around we secured the job for Judas but couldn't get Scobie a job but we thought it was only a matter of time for him as most of his brothers were at sea and were well liked and informed of what was going down. Our last night in port was spent in Gaddies bar listening to The Who, The Small Faces, and the Beatles of course. There was also an iconic and very profound song playing regular, Thunderclap Newman's *Something in the Air*. Read or listen to the lyrics of this song which was released in July nineteen sixty nine, unfortunately I cant copy the lyrics but its so much of its time, Belfast time. It was like a pre cursor of what was to come in the great city of Belfast. As other rock songs belted out and the sounds filtered through the crowd from the famous Roc Ola jukebox, I was getting drunker. I again wondered would it all go well, would we actually sail next morning or would we get the sack. We had been told the turn over in crew was quite big even while *The Cross* was in dock. So we returned to the ship and got something to eat from the night plate. This was left out for sailors on watch, ham cheese and some bread. It was great, you got food literally on demand and as we lashed it into us as drunken men do, we then made our way to our cabin for a nights sleep.

The next day we awoke and it was sailing day. We were going to be off in an hour or so and me being me was still a bit apprehensive about how fate dealt me a bad hand, or was it. I waited patiently for the sound of the ships horns as *The Cross* blew for tugs. I was irritable and discontent all my life and it was now starting to show. "What if" There in front of me, was the gun port doors, they were open and I could jump and land on the quayside but I wanted this trip more than anything in my life, at that time. The gun port doors were large openings on the side of the ship, used for loading stores and such like but we were to use them for other things later in the trip. Dumping rubbish and when the plates got too much for us those as well.

The Southern Cross was like no other ship and was the first passenger ship to have the engines built in the after end so providing much more comfort for the passengers but they forgot about the crew. The passengers were more commonly known as bloods but they were not tipping passengers so they weren't really bloods that had plenty of money and cruised half the year. She looked majestic with her art nouveau exterior and art deco interior and at fourteen years old the ship was as new as the day she done her maiden voyage in nineteen fifty-five. She was built in my hometown by Harland and Wolff and was something of a triumph with her futuristic design. She had air-conditioning in all her passenger cabins, but what about us the crew. We didn't have it and our cabins were like sweat boxes later on as we went to sunnier climes. All her public rooms had it as well and the lights in the passenger cabins came on dimly at first light in the morning, thus giving the effect of sunrise. Pity we had none of those luxuries. We had to make do with a six-berth cabin in the front of the ship, the forecastle head. This was at the bows of the ship were all the noise happened as the ship ploughed through the seas. She was twenty thousand tons and carried a little over a thousand passengers and a crew of near four hundred, the mind boggled. Where were they all going to eat sleep and make merry. Well I was to get the answers as I came to know the ship better. There were three swimming pools, two out doors on deck, and one in doors. It also had a cinema, dance hall, two restaurants or saloons as they were called, one fore and the other aft. This was a floating town of its time and I had never seen anything like it but had heard many stories of adventures and how twenty of the crew mostly from Belfast jumped ship in Australia and New Zealand some years previous.

She was also known as a troublesome ship, meaning she was crewed by guys who had received DRs from other ships. When you received a DR in your discharge book it meant a captain had declined to give a report on your behaviour and it was taken as a bad reference. It made it difficult to obtain work on other ships and here I was on a ship that had lots of DRs among the crew and also gave a lot of them out. As I looked out the gun port door I watched in amazement at the comings and going of people, shore side crew, passengers, or people bidding there loved ones a bon voyage or farewell. There were fathers, mothers, grandfathers, uncles and aunts all looking on and probably thinking they would never see there loved ones again. They were sailing for far of lands, Australia, New Zealand and South Africa beckoned, for this ship was a mass transporter of people in search of a new and exciting life offered to them in shiny brochures littered all over the country. These were some of our ports of call and to me it was the only way I had a chance of visiting them but one wonders how many or what percentage of the people that emigrated to these countries stayed.

As the festival like hullabaloo was taking place on the quayside, some of the crew were been being waved at by there loved ones who had come to see them off as the band played. Suddenly a large rope fell splashing into the water, then another, there was no turning back now as we nudged ever so slightly from the now crowded quayside of Southampton docks. We were gone. I ran up onto the deck to have a better look. You couldn't get sacked now and I looked at the fanfare as we pulled away and I wondered again, what if. I said to myself, "what the fuck if, we are gone, we were sailing now, wise up." That was another great American saying adopted by our lads around our corner. Then I thought this would be fun so make the best of it. It was the twenty-fifth of September nineteen sixty nine; the troubles back home had abated albeit for a short time. I was on my way around the world not in eighty days but just a little more eighty-three.

That night I visited the Pig after washing more plates than my Ma had ever washed in her whole lifetime and there were twelve in total in our family. I made my way to the meeting place to see whom I knew among the crew. First I had to acquire my pint pot and it was on a first come first served basis and I got my first pint of the worst beer I ever tasted in my life, "Allsopps" or as it became quickly known as "all slops". I settled down to enjoy a well-earned pint and was joined by Desi and we sat together. After an hour or so Desi decided to turn in as we had an early start next morning. I wasn't bothered about turning in, as I knew I either had to get drunk or lay awake all-night. The next fellow I met in the pig was Tommy "Rocky" Magee a deck hand. Then Barney Sullivan joined the company and we got to know each other. Rocky and Barney were what I called real seamen and had been going to sea most of their adult life. After getting some gen on how it all worked at sea from Rocky and Barney I decided I would turn in and get ready for a busy day tomorrow. We had washed the cutlery for one sitting today what was it going to be like when things were in full flow, breakfast, lunch, and dinner, and the odd afternoon tea thrown in.

Next morning our glory hole, called us all. It was time for the plate men, Desi, Dinky and myself and some English guy, so we headed for breakfast. There was plenty on offer, bacon, eggs, sausages, and plenty of cereals and toast and this all seemed great. So after a nice bit of breakfast we headed for our work stations Dinky and me in the aft and Desi in the fore plate houses. As I started our machine up I decided I would load and my partner would scrape the plates and stack them up for me so as I could drill them through the machine and he would take them off clean and stack them away. As waiter after waiter returned from the restaurant with what seemed never ending plates, cups and saucers, and side-plates, I wondered when would this ever end. After breakfast was over we done our scrub out which entailed helping to wash down all our stainless steel presses and then scrub the deck and then we could go and have a wee kip and prepare for lunch. As we made our way down below I asked Desi, as he had already been deep sea hence the nick name "Desi Deep." Was this all the passengers done on board, eat and sleep. Desi just laughed and told me we would be in Las Palmas in a couple of days and just to take it as it comes.

A couple of days later I had got the hang of letting the plates do the work as I lifted them six or seven at a time and let them roll into the plate washing machine tray without a hiccup. The bosses didn't like this as in some cases it damaged the rim of the plates so it was only done when they weren't about. That was for a wee while anyway, after a few days it was "fuck them." I'm doing it my way. Next day we would be in Las Palmas in the Canaries with some shore leave and a bit of drinking and anything else that came to mind.

The night before I had been talking to a guy called Rooney from Norfolk Street and he told me that he was doing his first trip back to sea after some years ashore. As we talked about the events of the previous month and how his house was so close to the **pogroms** inflicted on our community by loyalist mobs accompanied by the RUC and the B specials, he told me it was a real bad night and his family were close to being burned out as well. His street bordered on the Streets that were burned. Next morning as we pulled into the port I saw a beautiful sunny place like nothing I ever saw before and thought here's number one on the itinerary and wondered would I receive some mail but then I thought I'm only away a meal hour. As I peered out the porthole in the plate house I could feel the heat, which was now reaching the nineties in the galley I couldn't wait to get ashore. I was about to discover a world that I had never seen before. A few hours later I was in a pub along with the guy Rooney from Norfolk Street and I asked first for a glass of water and the barmaid informed me after I drank it that it was ten pesetas so the next drink was a seaman's special, a Bacardi and coke. After a few I wandered around some other pubs and some guys visited the yellow doors as they were called. I declined thinking I won't be paying for it. I was too young to have to visit a lady of the night or in this case a lady of the day. After getting a few drinks maybe even a few too many some of us headed back to the ship and started work as we prepared for our next port, Cape Town in South Africa. Sometimes I didn't know if it was New Year or New York and just got on with it all. It was a ten-day trip at sea to South Africa. Las Palmas was really only a bunker port for taking on cheaper oil and stores but being from Belfast it was like heaven, a new world but what would South Africa be like?

During the next seven days at sea my drinking got worse and the ships doctor prescribed me Valium. In later years I would hear it mentioned on a daily routine but simply called by its trade name Roche. As I left the doctor, a young man who probably had just qualified, with a little package of wee yellow tablets with the instructions that I take one in the morning and one at night. I didn't give it a second thought as to what type of medication it was I just wanted a good night sleep and be able to turn my bunk light off in the cabin and let others get to sleep as well. I was laying awake at night listening to my heart beat like the thunder of galloping horses that I watched as a kid in western films, or the sound of Thunderclap Newman. Thump, thump, then a miss, and I was only nineteen what did the future hold?

The one thing I never blamed it on was drink but nearly every job I had before and after this, I lost through drink. Anyway things on board I started to settle and I enquired about the guy Rooney and was told he was one of about twenty who had missed the ship in Las Palmas. All the other Belfast men had got back all right and it was time to get my head down and get on with washing plates and try and enjoy the trip.

The next few days the weather was fantastic and it was the warmest I had ever experienced and every afternoon we went to the forecastle head to bronzy. There I met a guy called Hugh Mc Geown who was holding his hands out and peering over the bows and I got talking to him. His theory was that his hands and face were the only places he needed bronzed, as its all people would see. I nodded and I had made a new friend on board. That night in the pig all the Belfast men got together as they usually do and I think Rocky became our leader even though he didn't know it or act it out. Another guy joined our company, Christy Hughes from Greencastle outside Belfast. The group was starting to grow. Then another guy joined, Joe Fireworks McMullan and the two-scouce guys, who ran the laundry, Mick Browne, and Billy Kilcource. The gang was complete. Most worked in different departments, Rocky on deck, Christy in the saloon, Joe was the lift operator, Barney worked down below in the engine room for a while, Judas in the laundry, and Dinky, Desi, Hugh, and me in the galley. There were a few other Belfast lads who didn't bother much and just got on with their work, the last thing on my mind. For ten days it was work, drink, bronzy, eat and sleep when possible. I never turned-in in the afternoon as most seamen did I wanted to sleep at night so I ran about the ship or lay up on deck listening to music.

After a few days at sea the weather was great and I spent some time in the crew swimming pool, a large square box affair lined with canvas. It was opened for us so we could cool of as the heat reached the nineties. The next day was Cape Town and as I went asleep I wondered what this big city was going to be like. I woke early and went up on deck and we seemed to be sailing under the Tablet top Mountain. A sight I never witnessed before. It was surreal, it was like the ship was sailing into the mountain and as I looked to port side I noticed ships beached on rocks and when I looked to starboard, that's left and right for the uninitiated, I saw similar ships sitting perched on cragged rocks. Having discussed a few nights before with my mates it was decided we would go to the Spurs Club in Cape Town, the first place most seamen went to for *entertainment* and to drink some cape brandy. That night we headed to the Spurs Club and it was something else. I had never experienced anything like it but as soon as I walked in I was in heaven or so I thought. The bar stools were made with a cowboy or western saddle seat. I then realised how it got its name. Before we had gone ashore a notice had been placed in our mess room and it warned of the consequences of mixing with the African people or more to the point the blacks. A term of two years in prison was the penalty for being caught in flagrante with a black or Cape Coloured female. It was their country and we couldn't associate with them. What a joke, but more was to be revealed when we went ashore.

Chapter 28

Apartheid in South Africa

After we tied up, the ship was suddenly filled with blacks trying to etch out a living by doing my job or anyone else's job and all they wanted was the food that came back from the restaurant. For that they would do your job for you. I had just come from a country filled with hate, sectarianism, and gerrymandering, but what I would witness here would blow me away. When we went ashore and walked on the cribby (sic) or sidewalk, or footpath, take your pick. I noticed signs on the flagstones saying whites only. This meant that the poor blacks were only allowed to walk on the street nearest the road. That was bad, this was apartheid. This was a modern country were the native inhabitants had no say in the day to day running and in fact were treated a little, but just a little, better than slaves. I was young and on reflection it resonated with me, but what could I do about it. On reflection it was ugly and crass. I will cover this more as I spent some more time in South Africa when I worked aboard *The Edinburgh Castle* a ship belonging to the Union Castle Line when I was a little older and wiser and a bit more politically aware.

Cape town was a beautiful place, where the sun shone and the place seemed for all intent and purposes immaculate. This was a happy place for the whites, but not for anyone unfortunate to be born black, in Africa. The night we went to the *Spurs Club* and as we entered into my first real nightclub it was fantastic. We had had a few drinks that day in it but it was just like a large bar room with no entertainment but it was now transformed into a place that made the Plaza in Belfast seem so old and dated. After a few bottles of the local brandy it was just like anywhere else. A place to get drunk and flake out, or touch for a girl.

Later that night we did what we shouldn't have done and visited one of the districts that were numbered ghettoes. It was district six where the poor blacks lived. They were no better than interment camps, but these people lived like internees. They hadn't committed any crime. The only crime they had committed was to be born black, a crime one asks, no, but the whites undoubtedly treated them worse than criminals in their own country. Me and some other guy were courting two black girls we had met as we wondered drunkenly around Cape Town. The place was so dark you couldn't see a thing in front of you. The district had no electric lighting and it was scary. As the night went into morning and I started to sober up and get my senses about me I called quietly for my mate and we made a hasty getaway to the safety of downtown were we got a taxi back to the ship?

The next day Christy had arranged a football match with the South African customs men and a bus was led on for us all to go and watch our play whatever the case may be. When we arrived at the venue I looked at the opposing side and most of them had no boots on and I wondered what were they going to do. I soon learned that those guys could kick a ball better than any guy I ever saw in football boots and they beat our team hands down. Christy was a great organiser and loved football and golf but this was another reason for a good drinking session and we didn't travel light. We brought a very big carry out with us. Again I had learned something; some guys can kick a ball as hard as the next even without boots.

The next night as we headed back to the ship after a drinking session we hopped across the train lines in the docks I saw a giant crab like animal running in front of me and Desi informed me it was a cockroach. I said are you're sure and he told me to be quiet for a minute and see what happens. It then turned into what only described as a mini grand national. They were every where jumping over train lines as they made there way to greener pastures, trying to get on the ship in their quest for food. You will see them on the ship I was reliably informed by Desi, they just might not be as big but you can bet the ships full of them. He was right, the ship had to be fumigated before it left for Australia the next day. I think all the ships had too, as Australia was hell bent on keeping out strangers of the creepy crawly type.

Although the **Cross**-was described as one of the lesser grand ships for crew grub it was a million miles from what we ate in Belfast and it was plentiful and it done the job well. The one thing I hated about the ship was the Allsopps beer and after leaving Cape Town it was the only thing available.

Typical English beer, which did nothing for me, but must do, is a good master. So it played its part until we arrived on the Aussie coast.

We would be at sea ten days and it was the only time I ever went to bed on a Thursday night and woke up on Thursday morning the very next day. As we made our way to Australia the ships captain put two or three hours a day on the clock and the night we crossed the International Date Line we had two Thursdays one after another. The weather was now so warm and all we wanted to do when we finished work was to go up and deck and watch as dolphins lead the ship on her steady course.

This for someone from the Falls Road or any other working class part of Belfast was a sight to behold as the Cross-cut a dash through the seas and the dolphins leapt out of the water and looked at us as we peered over the deck. It was if they were saying look at us, and we did. We were in awe of them. Some clever fellow who had been at sea a while said wait till you see the flying fish and I looked at him as if he was mad. After all when I was a kid and just left school people would have sent me for a long weight, a bucket of blue steam, or a skyhook. I wasn't going to get caught out with, "flying fish." After watching the dolphins or porpoises some clever dick shouted did you see the flying fish and I ignored him but me being I sneaked a look and low and behold, there were fish flying out of the water in front of the bows. I was amazed to say the least. Imagine if I went home and told the boys at the corner about this they'd say I was crazy just like I thought the guy was that first told me was.

This guy worked in the spud locker was called Billy Budd and his job was peeling potatoes and he told me if you caught one and boiled it the skeleton was identical to the crucifix. I wasn't going to argue and that night in the galley he boiled a flying fish that some one had caught and yes true enough the skeletal shape was identical to a crucifix. I was beginning to learn that the world didn't stop or start on the Falls Road and that the world was much bigger and interesting than I could even stretch my imagination too. I was a young man who had a lot to learn.

A few days later the sleek *Cross*-sailed under Sydney Bridge, a strange looking building was under construction the like I had never seen before.

It was the Sydney opera house and it had been in the planning stage for about twenty years and building process about six. It was an odd looking building with which can only be described as sea-shell like domes offset from each other and looking like a large feast of oysters that giants had eaten and left open in a style that could have been taken from art deco or even stuccoed style houses in London's Eaton square. It may have blended in well but stuck at the entrance to Sydney harbour it looked a folly. As we got closer I saw what the architects were maybe trying to do but in all honesty the word opera house to me was linked with snobbery and it wasn't for the ordinary Joe Blogs. This was more for those that suffered from the tall poppy syndrome, as the Australians call it. But it was home for a few weeks a year to some great opera singers of the day and other forms of entertainment.

At this time all the culture I held was from the Belfast and it didn't amount to much. Anything that didn't lock into my style of thinking got blocked out and that was that. How wrong was I, to think so. But it did take a thirty-year war to bring out a rich gold vein of artists, both visual, and literary from our road and many other working class areas in the North of Ireland. Now I'm not saying I'm one of them but time has proven that there are some gifted people who may never have had a chance except for the revolution of thought in our city, to bring to the nation their artistic gifts. The arts belong to everyone, not the select few and the Sydney Opera house is open to anyone wishing to visit it.

After work that day Judas Nolan and me and some others went ashore to a strange world where butchers and bakers advertised their wares through a small PA system. I had seen a few shops do that in Cape Town but it seemed every shop had it here. After finding a pub were most of the crew had met I witnessed a new strange phenomenon. Jugs of ice-cold beer served to the customers along with small glasses. I ordered jug and was informed it was called a schooner and as I sat down it seemed with the small glasses you could drink this to the cows came home, or in this case the ship sailed. The large jug was covered in a mist of ice coldness and as I lashed it into me I thought what would happen if they sold drink like this in Belfast. One answer to that was, the greediest would get the most of it and would cause more fights than enough. So I settled down to drink this cold beautiful beer and switch off for a while before I headed back to the ship and wash dishes that seemed to continue forever and ever.

That night in the galley I was working in the forward plate house as most of the passengers had disembarked for the new life when there was a loud commotion coming from the saloon and as the doors flew open there was Joe Fireworks McMullan in full flight. He was drunk as a skunk and the chief steward was telling him be had to wear a shirt under his white coat if it wasn't buttoned up but Joe was having none of it. As Desi and I tried to cool Joe down he turned on us. He was totally out of his head and he made a go for me and I had twelve large diner plates in my hand. Joe got them thrown at him and unfortunately he cut his face. You could have given yourself a bigger cut shaving. The sight of blood sent Joe haywire and that was the night he gained the name "Fireworks'. After a few of the lads got him settled and brought him down to his bunk all went quiet and Desi and I went and got showered and headed for the big smoke of Sydney. We done the bars and clubs and headed back to the ship, which was heading for Melbourne the next day.

The next day as we headed for Melbourne I awoke with a headache like I never had before. Some of the older guys told me it was a result of drinking the chemical lager, which I had thought was as good as anything I had ever, drank. The moral of the story was drink too much and you pay the penalty with a big hangover, but it was ten times better than the ships beer. As we steamed for Melbourne the heat was now in the nineties again and much more time was spent on deck during our free time. The pool was in full use and the music wafted on the forecastle head as more and more of the crew became bronzy kings and escaped from their hot and steamy cabins that had little or no air.

A few days later we docked in Melbourne and I went ashore to buy a book for a friend of mine called, Sean Hack Kerr who had asked me to get it for him: **The Standard Bred Horse**. Trotting had come to Belfast and this was the bible and was unavailable so I went and bought the book at the princely sum of twenty-five dollars, a week's wages. Then my mind wondered back to happy days working in Henry Kane's yard were Hack was foreman and how well he treated me, so it was no big deal. Anyway after getting the book I went back too the **Cross**-and a ship called the **Ocean Monarch** was berthed in front of us and there standing on the after end was my cousin Eamon Walsh. I shouted at him and then went aboard the ship, which in some ways resembled the **Cross**. We then decided to go and get drunk. We went ashore and went to Young and Jacksons, a world famous pub, come hotel, on Flinders Street and had a great nights craic. Next morning we bid our farewells as we were sailing the next day for Perth, the port of Fremantle, another city in my travels of revelation in this strange and beautiful world I was been paid to see and visit. The trip went on uneventful and as we left the Australian coast we headed next for New Zealand, another beautiful place not unlike Ireland.

It had a better climate with no dampness that most of the Belfast people had to endure. It was a three hundred and sixty degree turn around for me, from a cold damp house to a hot cabin to sunning outdoors in November. This was all new and exciting and in some ways it showed me how the other half of the world lived and at times beggared the question should I jump ship like the twenty odd crewmen from **The Cross** had done some years ago. I now understood why. This was heaven in comparison to Belfast, but what ever the world threw at me there was only one place for me to live and that was the Falls Road in Belfast.

As the **Cross**-sailed into Wellington it was a bright and sunny, a beautiful day reminiscence of one of our great summer days that we occasionally had in Belfast. As we tied up and we cleared up the plate house as we had a full day ashore ahead of us. As we got showered and spruced, we headed ashore to explore this beautiful country. After having a milk shake in the terminal Judas, Desi, Mick Browne, Billy Kilcourse and me headed to the town to see what it had to offer.

After a few hours I decided I wanted to go horse riding and we went to a riding school and hired out some horses and headed into the mountains. Again this reminded me of Tornaroy and days when I went camping there and maybe rode one of Joe Hughes horses to get there. A young lady led the way as we tracked up the mountain and gazed down on the beach and in some ways thought of my days when I first started riding horses in Joe's yard and thought I was Roy Rodgers or Gene Autry. This was a good as it gets and after some deliberation we decided to head for the beach and some fast riding. As we headed to the beach and the tide ebbed in around the hoofs of our steeds I decided to go for a gallop as the waves lapped around my horses forearms and touched my feet. Later I was galloping back on my big grey steed when all of a sudden my horse went from below me and I was struggling in the seawater. Everything was in slow motion as I tried to swim and the tide washed over and back I realised I was okay. After securing my horse and shaking my self down amid the laughter of my mates, I decided I had to throw my leg over my horse again knowing if I didn't I may loose my bottle and have trouble mounting a horse again. After a timid gallop down the beach again I learned that when the tide came in it loosened the compactness of the sand and my horse had lost its footing. As usual I wondered what if he had rolled on me, as he was a big thick type of horse. I put it out of my mind and galloped freely down the beach like the proverbial pro rider as none of the other guys had ridden before so I had to carry the flag for us.

The girl who was in charge of the riding school invited us to a party that night in the outskirts of the city. After riding back to the stables we headed back to the ship to get spruced up for the party. When we arrived at the party Judas and I were drunk and we were refused admission and in the melee a window was broken and the cops were called. One of the gang was arrested and the next day was fined twenty dollars for the window and the nice girl who invited us to the party became a memory. It was a good memory that stayed with me for a long time in my mind. Next day we were sailing and we had to turn too as normal and I was feeling the effects of too much drink. The next stop was somewhere I had never heard of in the Indian Ocean, Tonga or Rarotonga but we didn't get ashore but the locals sailed out on small raft like boats to see there wares and after a few hours we were on our way again. A similar call was to Fiji were the locals came out on small boats and you could trade soap and other ships belongings for trinkets.

After visiting Bermuda our next stop was Fort Lauderdale and we couldn't wait to get ashore. This time Judas and me went alone as we were going to hitch a lift into Florida. After a few lifts in different cars, every one of them had some claim to an Irish ancestry. One man who claimed he was Irish blood was actually telling us his people were from Leeds. We tried to explain to him that Leeds was in England but all to no avail.

Our next lift was from an American record producer who told us he could get us tickets to see the Rolling Stones who where playing close by. How close we didn't know and our ship was sailing in a few hours. After some small talk he decided to bring us to a then modern disco tech and believe it or not it was housed in an old B52 airplane. We had never saw anything like it then or since. It was unbelievable. A large airplane converted into a dance hall. After about half an hour he decided to leave us into Miami. As we wondered around Miami we started to get a bit worried about how to get back to the ship. As we were walking down the street a little old lady and her husband passed us and I asked her the time. He was dressed like Humphrey Bogart and she was dressed like Lauren Bacall although the sun was splitting the trees. Her husband walked on a little and she called him back. She then asked me to say something to them, which I found to be an unusual request. She was amazed at my accent as she was originally from Ireland but left as a child. Although her hubby wasn't that amazed he stood as we had a chat, both were very nice people. After telling her of our plight she reached into her purse and gave us five dollars each. She then told us to go and get ourselves a burger but not to go to Howard Johnston's place, as it was too expensive. After thanking them both we got the thumbs out and within minutes were on our way back to the ship.

Our next lift left us back near the Cross and we saw two phenomena that day. As we walked down the street it was raining on one side of the street but not the other. We had never saw anything like that in Belfast or anywhere else on our travels for that matter. We then came across the second. **The Queen Elizabeth** berthed in a permanent spot; she had been turned into museum of sorts. As I looked at her she made the **Cross** look like a pond yacht. She was enormous. I wondered what it must have been like to sail on her, she looked so grand but I had heard all the stories. I just pictured it in my minds eye what it must have been like to sail on her. That night we left America for our journey back to Southampton.

Chapter 29

Big trip is over

It was now the eleventh of December as the *Cross*-sails its way up the channel and I awoke with some enthusiasm for once even though I was blind drunk the night before. Channel Night is a celebration at the end of the trip and we had some night. It had been a life changer for me, and one I wouldn't forget easily. I had just seen the world. All be it from the inside of some good pubs and bars but I had also had a life experience that I couldn't have bought or gained at a degree receiving ceremony. I had just experienced my longest term in a totally alien place to me, a world where I learned a lot about my life and me. It's a pity I didn't endorse it at that time, but it was there to be looked at and it was tangible but I had never had time to embrace it.

Next morning as I gathered my self and looked at the breakfast being prepared in the galley I thought this is the last of this as I made my way to the plate house and finished off my last wash. Dinky and me washed up all the breakfast ware and then a small scrub out. We then went up on deck as the *Cross*-pulled in along side the wall at Southampton harbour. As I poked my head over the wall on the after end I noticed it was cold and dark and having just made our way from the southern hemisphere I asked myself why didn't you jump ship in that warm beautiful country New Zealand.

The first man I met when the ship had berthed was Ducksey Rooney who had boarded the ship to meet some friends and try and earn a few quid carrying cases or wilking as it was called. Anyway a few hours later I was going up to pay off and get my money, one hundred and twelve quid after twelve weeks of relatively hard work. As I signed off I received a note, as did most of the crew that we would not be invited back for the next cruise. I thought I had behaved very well during the trip but the bosses didn't agree and that was that. It would be my twentieth birthday in a few days and it was near Christmas so I thought I would head home in the next day or so.

Around about eleven o'clock I headed ashore and met my cousin Anthony Walsh and his brother Robert who I hadn't seen in a few years. He had moved down to the Hamp from Birmingham. After having a few drinks and giving a few quid to those that were good to me when I arrived in the Hamp I was literally skint. I then decided to go home on what was going to be a longer journey to Belfast on the train and then the Heysham boat. Desi and Judas and me headed for the train and the long trip to Heysham to catch the boat for Belfast. As we boarded the boat and settled in the bar for the night someone produced a deck of cards and we started playing pontoon. By now Rocky, Hugh Mc Geown and some others had joined us and a good card school ensued. This was the strangest card school I had ever been in. A new coin was being thrown in the middle with out much value been put on it. This was our first experience of the new half a quid or the fifty pence piece. Before we had left on the *Cross* the ten bob note was a worthy piece of paper to have in your pocket and was treasured. But now a coin had taken its place and didn't represent the same value or importance. After two hours we decided to call the card school a miss and we all got our head down. I won about fifty quid, half of what I had earned on the three month trip and I was in my element not for winning the money but because I won. My ego was stronger than the money, a stupid thing of course but then I was a probably full of it at the time. I was twenty in two days and believed I had the full knowledge of the world and I suppose that was my youth taking over.

The next morning we arrived in Belfast, cold, dark, and very uninviting. I was back in the real world; my real world and it didn't look good. After bidding Rocky and Hugh good luck Desi Judas and me headed home in a taxi. Judas lived next door to me and as we got out of the taxi I told Desi I would catch up with him later. As I walked in the door of our house it was like Royal Avenue as the rest of the family prepared for work and school. I felt so claustrophobic after coming of the *Cross* into our now what seemed so cramped kitchen or as it now would be called, the living room. After giving my Ma her few quid and gave the rest of the family some presents, Kola bears, spears, a coffee table made out of the middle cut of a tree and some other trinkets. I couldn't wait to get back to the corner and then came the realization, "when I was in Sidney I wanted to be at the corner in

Belfast" and now I wished I was back in the warmth of Australia. I should have realised that I would never be happy, no matter where I was.

I was irritable and discontent and it was the start of a long battle to achieve some modicum of contentment. It would be a long hard search with lots of ill feeling, disillusion and trepidation. This would hunt me for the rest of my adult life. A few hours latter I called around to Desi's house and he invited me in and his mother made us a cup of tea, then my irritability set in. as they say in Belfast. I couldn't sit a pace. "Sic."

A few hours later I was drunk and heading to my girls house and I thought I looked the bees knees. I had bought a leather James Dean jacket, or bikers jacket as it was also called, that you just couldn't get in Belfast and had my scrubbed out jeans on, I had arrived. As I knocked the door of Armstrong's house her little frail granny invited me in which was unusual. As I made my way in I fell over their small settee and near knocked the granny to the ground. Eileen then informed me that she would not be going out with me in that state. As I followed her drunkenly down the scullery I hit the stove and near knocked it out of the lead-piping socket it was connected to. It took years and years to work out that Eileen was not talking about my attire but my drunken state.

The next day I went down to Burtons and asked them to transfer a gold coloured mohair suit I had ordered in their Southampton shop to Belfast. Again mistaken that Eileen was on about my attire I thought I would sicken her with this new suit, which in its day was class. A few days later Chip who was my drinking partner and I went to Burtons in Ann Street to try on my new suit, and it fitted perfectly. It was a suit that would cause me some trouble in later times, as the trousers were what was called, "cut neat". Anyway a few days later I'm walking past Saint Comgall's School in Divis Street investigating the loyalist mobs handy work when I bumped into Eileen. I was suited and booted and she didn't even blink an eye but I was out with her again that night and all seemed rosy in the garden. Had the suit worked or was it my drunken foolishness that caused the rejection.

By this time I had become very fond of drink and teamed up with some of my old drinking buddies whom I worked with in Henry Kane's yard. I was now back drinking in Sean McGeowns pub at the corner of Lemon Street . McGeowns was the original **Decent Mans** pub a title later relinquished to Paddy Gilmartin who owned a pub a hundred yards up at the corner of Peel Street. Chip and myself drank with Bud Dorrian, Danny Braniff, Jacky McBurney, Paddy Darling, and the one and only John Manning or Sullivan John, as he liked to be called when he was drinking. Chip and myself were actually too young for this company. For example Bud and Danny were at least fifteen years older that us but we were I suppose older than our years.

Chips parents Kitty and Paddy also drank in the company when we moved to the lounge at the weekend. The lounge was a big room situated at the back of the public bar and I would say it was as big as most bars I had ever been in on the road. At this time the whole conversation in our company was horses and more horses, no mention of football or any other activities. It was now my birthday. I was twenty. The day passed without any importance being placed upon it, as some one coined the phrase "its just another day" and I thought I was the epicentre of the world. You must be joking I said to myself. Christmas also came and went in a haze of drink and became a non-important event. We were now moving into a new year nineteen seventy and events would change almost as if it was sixty-nine all over again.

One night a group of or gang were standing at Raymond O'Neil's butchers shop at the corner of Osman and Servia Street when I was beckoned by a man wearing a grey Dexter and a black beret looking like something that had dropped in from the nineteen sixteen Easter rising. As I made my way a few yards up Osman Street, the man asked in a southern brogue how he could meet a leading republican of the day as he was sent up from Dublin. It just so happened that the man he was looking for was the brother of one of our gang. I called him up and we told the man to walk along Servia Street for a hundred yards then turn back and we would try to get the meet organised. As the man slowly walked up the street you're mans brother and me walked over and rapped the door of a house where some of the newly formed Provisional Irish Republican Army were having a meeting. The houses were then titled, "Call Houses", and there were to be many of such houses over the years in the Falls. After some discussion and maybe a telling off the guy agreed to meet the man and made his way to the corner and waited apprehensively on the man to approach. It was a winter's night and the lighting wasn't so good and as the man started to talk to the guy he then revealed himself to be none other than the Jimmy Ward better known as the Guv. Talk about embarrassment. After some deliberation we saw the funny side of it and congratulated the Guv on his Oscar winning performance but the Ra man didn't see the funny side of it till some time later as he had been disturbed at an army meeting and in some way the call house had been compromised.

In all honesty it was a sterling bit of acting by the Guv who over the years had played his part like some Shakespearian actor, with some actual events thrown in as well. As the troubles or war started gaining some momentum the Guvs house was a focal point for lots of activity. It was one of the few houses in the district that had a phone and it was the place general Harry Freeman rang when in negotiation with the local Official IRA man Jimmy Solo Sullivan about what was going on in the districts and so on.

At this time the British army were half acceptable to the nationalist people as they acted as protectors from invading loyalist mobs and for a brief time were received well and in some cases got their tea from residents from the road. All that would change and like a double-edged sword the Falls Road became a place were no British soldier was safe at any time, day or night.

After a few months working and messing about Henry Kane's yard the troubles had taken a sort of lull and I decided that I would try for another ship so I set sail for Southampton again. The land of milk and honey and I can assure you at this time drink flowed and it was what I call an easy town. There wasn't many times that one failed to get a drink in this home of seafarers. Some ship with a friend on it was either tying up or letting go and both were a cause for heavy drinking and celebration.

As I waited to get a job on a ship I was on the beach as it was called. That's when you were shore side with out a ship. I was offered a job in Dimplex, a large electrical company and was to go one night and start on the night shift. It had all been arranged by a guy who was a foreman in the factory, who I think was called Gerry McAllister. After a few drinks and giving it some thought I decided to tell Jimmy Prenter to go and he would probably get the job, and so he did, hence his new nickname Jimmy Dimplex.

On another occasion on a lighter note I remember going to a darts match in a pub in the same area and watching the dart match without any real interest as we waited patiently until it was over then the grub was handed around. As we had no money we were waiting on the food coming around as was normal after the match and we filled our pockets with baked jacket potatoes and left before the two teams noticed. We didn't leave much for the two teams that were actually playing on the night. After a few weeks drinking and generally acting the idiot I went to the pool but didn't get a ship.

After dossing about Southampton for a few weeks drinking the piece out I got a job on the **Edinburgh Castle**, one of the Union Castle Saf Marine ships that sailed like clock work to and fro to the South African coast in a trip that lasted six weeks. I got the last job I wanted but was glad to get away and get a bit of sunshine and I signed on as crew steward. This job entailed looking after the deckhands and the down below men, and making sure their mess room had plenty of bread butter and preservatives and fetching their dinner when they were on watch. It was a long haul carrying eight dinners from the galley to the forecastle head of the ship and was difficult trying to keep them warm, but I was fit, built like a greyhound so it never became a problem unless it was after a hard nights drinking.

This trip was going to take me back to Las Palmas, Cape Town, Durban were I had visited before on the **Cross** with two unknown destinations thrown in, Port Elizabeth and East London. After leaving Southampton on a nice warm Thursday afternoon with some drink taken I set about finding my way on board the Edinburgh Castle a ship also built in my home town Belfast. After feeling my way around the ship I started looking to find out if there were any Belfast men among the crew. There was always someone from Belfast aboard these passenger ships as lads like myself found it a way to see the world, get paid for it and even immigrate by jumping in the favourite port.

That night in the pig I met some Belfast lads and I settled down for the trip. As I suffered form irritability and discontent it made trips at sea very difficult for me and coupled with my new found love affair with alcohol made for many sleepless nights. If I got drunk I slept and if I got too drunk I couldn't get out of my bunk in the morning so I was in a catch twenty-two situation. First port of call was Las Palmas and two things were on my mind drink and a bottle of Bacardi and a Cauny watch. Bacardi was ten bob a bottle and a Cauny watch. This was a square faced watch that cost four pounds in Las Palmas. It was a must have and started another love affair for most of the sea faring guys from around Belfast had developed. As I went ashore in Las Palmas I found the jewellers and purchase my watch and then a bottle of Bacardi and found a nice little pub not far from the ship. It was the normal or done thing to get drunk in Las Palmas as it was ten days before our next stop, Cape Town. On arrival in Cape Town the ship tied up and masses of the local black population boarded the ship in gangs of ten or twenty lead by a black man with a stick some what resembling an ash plant from back home.

They all carried catering cans with a wire handle fixed to them. These cans that once held peaches, dried custard, and other foods used on a ship or in a hotel. I wondered why they carried these and I was soon to find out that they were the only means they had of carrying any food they foraged from the ship to their home to feed their families. They worked in the galley and engine rooms, painting, scrubbing and generally doing what we the crew usually done. At this time I realised that for a small token, no money involved a black man would carry out your menial tasks up and down the coast for the simple reward of something to eat. They would sleep up on deck and travel with the ship and do every job available to them with help of the persuader the big stick carried by their black bosses. I was only becoming politically aware but I soon learned that was the way in South Africa

and if one was foolish enough to try and redress the situation it was met with stiff opposition from all sides. So everyone fell into the way of, when in Rome do as the Romans do. Apartheid was part and parcel of this beautiful country and God help anyone who tried to change it.

After tiding up my mess room I headed ashore with one of my new found friends Gavin Todd "a mush, as Southampton people were called." His father's people were Irish so he had a Belfast connection. As we made our way up town I noticed nothing had changed the flagging and kerb stones whites only engraved on the pavements and I needed no explanation I knew what it meant. After some explanation I came to realise that although the vast majority of the. They couldn't ride down stairs on a bus, eat in restaurants, or use the same taxis or toilets and we thought Belfast and its gerrymandering was bad. This was an uneventful trip except I met Francey Walsh again and the usual followed, **The Spurs Club** and the cape brandy and all the other things that go with it. I suppose a better description would be wine women and song . I also became friendly with some Scouse lads who in some ways were like Belfast men. They were the ones that had set the fashion earlier of mohair suits and they also wore shoes called Dino's. They never caught on in Belfast, which was a Chelsea boot and Oxford shoes place. The Scousers had a sort of affinity with Ireland as someone once said, "What's the capital of Ireland? Dublin I replied, only to be told there was more Irish in Liverpool than the whole of Ireland." After I few visits to Liverpool I have to say I agree. Anyway after six weeks on the high seas on one of the fastest passenger ships around it was channel night and a good drinking session was had by all. The next day I signed off and headed back to Belfast for a week or so.

On my arrival back in Southampton a few weeks later I got a job on a ship I had heard so many stories about. I knew it like my brother or sister, **The Rena Del Mar**, the queen of the seas. Again I got a bad job, officer steward and I prepared myself for the cruise. To be truthful the Belfast guys didn't really work that hard in the galley but I was officer steward and had to be at there back and call. Anyway that night I got drunk and the next morning was in a mess but got on with things all be it a bit late. But when officers are on watch they need their meals on time so they can get back on their four-hour watches. The next few days were uneventful and then we arrived in Lisbon and we played a match up at Benfica's training ground and it was Christy Hughes the guy I had sailed with on the **Cross** who organised it. It was like all other sporting things I got involved in, it was a good excuse for a drink, like I really needed one. That night I went to the American bar in

194

Lisbon and finished in an apartment there with some girl I met in the bar. There whole way of life was not dissimilar to ours and the family bond was so much like ours back in Belfast where the granny, granda, uncle, or aunt lived with a young family under one roof. The next day we arrived in Naples and I got drunk and bought a chronograph watch for about a tenner a lot of money and headed back to the ship.

The next morning I woke up half drunk and my arm was black. The watch was brass and not worth ten bob. I planned my revenge on those fly fuckers in Naples and I got dressed like a tourist and headed up into the shopping area where literally you could buy a tank. You have to remember anywhere the yanks are you can buy anything that they use. After all it's a capitalist army run by capitalist men who have an eye for a fast buck. After getting myself prepared I walked into a large shop that sold tea sets and fancy wares and most other things seamen brought home as presents. It was maybe our way of showing that someone travelled the world in the house. A hark back to the grand tours travelled by aristocrats in the previous century when they brought back items unavailable in these lands. But I know one thing every house that had a Japanese tea set, you didn't have to ask were it came from. You only had to ask what boat the males of the family sailed on. After flashing the watch on my wrist I asked the guy how much a set of coloured glass was and some other goods. I calculated the cost against my watch I asked him to do a changy, changy, as we called it. He asked to inspect the watch and after some investigation he sent an errand boy to have it checked out as I stood edgily waiting a result. After a few minutes the boy returned and I noticed he nodded in the affirmative. The guy behind the counter offered me two of the items I had asked for and I said no, the four items or nothing. So he wrapped all the items up and happily done the swap. Frankie Short had been waiting in the background and as we got into a taxi we laughed our balls off as we headed back to the ship. I just had got one over on the shrewd men of Naples; it was just getting even.

The next day we arrived in Gibraltar and **The Rena,** as she was affectionately known sailed in to Gib and I thought what a place. A big rock stuck in the middle of the Medy. After getting my work done a gang of us headed for the town and when I got there I was amazed. Here was another little bastion of English domination about the size of a two-penny stamp. But it was great; Spain with English speaking publicans, music blaring from juke boxes or reel to reel tape recorders. This was Omeath in the middle of the ocean, with sun, sea, cheap booze and fags. What more could a man want. After a visit up to the top of the rock to see the famous Gibraltar apes or monkeys and watched as they terrorised some of the ships tourists, Short, Frankie Bouncy Henry and me made our way to the Fox and Hounds public house. It was so English you may have closed your eyes and thought you were back in the Hamp but the difference was the price of the booze. Bouncy now there was a character. He got the name because of his make and shape and was an ex boxer who like myself loved the drink. After a lot of drinking Bouncy called a cab and we made our way down town towards the boat stopping of at one of the many gift shops in the narrow streets of Gib. I got out of the taxi as it was rather warm and said to Bouncy how much I liked the place and wouldn't mind staying a while. How prophetic that statement would become some time later.

After a few minutes I got back in the taxi and Bouncy walked out of the shop with large what later became known as a ghetto blaster and handed it to me. He said to bring it back to the ship and not to ask any questions. I told the taxi driver to drive on and Bouncy walked off in the direction of the ship. Try as I might I couldn't turn the thing of and the music could be heard far and near as it blasted out a Tamla Motown record. After paying the not so bemused taxi driver I made my way to my cabin with this large monstrosity and wondered what the hell he wanted it for. I thought, I suppose it was so cheap in a duty free shop and he just bought it for to play on the ship but as I was drunk it didn't really matter to me.

That night when I was working, Bouncy came to see me. I was now sober and I asked him what the score was with the blaster and then he told me to keep it. I thought thanks very much and then he laughed and said, "Well you stole it". What I didn't know was he had asked the shopkeeper could he take it outside to listen to it handed it to me and bobs your uncle. It was a piece of equipment no one had around our way and I looked forward to playing on our corner when I went home. But like every thing that comes the wrong road it got smashed in the pig some days later during a fight. So much for that, but it was back to drinking and the usual and then came channel night and the crew were putting on a sods opera as it was called, more a night of cabaret. After some deliberation on Short and Bouncy's behalf it was decided I would sing at the opera attended by the captain and some of his fellow officers. Short dressed me in his tank top and I pressed my black strides and up we went to the pig where we met some fellow crewmembers. After a night of drinking I was called to sing and without further ado I was on the makeshift stage belting out some rock and roll numbers to a very good applause. It was decided, but I don't know why that they would put me forward for opportunity knocks to which I just laughed but the guy who was previously picked wasn't too pleased and showed his resentment and let it be known that he had been already picked. After some discussion he agreed I should go forward. After been introduced to the captain and been congratulated on my singing the opera ended and it was down to some good drinking. The captain and his fellow officers made their exit and everyone else got blootered. Short and Bouncy worked as KPs in the galley so they could lie on most mornings but I was officer steward and you had to be on the ball.

Next morning I was being called by the glory hole and I fell through a term used for not turning up for work. I was informed I was going to be logged. So at twelve noon I appeared in front of the captain in what was literally a court at sea. I walked up on to the bridge and the captain was sitting behind a desk draped with a union jack flanked by two officers and an MA or master at arms standing to attention. As I stood in front of the captain he asked me my name and discharge book number and asked had I any mitigation circumstances. After I told him that I got drunk and wasn't fit to get up out of my bunk, he then said to me. "Your face looks rather familiar. Have I met you before on board my ship?' I looked sheepishly at him much the wear for drink and told him he had met me the night before. After some deliberation he asked me was I the guy who sang? To which I replied "yes." He was dumbfounded and told me he couldn't understand the transformation that had taken place from a bright young fellow to a half drunk man with two eyes that looked like piss holes in the snow. A reference to my red eyes a side effect of my drinking. He told me he enjoyed me the night before and logged me one days pay and told me to watch my behaviour in future but there was to be no future. A few days later as we docked in Southampton the inevitable happened. I was sacked off the one ship I always wanted to be on, **The Rena Del Mar**. I had lasted all of two weeks and things looked bleak with the Union Castle line for any future employment. After paying of with a measly twenty quid I decided to head back home to see if I had missed anything in the most important place in my life, The Falls.

Chapter 30

The curfew

After being back for about a fortnight in the district things had now changed and our people had become polarised into factions of both the Provisional and Official Irish republican armies. Better known as the Provo's and the Stickies respectively and again peoples thoughts and actions would take us to a new level in a very eventful period of the war. I was standing outside Willie Darks shop on the corner of Osman and Sultan Street along with some mates waiting to get a card school going and eventually go for a drink in the Burning Embers pub in Sultan Street or some of the other bars that dotted most corners in all districts in the city, at least in working class Belfast. The army was raiding Sticky Maguire's house in Balkan street and had uncovered a large arms dump belonging to the Official IRA.

It was a nice summer day but things could change in Belfast in minutes and it did. Rioting started and CS gas was fired at the residents without any concern for young or old, sick or infirm. It seeped in people houses, into the living rooms and kitchens and even the bedrooms. A lot of people suffered from the results of damp housing and were prone to chest complains this only made matters worse for them. The people of the district were very resilient and buckets of water were placed out side most front doors and the houses had become open to all and sundry while evading the clutches of the British army. If only our people had sustained that camaraderie we wouldn't have had such futile feuds that in hindsight were probably the work of the dirty tricks department operated by MI5 or some other shadowy British group who used the war in the north of Ireland as their personal playing field.

By now the rioters were giving the Brits all they wanted and hand-to-hand battles were fought along Raglan Street and the immediate area. To combat the effects of CS gas we got hankies and old pieces of rag and dipped them in buckets of water, which had vinegar, added. These were strategically placed in the hallway of most houses in the riot torn area. The vinegar supposedly numbed the effect of the CS gas. The polarisation had been set aside or dropped temporarily and the people fought as one to defend their homes and district from a now invading army that less and a year previous had been welcomed with open arms by some of the community.

After the rioting intensified in one area a new front was formed. One such front was off Leeson Street in and around Abercorn Street North, as the Brits were now in the Dunville Park and they probably thought that they would have things under control with in the hour. Were they in for a surprise? They didn't understand that the people of the Falls Road had been reared on harsh times often inflicted on them by the infamous RUC and B specials and many young people had broken their teeth at the Divis Street riots in nineteen sixty-four. That trouble was brought about by the one and only Ian Paisley the leader of the free Presbyterian Church. He personally swore he would remove a tricolour from the window of a shop that was acting as Billy McMillen's election headquarters. That probably was the start but it wasn't then end.

As the rioting continued a crowd made their way down towards the brits and a small group of young volunteers from the Provisional IRA stepped out of the crowd and produced a Garand rifle. A large rifle not unlike a three o three as I later learned by watching the odd documentary. The Garand was used by the Americans in the Korean War and was an old but effective weapon. After some deliberation between the young men one informed the others that he had been to confession that day and he felt he was the one to fire on the Brits. I supposed he looked at it if he was shot dead he was in a state of grace, so no better man. After a few seconds I was standing beside him as he got down on one knee and fired one very loud shot into Dunville Park. I had never heard or seen anything like it before, as the crowd retreated, a gun battle began to take place. To my knowledge that was the first shot fired by republican forces in the curfew on Friday July the Third nineteen seventy.

The rioting continued unabated for a few hours and out of nowhere a helicopter appeared overhead. A loud hailer attached to it announced that the area was now under Curfew. An infamous day in the history of Belfast and Ireland as a whole. The announcements coming from the helicopter made it clear that anyone caught out in the said streets would be detained and that all residents should make their way home or suffer the consequences. This of course was an illegal curfew. Unfortunately four entirely innocent people died that night in the ensuing battle, their lives taken by trigger-happy Brits that literally thought in their eyes they could fire at will at anyone they saw in the street during the curfew. The people that died were not members of either the Provos or the Stickies. One was a photographer called Zbigniew Uglik who had just moved to London from Poland and was in Belfast to photograph the riots, Charles O'Neil who was killed by a Saracen armoured car, William Burns and Patrick Elliman who were shot dead, all innocent victims of the Brits, driving around shooting indiscriminately around the small streets of the Falls.

The rioting by now had turned into a full-scale gun battle and three thousand Brits were kept at bay by a handful of active republicans. Nightfall came and I made my way to a house in Sultan Street as the Brits made inroads to the heart of the district and we couldn't walk home for fear of being shot.

As I entered the house I was forewarned that there wasn't much room and to my amazement there was sixteen men in the house. It was going to be along night as we sat listening to continuous gunfire and every one tried to second-guess the type of guns being fired. I have to say there were some experts present or so they thought. A few yarns started and as the night went on it became clear that the Brits were now within hearing distance and we lowered our voiced as we heard brits barking out orders as they burst in door after door in search of guns and the people that had been firing them. As time went on and boredom set in we decided to make some tea but found that there was no milk in the house. As we went to the stove we could see the soldiers on the backyard wall of the house. The Brits had came up a wee back entry in Sultan Street and had gained entry to some houses by both the front and back doors. It was only a matter of time before our billet would be raided. I have to say that all the people in the house had been caught up in the curfew and were not members of any organisation.

About seven o'clock the next morning the brits started banging the front door of the now dark and lifeless house as we all sat still and motionless hoping the soldiers would move on. But the hammering was relentless and it was only a matter of time before they came in on top of us. Some of us went to check the back and soldiers were crouched on the wall, armed with SLR rifles and sterling sub machine guns. They had it covered. This was an invasion of no small portions and resembled films we watched as kids in the Clonard and Broadway picture houses where we cheered at the sight of a holy statue or the star blessing him or her self. This was real, soldiers intent on wreck and ruin and statues of our lady or other catholic saints held no special place in their hearts as they wrecked all in front of them.

After some deliberation we decided to open the door and save the owner of the house the hostilities that may have befell us if the door remained shut. One of the guys decided to open the door and we filed out one by one, sixteen of us in all. As the brits lined us up against the wall one officer started at the top of the line and asked the first person where they lived and why they had broken the curfew. The guy replied with the same unhelpful answer which fifteen of us gave that we had been out for ten park drive and had got caught up in the curfew and he was over twenty-one. Sultan Street had become something of a battlefield with soldiers and military vehicles everywhere and men and women in the arrest position, standing against the wall hands leant to fingertips and feet spread apart. After some time the officer told us to stand at ease or stand facing the wall but one of our gang Jimmy D refused and remained in the crab like position until the three ton lorries or trucks appeared and we were marched off to Osman Street to be loaded on to them.

As we arrived in Osman Street, a few yards away, a real cheeky old army man met us. He was small, low set with greying hair. He had probably served in some of the British armies other disastrous campaigns around the world and he wasn't taking any shit. As we waited to get loaded like cattle onto the trucks the Gillen twins appeared from around the front of the truck and they were told to get in the back. Now the two twins were thirty stone in weight, about five foot eight in height, not very agile and we were asked to give them a heave up. After all the usual quips like, " Is there a crane handy?" and not really wanting to get them in the truck the Brits got serious and about ten of us managed to get them in the back of the truck. This was all done under coercion at gunpoint, with the threat of being shot if we refused. As the rest of us jumped in the back of the truck we wondered what next. In a few minutes we were soon to find out. Our first stop was Springfield Road barracks and we were told after alighting from the trucks at gunpoint by the cheeky Brit to get down on our knees as he ran about pointing a browning pistol at us, one by one. A small crowd of people had gathered across the road at Colligan Street and were shouting obscenities at the Brits when a guy jumped out from around the corner and opened fire on the Brits and the wee cheeky Brit I think shit himself and we didn't see him again. Hero to zero in one act as the saying goes. It was all right giving us unarmed civilians a hard time at gunpoint but when a republican opened up on him it was a different story.

After a few minutes we were reloaded into the canvas backed trucks and we headed into the unknown and hoped that none of the boys opened up as we passed through republican areas. As some of the bigger fellows peeked out of the canvas covering they gave a bow by blow account of where we were going and then one of them said we are heading up the Shankill Road, a notorious place where most of the people who burned our houses a year previous in the pogroms of nineteen sixty nine lived.

My mind went into a bit of frenzy and I wondered what was happening, as we headed into the unknown. Willie Dark who was in our lorry started asking the brits guarding us at gunpoint what the fuck was happening and poor Jersey Joe Mulvenna got beat over the head with a large baton in mistake for him. The brit thought it was him who was complaining and all the while it was Willie Dark. Suddenly the trucks stopped and we drove into a large yard very non-descript with lots of concrete walls. Cars were parked and it looked like the back of a factory. As we piled out of the back of the trucks we noticed the name "Tennant Street RUC Station." We then realised we were right in the heart of the Shankill, a place that we didn't feel at all comfortable in. We were then marched into the barracks and placed in the cells that were for drunks or people who committed misdemeanours and were held over night in, the drunk tank.

There were now forty of us in the cell, "designed for two persons", including the two Gillen twins who took up the space of six people. It wasn't very comfortable, but then again it wasn't meant to be. We were treated like cattle. After we settled in the cell the slagging started and the assumptions began. Someone told us we would all be interned and he had to tell some of our cell mates what he meant as they didn't understand what internment was. A few months later they would not only know what it meant, but actually experience it. Internment became the futile weapon of the British Establishment and was a disaster showing that they didn't think it out to well before implementing it. It was more of a knee jerk decision and a very stupid one.

After a few hours we were allowed out in to a now barbed wire enclosed yard and Hugo Mc Donnell asked could he use the toilet and a Brit threw a large galvanised bucket at him and said, "Use that you Irish bastard" one of our mob threw it back at him telling him what to do with it. It now was becoming clear to the Brits that they had lifted the wrong people and I think the chief of staffs had realised they had acted illegally and the curfew was a shear act of murder, madness, and mayhem. Four innocent people died at the hands of the invading army and no one knows how many brits were killed or injured. Better still how many people of the Falls were injured both physically and mentally? It was now late Saturday we had been lifted at about six o'clock in the morning went and about seven o'clock that night it must have been decided that it was time to release us. This wouldn't be a straightforward job as our homes were still under the illegal curfew and anyone out on the street was fired upon indiscriminately as soldiers were nervous and trigger-happy. As we were reloaded onto the trucks again and driven out of Tennent Street, a large lynch mob had appeared in the street. As we drove by they heckled us as we got down low and took cover just in case one of them opened up on the military truck as it passed. Willie Mervyn who had a slight stoppage and was a big man and was known as abut, abut. He could see out side the truck and he gave a running if abbreviated commentary with the odd abut, abut interspersed as he described how crowds of loyalists men were standing at every corner we passed.

After what seemed hours we arrived home, which was now reminiscent of a town in France or Germany during the Second World War with soldiers everywhere. There were sandbag emplacements with general-purpose machine guns, **GPMG**s manned by members of the infamous Black Watch battalion of the British army and military vehicles parked at every vantage point. It was a real war zone now and there was no doubt in anyone's mind now if there had been previously, they could now see the hole in the hands that a war had started. The next question was how long was it going to last? After been handed over to the military police who were accompanied by the Black watch in Leeson Street we were marched in twos and threes to our homes. Jim O'Reilly and myself were the last two and as we walked to our respective homes in Servia Street I'm sure we both wondered what if. This was as real as it gets.

As I walked in the door of our house my brother Oliver was sitting watching television and biding his time as he was leaving for Australia in a couple of days. I ran out to the scullery and asked my Ma was there anything to eat. She informed me that no one had been out of their homes for two days and the cupboards were bare, to coin a phrase. I was starving but had to do with a round of bread toasted at the open fire in the living room and a cup of tea. Most people bought their rations, now called grocery shopping every Saturday and my Ma and every other parent and resident of the Falls couldn't go to the shops having been penned in illegally for two days, so all and sundry starved.

The illegal curfew was ended by the courageous action of the women from Ballymurphy and surrounding areas in Belfast, including Andersonstown, St James, Kashmir and lots of other districts . Maura Drumm and Blue "Buckoo" Kelly's mother Harriet led them. He also had been in our lorry and all he said to me was remember this McCartney for future reference. Some very brave women who risked their lives and confronted the might of the British Army that day and they memory stayed and lived in our minds for years to come.

The next day the shops opened and were sold out of groceries within the hour even though the women led by Maura Drumm hadn't arrived empty handed, but laden with food. I don't think they left empty handed either, as most of them secreted out some of the guns used in the defence of the road during the curfew.

The following Monday things sort of returned to "Normal" or what we now presumed to be normal and life trudged on and the Brits now became more alienated. As the people of the Falls set about burying its innocent victims of the curfew a few days' later things had changed and the Brits were now looked upon as the enemy rather than the peacekeepers and our district got more polarised as people took sides. It was all supposed to be about politics but in hindsight one may ask, "why was it parts of certain districts went one way and the same old friends who lived a few streets away went the other". Was it more a geographical split with political reasoning being determined by where you lived and whom you ran about with and what organisation your father, mother, brother, sister supported. Or were the splits that occurred regularly in The North of Ireland politics the work of a sinister element called, The British dirty tricks brigade. I think some of the splits need to be examined objectively and maybe someone will put there hands up and say, we were duped and I'm not saying that it would or should be one sided look at our past in detail. We may learn maybe by our mistakes. If you have no history you can have no future. Time was moving on and as the district settled down I decided on another trip on the boats.

Chapter 31

Next stop Wales

I got itchy feet again and decided to go to the pool and try for another boat and to my amazement I got a job on ferry that had been taken out of mothballs, ***The Saint David***. This ship was brought out of the proverbial mothballs to supplement the continuous tourist traffic flow to the republic. A bridge had came down in Wales and for some reason the need for another ship was a given.

So of I set to Holyhead in Wales to join the ship. On my way I bumped into a fellow on the train whose face I recognised and after a couple of beers on the train I went over and asked him was he from Belfast. Sure as there's an eye in a buck goat he was and he was on his way to join ***The Saint David***. After a few name swaps I found that he was the nephew of the former world champion boxer Rinty and his name was Bobby Monaghan. He would be later murdered by a death squad in Rathcoole, a staunchly loyalist area of greater Belfast.

After a few more drinks and some sea dog talk peppered with questions about his famous uncle we arrived at the train station in Holyhead. This was my first trip to Wales. We decided to try the hostelry in the town and found that once we opened our mouths the other customers decided to speak in their native Cymraeg tongue. So after two drinks we left and made our way to the ship only to find an old-fashioned dilapidated ship wreck, which hadn't, ran commercially for years. After finding a cabin in the passenger accommodation, as the crew accommodation was uninhabitable, I unpacked my gear and headed for an assembly in the galley, which was now full of an angry crew who were ready to go on strike.

Most of the crew came from Liverpool and I took that as meaning they didn't stand for any shit and were union mad and fought for their rights. The cook was a large mixed race Chinese Scouser who was complaining about the stove. He said hadn't used a coal fired stove in over twenty years or saw a kitchen so bad, which he referred to as being something from the "Bounty" and the crew were ready for a mutiny. After a few hours negotiation the crew were enticed by the pound note and were promised a better wage than any of them had ever had at sea before. Most agreed to sail on the rust bucket, myself, and Bobby included. After getting the head down for a few hours in a damp mildew ridden cabin I was awakened the next morning to turn too in this foul smelling damp, badly lit ship. It didn't even have any stores on-board. Anyway the big cook and a few of his followers walked of and I looked around at what was left of this crew and I asked myself "what if". Maybe they couldn't get a job on another ship as I was surprised to get a job so quickly myself. That's when I realised it was a bad job that no one else wanted.

After a few hours we were ready to sail and we prepared for passengers who would be boarding the next day. In all fairness she didn't look too bad after a good clean up. Next day about a thousand passengers, a lot more than the ship was registered to carry, boarded and we set sail for Dun Laogharie just outside Dublin.

A few hours out and it was bedlam when a storm rose and every man woman and child seems to be seasick and the place was awash with vomit. So it was mops buckets and sugie clothes to the ready. Along with the toilets being blocked and water running everywhere it had to be the worst trip I had ever been on. Kids cried and mothers looked as if they were on the trip to hell. Some hours later behind schedule we tied up in Dun Laogharie and the passengers alighted with some saying they would never sail on a boat again. Now it was time to clean the ship for the returning passengers and I can tell you it was the biggest work up I ever experienced on any ship I ever sailed on? It reminded me of flood-hit Belfast years earlier only this was different ball game.

Everywhere you looked some poor unfortunate had been sick and the contents of the toilets were now running down the alleyways to meet us. I have to say a lot of the crew were sick as well, not sea sick but sick from the sight that befell them as we set about a mass clean up with every member of the crew barring the captain and his officers helping. After a few days things started to pan out and the ship started operating at a normal level and everything seemed to be all ship shape and Bristol Fashion.

One day, I was working in the saloon and I chatted up some girls who were having a meal. Me, and some of my crewmates decided to ask them down to our cabin for a drink. I had been working for all of two weeks on the Saint David but it was about to end in tears. The girls were supposed to disembark at Dun Laoghaire but through a chain of events, the girls and some of us got drunk and they missed disembarking. About a half hour out at sea someone saw one of the girls on board, as the ship was supposed to be now devoid of passengers. The captain came down and saw the six girls and it was decided that the ship would have to turn back and let the girls get off. Some one else had to join them and after some deliberation between my mates, I decided to take the fall. I was single and the rest of the guys were married. So I took the rap even though the captain told me that he knew I wasn't the guilty party, he would let me go without a blemish on my sea book. He also told me that under normal circumstances he would have sacked the whole catering staff but it had been very difficult to crew the ship in the first instance. Now I knew why I got the job, quickly I realised that not reporting to the pool on a regular basis meant you were looked over for a good job. As I walked down the gangplank some of my mates gave me a few quid for taking the rap and thanked me as I made my way first to Dublin and then back home and normality. It seemed by now I wasn't cut out for long term employment or commitment and I suppose that's the story of my life. A lot of ifs buts and maybes and there were lots.

Chapter 32

The Rena Del Mar

My next move brought me back to Southampton and getting back to what I knew best drinking and dossing. One day Walsh and I were sitting in the Oxford, a pub that we didn't really frequent when some one came in in and told Walsh that there was two strange looking guys outside asking for him. He just gave me a nod and told me to go and see who they were. We were actually waiting on the Carmania coming in as we had a few friends on it. Mickey Mc Quade and Frankie Donnelly who we hadn't saw in a while and I was looking forward to a good dinking session. As usual I bounced out and the two guys were standing a few feet from the pub entrance. Both had long hair and one had a beard and was wearing canvas like trousers or jeans and they were like a red colour and he had a three quarter length leather jacket on. Very mod looking, trendy and the other guy was much the same. So I approached with caution. One of them turned around and it was none other than Joe McDonnell who had came down from London to see Walsh and the boys. The other guy was from Ballymoney, he was called Ricky and was a protestant who I came to meet regular, later on in my life and became friendly with him. I'm telling his religion to show that it didn't matter what religion you were in England you were iris and that was it "Where's Walsh Fra" Joe asked and I pointed to the pub and he followed me in. After a few drinks, Mickey and Frankie came in some time later and after a lot of catching up and slagging we all got gargled. Two o'clock came around very quickly and the pub was closing so we got a few beers to go along with the bottles of Bacardi that Mickey and Frankie had taken ashore from the Carmania. They were called docking bottles. Now we had to go to somewhere to drink the carryout and we finished in Katsie and Tony Maddens house were we all got steaming drunk. I don't remember much after that but Mickey and Frankie re-joined their ship again and Joe and Ricky headed back to London and I was as sick as a pig having drunk and smoked a lot.

A few days later I decided after dossing about the Hamp to try and get a job. I had got barred in three pubs in one night in Southampton when a young friend Colum Tohill who was visiting his brother don came down to see me and we were steaming. This was a time when it was difficult to get barred, as it was a little piece of Belfast around the area of Saint Mary's. The first pub we got evicted from was the Kingsland for I poured a pint over a barpersons head. Then we went to the Joiners Arms and got barred for rearing up there. The next pub was the Angel and after being thrown out of there I remember throwing a brick at the windows egged on by Anthony Walsh. Much as I tried, I couldn't break them. I had this feeling that I was going to make the residents of the Hamp receive a bit of their own medicine so to speak, after all their soldiers had ruined our lives. That night Tohill left and it was some time before I saw him again back in Belfast.

After a few weeks drinking and generally acting the idiot I went to the pool and to my surprise I was offered a job on my favourite ship, **The Rena Del Mar,** the ship I had heard so much about at our corner years before and the one I done a two week trip on, only to be sacked. Anyway down I went and signed on. Much to my amazement the chief steward hadn't remembered sacking me and I dandered down to my cabin. There I met by Frankie Short and Bouncy Henry. The first thing Short asked me was what job I got and I told him I was a "KP" or kitchen porter. He looked at Bouncy in amazement and asked me would I not rather work in the scullery and I my reply was, "Why"? As we sailed that night I was introduced to the galley and then the bombshell hit me. Both Short and Bouncy expected me to do the work. Were they in for a surprise! Short and me had went to school together and ran about most of our early days together along with Buster Crossin so we new each other well. Short was about five foot six, well built, with the agility of a cheetah and a heart like a lion. Bouncy was a little bigger and was round and fat and like Short had been very good amateur boxer. They ran the Rena and it was all about the survival of the fittest and I was here disrupting their little ways. What it boiled down to was that they would rather have had an English man who they could rely on to do the work in the galley. So they tried unsuccessfully to coerce me into being what was termed in a funny sort of way, a galley slave.

They must have been joking. I was five foot seven and skinny as a rake but it was all the better if your peers were hard men you had nothing to loose by standing up to them. After all you're not expected to win. As a KP your only tool was a three foot long piece of thin rope with a hook on the end which snuggled nicely into the handles of the large pots and deep frying trays that had to be moved from one side of the galley to the other to be washed by the guys in the scullery. I think Jamesy Kane supplied the rope.

That night as per normal on the boats we went to the pig and got drunk. I consumed a large amount of drink and after an hour or so found my cabin down the working alleyway that resembled a dark back entry in Belfast. After getting into my bunk I fell fast asleep only to be aroused by the glory hole calling us for work. Another little guy shared the cabin with us called Chick Connolly, a little waif like guy from Glasgow who didn't drink as much as us, so he was up and on the ball. As I looked over at Bouncy he nodded to me to get out of my bunk and I thought I will turn too as I was only back on the ship after been previously sacked. So on with my jeans, tee shirt and flip-flops. I made my way up to the mess room and had breakfast thinking Short and Bouncy would follow. After breakfast I made my way to the galley and cleared up the mess, which wasn't much as breakfast wasn't a big cook up. After doing a scrub down with the help of some cooks I wondered where the other two had gone and I made my way down to my cabin to get a shower and get changed. I was now free for a couple of hours and I was going to have a wee nap up on deck. As I opened the cabin door, I turned on the light as it was still in darkness and Short beckoned me to be quiet as he and Bouncy were sleeping. It was the roughest cabin on the ship and after two days the glory hole that also cleaned out your cabin refused to enter the place. He was a big guy from Leeson Street called Gerry Kettle who was actually a friend of my older brothers as well as Jimmy Short, Frankie's older brother. It caused a little friction but the status quo remained and we didn't see much of him and we just treated the cabin as a doss house and every thing was just thrown at your arse as they say in Belfast. It was a different story on captain's inspection day and we usually spend a few hours cleaning our cabin, which was now called "The dug out".

By now I was getting the feel of the ship as we headed into the glorious Mediterranean and we became sun gods and I spent a lot of time up on deck bronzing my pale skin. After our first port of call I decided it was time for rebellion on my behalf. If the other two thought they had a galley slave they had another thing coming.

The Mediterranean was a very warm place not that any of us needed an excuse for heavy drinking but you could rationalise it with "it's the heat" and so the pints flowed. It was then the fun started and in the morning it was game of cat and mouse between the three of us cabin mates. One would say "it's your turn to get up early" and vice versa and it became like a ritual as each of us put one leg out of bed only for the others to jump back in to bed.

One morning the ships cook actually came down to the cabin and pleaded with us to at least come up and show our faces as the work was almost done. After some deliberation we decided that it might be better if one of us got up and went up to the galley just to appease a now frustrated cook. So as the trip developed on and I got the hang of things I decided if they were cruising, so was I, much to the annoyance of Short and Bouncy. So it was if you do some work, I will do the same. It was all done in fun but I do know the pair would have rather have had some English man who they could manipulate and take it easy.

After visiting a few ports I visited my favourite port Gibraltar. One night we explored Gib and got drunk in a little pub of the main street and we met a guy whose surname was Salmon. Was he sorry he told us that? He became John West, pink, or smoked and any or name associated with the fish. After about and hour of Short and me torturing him about his name he got up to leave. As we were sitting on a type of gallery he turned to tell us where to get off and he fell like a stunt man in a movie hitting every stair and balustrade on his way down the stairs. The funny side of it was that he didn't spill a drop from the glass he had in his hand and how he never broke his neck I will never know how. Maybe there's a message in there that the drink is more precious than life itself at times.

After that the trip sailed along with out any major events and when we arrived back in Southampton Bouncy decided to take some leave. Now hopefully Short and me would get our own galley slave. This was a normal thing in the merchant navy and in some cases it was done on a rota basis, day of day on and the **Rena** was a very easy ship especially when working in the galley. Chic also decided to take some leave and that meant two new KPs would be joining us. Now hopefully we would definitely get our own galley slave this time.

A new guy signed on and guess whom the new guy in the cabin was, Francey Hogg a guy from Divis Street another Francey who definitely wouldn't play ball. It seemed inevitable that he would do his own thing as well. A couple of minutes later the head chef sent for me and asked me would I do one trip in the scullery along with Francey as the sculls as they were called didn't know the score. It was now the four fffffs for fuck sake I thought. To be honest the chef was a smashing guy called Paul King and I didn't refuse and he told me not to worry I would go back to being a KP next trip. I was now stuck in the scullery with the other eff and things went along swimmingly until we hit our first port. It was decided he would have the day off and I would get my day at the next port. Anyway after stowing everything away Francey and me headed for the cabin. I had to do lunch and then go ashore but he was free and he headed up town. After a few days at sea we hit another port and it was now my turn for the day off and it meant Francey had to clean up after lunch and dinner and I could go ashore after breakfast. Short told me that the **Carmania** was tied up across from us and a lot of Belfast men were on it. So we headed over and boarded her and the first man I met was Davy Mc Comb, then Danny Mc Quaid and believe it or not my cousin, wait for it, another one, Francey Walsh, the older brother of Eamon who I had met in Australia. So after a big piss up ashore then back to the **Carmania** and some more drinking I made my way back to the **Rena**. The first port of call after a feed of drink was always the galley for some grub and as I walked in I near fainted. Every pot, pan, or any other utensil used for cooking were strewn all over the galley. I nearly cried as the chef was standing along with the cook scratching their heads. Paul just looked at me and said, "it has to be done before breakfast in the morning and if you do it you will be back to KP tomorrow." As I got stuck in I was dropping pots and every now and then scalding myself with hot water. It was about four o'clock in the morning as I headed down to my cabin to turn in and I was knackered and was no sooner in my bunk than I fell asleep. Next day I was shattered and I fucked Francey Hogg off and told him, "You've got it all to yourself now. I'm a back to KPing, now just get on with it on your own." It took a while to renew the friendship but it was all right after a few drinks in the pig. He didn't last very long in the scullery and got the last card in the pack, "The Sack" the following trip.

Two weeks later we were back in Gibraltar and a team of us went ashore to enjoy the hostelry and have a laugh. I was wearing scrubbed out Levis' with fringed bottoms, a kaftan, a white sleeveless afghan, and a straw boater and pink coloured oddly shaped sunglasses. I stood like a sore thumb or beacon with my beads around my neck and my bright coloured baseball boots. After visiting The Fox and Hounds public house and downing a few vodkas or Bacardi's and coke we decided to move to the Gibraltar arms, which was more uptown. After a few minutes one of the guys "Ricky" who was with us bought a packet of nuts and accidentally spilled some on the recently carpeted floor. As he tried to clean up the mess some people had already trampled the nuts into the floor "after all it was a pub not a palace". The owner then arrived and made a whole scene over nothing and demanded that he be reimbursed for the cost of a new carpet. We all laughed at him and in no time he called for the cops and they duly arrived and started prodding us with batons. A couple of us maneuverer our way out of the situation, but a small cop about five foot one inch in height followed us to another part of the bar where he started reading the riot act and prodding us with his baton. Short was getting very annoyed at the situation and he asked me to just hold the cops hands and I duly obliged. Short gave him a few digs about the ribs and as he fell to the ground we made our way back towards the ship in a hurry. What we didn't know was we had committed a federal offence as far as they were concerned and they made a big thing of it. Reinforcements were called and this little keystone like cops saturated the main street in Gib.

As we made our way down the main street we all separated and I tried in vain to look salubrious and anonymous. How could I do that dressed the way I was and it wasn't long before a local pointed me out to a passing policeman who had over looked me among a crowd of tourists. I was arrested and taken to the barracks where on arrival I was informed that my cohort was in the cells and after giving my name, I was brought to the cells and doubled up with Short. After telling Short how I got caught he related to me his bit of an adventure. He never did anything in halves and he described how he ran down the main street like a mad man. As one of the keystone boys stepped out and called on him to halt, Short let a roar out of him and the cop fainted. This was to be proven right a month or so later when we appeared at court and the wee cop reported just as Short had said, at verbatim.

After we were in the cells a few hours some of the crew came to see us, Brian Mc Ilwee the guy who had introduced me into being an altar boy, Terry Moylan whom Short and me had went to school with all our life and a few others. After leaving us they were adamant, as were we that we would be released and driven back to the ship before it sailed at six o'clock. After a few interviews with the cops we were locked up in this draconian cell about three times the size of the one in Tennant Street barracks. As we sat and talked we wondered what was keeping them coming to release us. After all we didn't really do much except that Short had frightened a cop so much he fainted and we issued a few digs to another. As I looked at my watch it was five o'clock and we sat patiently waiting for the key to turn and our release.

A quarter to six and we listened as the **Rena**'s loud horn blew for tugs and the realisation that we were for staying crept in. Six o'clock and we could hear the **Rena** giving her last blow as she steamed away from my favourite port that I had told Bouncy I'd love to stay in for a while. That night we got something to eat and then a strange thing happened. We were told we had a visit. After looking at each other we came to the conclusion it must be the board of trade or shipping master as we were now distressed seamen as anyone who misses a ship is called. As we went into the visiting room we saw two big rough looking men and as we sat down at the table one of them informed us that Brian Mc Ilwee had told them of our plight and they decided to come and visit us. His name or one of them was John McCall a

Glasgow man now residing in Gib. He was an old friend of Jimmy Short, Frankie's older brother. After some chitchat John decided that he would bail us out if possible, but he wasn't ready for what the cops wanted for the bail. It was set at something like a grand each, which was about a year's wages for a labourer in Gib, in other words a lot of money. After some negotiation John found out to his and our relief that he didn't have to put any money up front and after signing some papers he was told we would be released after we met the harbour master who had to now get us somewhere to stay. A few hours later we were booked into a Spanish type hotel come villa and taken to a restaurant and told this is were we would get lunch and dinner for the duration of our time in Gib. We had only the clothes we stood in and about three quid between us, with no means of earning any money. Things looked bleak.

After settling into our new home we decided to go and visit John Mc Cauls pub to thank him and make our presence known. As we walked in I just felt at home as the Tamla Motown music belted out from a large reel-to-reel tape recorder resting upon the drinks shelves that beckoned me. After ordering some drinks we asked the barmaid if John was about. She was a bit vague with her answers. Then she asked us. Who we were and what we wanted him for. The alarm bells had rang with her and me as well. After a few gin and bitter lemon they stopped, the alarm bell that is. I was beyond wondering. This was the life, a King Edward cigar in one hand and a tall stool at the bar and no worries about where I was going to eat or sleep.

A few hours later John arrived along with his mates and he didn't even notice Short and me sitting at the bar drinking. I introduced myself as I was the more forward and he didn't even know who I was. I then I introduced him to Frankie and it all fell into place and he ordered us a drink which led onto a drunken night where we exchanged stories of Belfast and Southampton. We arranged to meet the next night and as we made our way to our lodging house I wondered was being in Gib a good idea. We were slowly running out of money and that meant long boring days on "The Rock" with little or no way of earning any.

After a few days we found or selves with ten bob to our names and it wouldn't have bought us an ice-lolly, so I had to get my thinking hat on. It was Saturday and I knew that the Prix De l'Arc De Triomphe was the next day and the greatest horse I ever saw was running in it. I suggested to Short who never had a real bet in his life that all we had to do was pick two other certainties and do the old Belfast bet, three two bob doubles and a four bob treble. All we needed was one other winner as Nijinsky was home and hosed and we would at least get our money back if the third one didn't win. After some arguing and debating Short said that it was the waste of our last ten bob and he wanted to go to a photo booth and get our pictures taken for prosperity. After some haranguing I won the argument and went and did the bet and waited and hoped.

As history will tell the horse got a bad ride from the greatest one, Lester Piggott and even if he had won the other two certainties I picked were also beaten. Demoralisation kicked in and I was reminded it was my entire fault. Short told me what we should have done with our precious ten bob. That night we went down to John Johnston's, he had two names, ostensibly looking for him but in reality we hung around hoping that someone would buy us a drink. Short wasn't really into it and kept going on about our infamous ten bob but I was worldlier in the drinking world and how it works. I knew it wouldn't be long before someone took pity on two distressed seamen. Just as we were about to leave John and his mates entered and as we pretended to leave he beckoned us to have a few drinks on the house. He had leased the bar we learned from two Gibraltarian brothers and he said he would be giving up the lease soon and it was coming of a broad board so to speak. One of John's mates was a builder and he talked about how difficult it was to get good tradesmen especially bricklayers in Gibraltar. He had no sooner finished his sentence when I said, "Look no further, Frankie's nick name is Silver Trowel back in Belfast". Short just laughed and after some questioning it was decided that Frankie would start the next day and his wages would be about sixty pounds a week. That was it. Our troubles were over.

Frankie was a bad riser in the morning, a habit I had myself but I decided that I would be his rapper up. A term used in Belfast when I was a kid for someone usually a woman with a loud voice who knocked on your door until you arose to go to work, all for a small fee. It was all agreed and we decided that it was time to go and get some shuteye. When we arrived at the lodgings I borrowed an alarm clock and set it for seven o'clock the next morning.

The next morning the alarm went off like the bell usually associated with a fire brigade or an old ambulance and I crawled out of bed and shook Short for ten minutes and got him wakened. I then gave him a bit of a giddy up, about how he was known as Silver Trowel and sent him off to work and I crawled back into bed. I wondered what I was going to do while he was at work and I decided I had to get my old thinking hat on again. After getting out of bed about ten o'clock I got a cup of tea and then headed to John's pub only to be surprisingly told that I had a slate and I could have what I wanted daily. "Fuck me" I had landed in heaven. After meekly asking for a bottle of beer and nursing it for what seemed an eternity I got another then bingo I ordered a gin and bitter lemon a King Edward and that was me until six o'clock when Short came in and we went and got dinner. All this was laid on by the harbour master, for us two distressed seamen well one anyway, I was enjoying it all. It was all I ever dreamt of. But watch what you pray for it may not be what you really wanted.

This went on for some weeks and in between the **Rena Del Mar** arrived back in port and we decided we had enough of The Rock and we were going to jump on the ship and make our way back to Southampton. After some planning the night before we decided that we would jump through the gun port doors that were always opened when the ship was docked. Then we would just get lost on the ship until it sailed and that would be our troubles over. The idea sounded great as we made our way to the ship on arrival at the ship it was surrounded by police cars and police officers on foot. We listened over the public address system that informed everyone that Short and myself were not allowed on board the ship under any circumstances. Did we rob a bank? Kill someone, or commit the crime of the century? No we had got involved in a drunken brawl, which usually involved a slap on the wrist, then taken maybe in cuffs to the ship and told never to set foot ashore again. No we were being treated like big time criminals.

Some of our friends that were still on the ship met us and told us that they had been warned not to try and take us on board. Bobby Lindbergh, Black

Tie that's all I knew him by, Terry Moylan and some others met us and we went and got drunk as our plans were scuppered and there was no chance of boarding the Rena Del Mar. After a few hours drinking the rest of the crew left to catch the Rena and it was decided that Short would start back to work the next morning. Well that was my decision as someone had to pay my bar bill and it wasn't going to be me.

A few weeks later we were at court and the case was put back until the next time the Rena was back in Gib and it all looked okay and Short assured me if we got a jail sentence he would knock out the two cops guarding us and we would make our way onto the Rena by hook or by crook and I agreed. Frankie would have been quite capable of what he said and was one of the toughest and bravest persons I ever met.

But it was back to the grindstone at least for him and back to the bar room stool for me as I drank daily awaiting Frankie to finish work. We then went to eat but on many occasions I was so drunk I didn't even eat the dinner. It was cooked in so much oil you'd have thought you were in Texas or Saudi Arabia. It was inedible for me when I was sick with drink but on occasions I was glad of it, most days anyway. One night in John's bar a few of his mates arrived for a bit of a party and then I sensed all wasn't what it was supposed to be. John introduced us to his partner; Pat a very attractive blonde who after some conversation I realised was a lady with plenty of worldly knowledge and may have even been the brains behind big John.

As the drink flowed the picture was now becoming very clear that John was behind with his rent and owed a few quid here and there and was for exiting The Rock in a hurry. As the conversation went on and the drink eased our minds the question was raised about could Frankie or me swim in deep water. Well I quickly informed the company that all I could do was a length of the local swimming bathes in Belfast but Frankie jumped in and told everyone he could swim for a few miles. The attention and focus quickly turned to him and one of the companies asked him could he swim with a wee package of diamonds around his waist. I jumped in and assured every one that Short could do it and it wouldn't be a problem. I was drunk by now and was more interested in chatting up big Johns partner. A few plans were brandished about and it was decided that a plan would be drawn up after our court case in a few weeks time. Not a lot changed over the next few weeks, Frankie went to work and I went to the pub and drank and he paid the bill on Friday night.

A few weeks later the Rena was back in Gib and that was the day we had to appear in court. We met all our mates who were still working on her in a pub in the centre of the town. Bobby Lindberg bought me a pair of shoes and a shirt, so I would look a bit more respectful in court. After a long chat and planning our defence and who was going to say what we headed for the petty sessions.

Black tie was there and a few other crewmembers and we decided that he was going to be our star witness. But we were in for a surprise. I never got his proper name but he was like a canary and he never shut up in the box. It became a laugh a minute as he told lie after lie, but at least he tried. He told story after story all nothing to do with the case and it became and embarrassment. After a few minutes the court went quiet and we waited with bated breath to hear how much we were going to be fined. Both of us had never been in trouble before and we told each other we would be back on the ship after we had a few drinks.

Chapter 33

Short spell inside

Then came the bombshell, we were sentenced to two months each in jail. Then came the announcement from the judge, "Take them down!" We were then handcuffed and placed in the back of a cop's car and driven to the jail which was right at the top of the rock and Short's escape scenario went through the proverbial window. As we pulled up outside the Victorian style draconian castle, that was to be home for the next lot of weeks. I wondered what lay ahead of us. As we marched into the guvnor's office handcuffed to two big cops this time, "no wee toy town cops this time." The guvnor took charge and we were now in his custody. After going through the usual paper work we were issued with our prison garb. The uniform had to be the most degrading clothes I've ever worn in my life and I felt like dirt.

The trousers I got belonged to either a big prison officer or cop as they had a truncheon pocket in them. I was then handed a piece of cord two tie around my waist to hold them up and a pair of brown gutties and a blue pinstripe shirt. Then a pair of socks was thrown playfully at me by the screw, who said to me, "You'll grow into that outfit," he laughed. I was less than nine stone and less impressed by his jokes. I was wearing a uniform that can only be described as for a big porter bellied screw, not a skinny wee runt like me. Short didn't do much better but we both decided it was time "pun intended", to get on with it and grin and bare it.

For the first two weeks you had to eat your food in your cell and then you gained a star, no not a gold star, you became what was called a star prisoner, Nothing to do with being a pop star or the like, I hasten to add. The food I have to say was crap; porridge for breakfast, no milk as it was scarce in Gib. There weren't many fields there for cows, if they even had any. You never got an egg or bacon and the bread was weighed and when you got chips they literally counted them. You also got cucumber, like who the fuck ate cucumber from Belfast in the nineteen seventies era. I don't think I'd ever seen one never mind ate one. Anyway it worked out well for me as Short loved it and I swapped him for his chips so it worked out in my favour. After two weeks we got a pair of boots to wear and mine were a size nine or ten and I only took a six. "What were they trying to do? Humiliate us" well if they were, it worked very well.

A few days later we were lining up for our dinner, like there were only twelve of us in total but you had to queue up and get served from a half door kitchen. We were all lined up but a new prisoner had arrived and he was from Tangiers we later learned. He walked in front of Short and me as he wasn't willing to queue up and was trying to bully us but he had made a big mistake. As we tried to put him in his place he threw one at me and spat in Shorts face. He was a big lump of a guy but Short just kicked him on the shin with his new boots and as he went down to feel his shin, yes he caught him with a right hook and knocked him clean out.

That was the last bother we had in the jail but in fairness the other guys were okay. There was one English lad who looked in desperate bad health, a couple from Canada, and a Gibraltarian who refused to do national service. In fact none of them really deserved to be in jail as they were in for smoking dope and the like and if you were sentenced to two years or more you were sent to England to do your time. Anyway time went by relatively fast in the jail which was visited by the Gibraltar apes who were the only form of entertainment available along with a table tennis table. There wasn't any radio or television just the odd book and in between times I use to get melody maker and the New Musical Express and I remember putting a big double page photograph of Dylan on the wall in my cell, much to the annoyance of the head screw a Mister Mena.

You were supposed to keep your cell neat and tidy and make your bed daily. Well as I said previously we had just come off a ship that we dossed on so we weren't going to change now we were in jail. After a dressing down the screw told me to tidy my cell up and to keep it tidy and make my bed every day. He said he would be checking up on me daily. In fairness the screws weren't bad and really didn't bother us much.

About the third week the guvnor informed us that we could write letters home if we so desired. In reality nobody in our families knew we were locked up, or so we thought. After a bit of deliberation the governor who was a nice man told me I was not the type of person whom he usually came across in jail. He then agreed upon our request that we could get our letters to be posted outside and our parents wouldn't be any the wiser as to us being in jail. So Frankie and myself wrote home telling our Mas how good the trip was going and that we would be home at Christmas. Little did we know the story had been printed in the News of the World and everyone knew we were in gaol? So we were hoodwinked and our parents played along with it all?

A few weeks later and it was time to be released and we were handed our belongings. Short had a wee bag of stuff and I had all my worldly belongings in a King Edward cigar box. As we got a taxi from the jail to go to the Board of Trade or Harbour Masters office were he told us that we could fly home the next day or we may have to wait for a ship to come in and we could go home on one as distressed seamen. I hated flying but I decided that I wasn't going to stay on the Rock by myself as my better half had declared he was going home on the plane, win lose or draw. So we went and had a few drinks and got what little stuff we had gathered up. I had my afghan and my yellow football pullover and my jeans on now as I stood in the pair of shoes Bobby Lindberg bought me. I hated them as they didn't fit into my hippy image, or so I thought. As the shoes were only for court I decide to leave them and go home as I came out of jail with my baseball boots on and the rest. So next day I got a lot of gin into me and I can't remember much about getting on the plane. But I do remember looking out the window and I saw it was a Trident made by Rolls Royce and as I was a bit of a car freak, "I said well that's half the battle." A few hours later we landed in London and I was steaming and the next thing I remember was walking into Gatties in the high street in the Hamp. Big Davy Neeson was the first person we met and he got us a drink and after a few more drinks and some slabbering about our time in jail I finished up sleeping in Anthony Walsh's house. How I got there I don't know, but I had made my mind up I was going back to Belfast. After a few days running around I got my fare off Walsh and headed to Belfast by boat. No more flying for me, well not in the mean time anyway. I had my stay in Gibraltar and in hindsight it was a good learning curve.

Chapter 34

Back in town

When I arrived back in Belfast it was December nineteen seventy and it was freezing, having just left the warmth of Gib a few days earlier. I had no gear, only what I was wearing. The afghan didn't really fit in but it looked class to me. Think Gerry Conlon in the film, **In the Name of the Father** when he arrives home from London and you have the picture. So after running around drinking and retelling some stories about Short and me it was time to get a few quid, as Christmas was beckoning.

I was reacquainting with my old mates, Josie Riley, Chip McFarlane, Billy Halligan, and Francey Walsh and I needed to start thinking about how I was going to get that now elusive few quid. I cuckooed into Chips house were I slept most nights in between sleeping in Walsh's house, my cousins in Osman Street. There was a carry out in Chips house every weekend accompanied by the usual sing song and I always gave an oul song accompanied by Paddy Dolan on his harmonica. He was Kitties cousin and although he didn't drink with us he was always at the singsongs. The craic was great, smoke filled the air, as we all smoked then and everyone had a great time and there was no shortage of drink. There was never a row among the older men as they drank bottles of stout and slagged each other. Some times Lazy Tom Clarke would put his head in, or Mickey Molloy it was just like the pub at the weekend. The Saturday night soup was there for us all to help ourselves. I was twenty-one at this time and Chip was a little older, talk about two wee old men. The others were twenty years older than us at least but there were no age barriers. On Sunday wee Kitty, Chips mum, would hire a car and we all went to Dundalk, Omeath and Carlingford for a drink and that included Chip and myself. The driver was Bud Dorrian, and Paddy and Kitty sat in the front, Chip, me, Jackie McBurney, or maybe Jim Robinson or Paddy Darling or Danny Braniff sat in the back. Sometimes all of the fore mentioned were there. We all piled in to the Morris Oxford usually about seven of us and away we went and no one complained about space. They were just glad to be going and they knew they would return drunk and in all honesty wee Kitty bought a lot of drink and paid for the car.

One night after a trip to the south Paddy decided that Kitty be left home and we would go to the Mandeville, a club in downtown Belfast where we met John Manning. As we were all half drunk we made our way to the front door but it wasn't a straightforward walk in. After some haggling the doorman decided to let us in but he said I was too young and that I could sit with him downstairs in the storeroom and wait on the others to finish. It was the longest night ever. The drink was dying in me and try as I might the doorman wouldn't believe I was twenty years old and there was no way he was going to change mind. After an hour or so we all left and headed home but I never forgot that doorman who I cursed all night. In fairness I only looked about sixteen so in a way he was right. Next week or so Chip got a job on the **Capetown Castle** and he was away and I had to find another place to put the head down and I decided to go back to sea as well but couldn't get a boat.

It was now early on in nineteen seventy-one and as usual I was at a loose end and looking something to do to get that easy few quid. One night Billy Halligan asked me to accompany him up to a new youth club he had joined, **The Rapid.** I looked at him as if he had two heads but went long with him anyway, like who wanted to join a youth club. As we walked up Panton Street I reminded him that this was Henry Kane's old scrap yard. He then told me that the Rapid Metals used to own it and that's where all the steel structures used in the construction of the barricades came from here.

As we walked through the wicket gate I looked around and it reminded me of the walls in Gibraltar jail. They were built so high they would be impossible to scale and this was only to keep thieves out from stealing scrap. After looking about the yard we walked into what was once the non-ferrous shed when it was a scrap yard. As soon as we walked in Billy took off his coat and got stuck into work. They were putting concrete floors in and Billy got himself a trowel and started rubbing the floors up. Just then the main man walked in: Nugget. We exchanged a bit of small talk. He then introduced me to a man who was wearing a suit collar and tie who was called Jim Fitzpatrick or as he became more commonly known too us as "Fitzy". Again after a bit of a chat Fitzy asked me, "Are you not going to give a hand Fra?" I looked at him with a little distain and was going to say are you not going to give a hand but I let it go. I think he sort of half read my mind and for a little time after there was little disagreements at times between him and me. Later on it morphed into a good friendship. Anyway I told Big Halligan I was going and he said he would see me at the weekend.

After a few weeks and a lot of hard work the Rapid opened up as a youth club and I became a member. It was full of kids who needed somewhere to go and get off the streets and feel safe. The Falls had become a place for constant daily gun battles and rioting. It was an experience to watch the kids grow up over time into manhood and most remained friends for years.

By this time Leaf became a member of the gang he and I formed a friendship. Some nights when I was sleeping in Walsh's settee he would be sleeping on the chair as we listened to Gasoline Alley by Rod Stewart. Leaf acquired his name from Frankie Short when one night he arrived at the corner dressed all in green. Frankie took one look at him and just said something like, "You're like a leaf that just fell out of a tree," and that was that. He was now known as Leaf.

After a few weeks my Ma was awarded a new house in Creeslough Park in the Lenadoon area. It was planned that they would move on Thursday but instead had to wait until Friday until wee Paddy Pudding Brady and his lorry Arkle became available. So they moved on Friday the 5th of March 1971 and Paddy brought the rest of the furniture up on Saturday. This was very important time in my life. In between, Eamon Walsh who was now working shore side had acquired twenty cases of a beer called Lowenbrau beer, which had been lying in Mc Kenna and Mc Kinleys, were he worked unnoticed for a few months. It later finished in my Mas old house and it was planned that we would have a party in a few days.

That night Billy Halligan, Francey Walsh, Josie Riley, a few others and me were drinking in the Burning Embers at the corner of Servia and Bosnia Street and the craic was great. The pub got its name from when it was mysteriously burned down but the owner got a few quid insurance and rekindled it into a nice wee pub with and upstairs lounge. The clue is in the last sentence to what really happened it when it went on fire. After a few drinks the night went on and all who thought they were the leading lights in the fight for an Irish Republic filled the pub. Later that night after wondering aimlessly about the corner with Francey Walsh we decided we go and call for Billy and go and get chips in the Chicken and Chip on the Falls Road. After getting the chips we walked down Peel Street and along Raglan Street and we came across a riot that was going on. In the mean time I was chatting to a girl I was seeing and we went for a lumber. So in between the lumbering and a bit of rioting the gunfire rang out from the paratroopers and everyone dispersed.

They had indiscriminately fired down Balaclava Street at unarmed people and it had a profound effect on others and me. A few hours later I met another friend Roy Smyth and we dandered down to Sultan Street to the Edel Quinn rooms that was acting as a first aid centre for those shot and injured to find out who had been injured.

A big Guy called Phil McMahon was badly shot up and was leaving in an ambulance to go to the royal Victoria hospital for treatment. A few minutes later we were talking to one of the Taggart's and were informed that Big Billy had been shot dead. This was too much to comprehend, as it was the first person we knew to suffer this fate in the troubles. Roy and myself had been in the same class at school as Billy and to be truthful neither of us believed what we were hearing. We then went into Taggart's house and Mrs. Taggart, her name was Sally, was very kind to us all, made us tea and toast as we listened to everyone retelling what happened Big Billy.

About a half hour later Roy and me left and wondered around the district totally in shock. As we wondered aimlessly we came closer to the Grosvenor Road so we decided to walk over to the Royal to find out for ourselves. We knew every blade of grass and most parts of the hospital inside, as it had been our playground at times as we searched for empty lemonade bottles, to get the three-dee reward when they were returned to the shop. As we walked along a corridor where all the wards ran off we met a porter from our district and he informed us that Billy's body was in the morgue. As we already knew where the morgue was we headed there to investigate for ourselves and see if we could find his body. You have to remember we were both in deep shock, "this wasn't a morbid thing". I know I was in total disbelief. As we gained entry into the morgue through a small window we were amazed at what we saw. There were bodies all covered in white sheets and we asked ourselves were do we start. After looking at some bodies we finally came across Billy's and as we rolled back the sheet all I saw was a large bandage wrapped around his forehead. It was a terrible thing to see and Roy and myself where definitely in deep shock now. This was real. As we looked at his feet there was a tag on it and a bandage on his ankle, which his Da later told me at the court hearing some years later that he was also shot in the ankle as he was falling. Just for the record Billy's father was awarded a small sum of money for the loss of his son and they don't award compensation to anyone they think were guilty of anything. But no money could ever replace the loss or compensate his parents for the loss of their twenty one year old son. He was a smashing fellow as well. Rest easy Billy it was a pleasure knowing you. A couple of day later after the funeral we went back to my Mas old house to have our own wake for Billy. As the night went on Roy and me retold the story of the morgue but deep down I felt guilty. Would Billy have come out that night if I hadn't called for him to go and get chips and fish? I often wonder and it brings an odd tear to my eye, like now. As the night went on and the drink flowed we were all startled by the sound of heavy gunfire. Little did we know that the Provisional IRA had gone into the **Burning Embers** and set it on fire with the customers who wouldn't leave still in it. The fire was started behind the bar so none of the punters were in danger. I believed and still do that it was a form of retribution against some members of the IRA that sat drinking as our young people were being shot dead in the street. A la Nero played as Rome burned. I was later on in years told my theory was wrong but I'm sticking to my side of things.

As the gunfire took a lull we decided to take a walk around the district to see what had happened. As we approached Leeson Street we noticed a Ford Cortina parked erratically outside the **Cracked Cup** with the doors lying open. As we moved tentatively towards it we met some guy who told us to get offside that a feud had started between the Stickies and the Provo's and we had best get off the streets. He also informed us that a guy called Charlie

Hughes had been shot dead in Cyprus Street. I knew Charlie from his uncle Joes yard and he was a neighbour who also lived in Servia Street. It was really time to get off side. So Roy went one way and I went back to my old house and told the rest of the lads who where still there that it was time to go, or they could stay all night as it was going to be hot and heavy and very dangerous. After a few days and Charlie's funeral the district got a bit quiet but it was never the same as people now sided with one army or the other which led to the break up of life long friendships.

Chapter 35

The grumpy rooms:
Willie Norney and Conn Connolly

A few days after dossing around the workmen came and blocked up my Ma's old house. People were now moving to different areas, like Lenadoon, Twinbrook, both large sprawling housing estates on the outskirts of Belfast where funnily enough we went to see the twin foals when it was, "Twinbrook Dairy Farm". One particular family was the McGeown's and I knew them quite well, especially the mother Josie, who should have been an actor. She could mimic anyone and was great for telling stories about what was going on in the district.

As she was flitting the local term for moving house, Leaf and myself saw an opportunity to get a wee house for ourselves which later was christened the **Grumpy Rooms**, a satirical take on the **Spanish Rooms** a well known drinking establishment that was famous or infamous for the sale of cider. As the Mc Geown family left, Leaf and I moved in.

This was to become our home for about eighteen months. All that was left in the house was a double bed, a gas fire, a mini main hot water machine, a wee chair, but it was ours. What more could one ask for, hot water, plenty of heat, all for free as the gas meter was opened and all you had to do was put a coin in, turn it and take it out of the cash box. After a few days we got a few bits of furniture and settled in to the Grumpy rooms.

Two very good friend lived a cross the street, Marie and Nugget Nugent and after a bit of negotiations Marie agreed that she would make us our dinner each day for the princely sum of thirty bob or one pound ten shillings a week. We already knew that she made good grub as we were never out of the house as Nugget was now the chairman of the Rapid Club. Sometimes their house was like an extension of the club holding committee meetings in the front kitchen before the club got its own room in their new premises. We were all familiar with each other and full of big ideas and some of them were achieved. Some said it was the best club in town and it probably was. Danny "Rocky" Radcliffe always told me it was the best club he was ever in and I'll gladly take his word for it.

After a week or two we decided we needed new furniture to add to what we had in the Grumpy rooms. We acquired the interior seating of a car before it was burned and it was now our living room suite. We had an eclectic mix in our own avant-garde way. A mix, between a cars interior, two wee chairs, a beer box for a coffee table and that was it. We also acquired a filing cabinet that became our larder. It fell off the back of some lorry but it was in great nick, it was new.

Many people visited us when we lived there and one even stayed. It was like a home for waifs and strays or those just passing through. Someone who had went on the drink and their wife had thrown them out, stayed over night. One night a guy called Jamesy Curley walked in with a Welsh man who we called, "John The Boy." He asked could we put him up for the night as he was homeless and he would be away the next day. "Does he think this is a hotel?" I asked myself as I looked at Leaf. True to his word he arrived on Monday and left on Tuesday - over a year later. It was now an ménage a trio` and it was time to renegotiate our contract with Marie, as it was now three dinners a day.

Weeks went by and the war euphemistically called the troubles was gathering momentum. It had become a long hot summer for everyone in more ways than one. One night we were watching television on our wee tuppence halfpenny set when we were interrupted by the sound of someone blowing whistles and a loud hailer informing us and everyone else in the district that the Brits where raiding the houses. These types of things were normal as the local women either rattled bin lids or blew whistles and the local dogs barked. Things were different now the Brits had taken a harder attitude towards our people. Suddenly a burst of gunfire was heard and we speculated as to what type of weapon it had been fired from. It wouldn't be long before we found out that the Brits had shot dead two innocent women and injured two other passengers in a car. As we ran out to see what happened we made our way up Cape Street. The Brits opened fire with rubber bullets at us and we hastily made our way back to safety. Two sisters Maura Meehan thirty-one, and her younger sister, nineteen year old Dorothy were now dead for the simple reason they were making the people aware that the district was being raided by the infamous Green Jackets.

A few nights later we were all sitting skint when some one rapped the door and asked could a French man stay the night as he was, wait for it "Cycling around the world". We invited him in along with his bike and he informed us in broken English that he had his own sleeping bag cooking utensils so all he needed was a lay down. As it was now late he started unpacking his meagre belonging and low and behold he had a wee primy stove just like the one we used when camping. Next he started pumping it. I had seen many of these stoves go on fire, so I moved well back from him. As he got it lit, he then got some water and filled his wee teapot and was making himself something to eat when I informed him that I had been in France once or twice but he was a bit stand offish and not really interested. He went on to tell us that Belfast was a very quiet place and the news had a way of exaggerating the facts and he talked it all down. Suddenly just as I was getting a bit annoyed at his attitude, we heard a bomb go off and the windows came in all around us. There was glass everywhere. I never saw anything like it. The wee French man jumped and packed his half lit primy stove and his utensils and left in a hurry. I think he learned something that night. The news wasn't exaggerated. It was all true and he had just experienced it, first hand. We never saw or heard of him again.

A few nights later I asked Leaf did he fancy dandering up to my Ma's, as I needed a bath and we were both starving. John the Boy would eat cold dripping bread and he was happy with that until things bettered. But it turned me watching him eating it especially after a feed of drink. So after telling him to mind the house we set of for Lenadoon. We didn't even have the money for the bus. We reached Broadway where just a few weeks earlier the Paras had got us.

They had put us up against Paddy Hinds pub wall and made us stand for what seemed an eternity, as they sat in their jeeps laughing at these two idiots standing in the fingertip position. We were very glad a few people got out of a taxi and asked what was going on as the Paras drove off laughing and shouting at us from their open top jeeps. That night was going to be a lot worse. A patrol of scots soldiers grabbed us and pulled us into an entry behind the now Culturlann building at Nansen Street to P check us. As they were half way through the P check someone opened fire on them and they used us as human shields with one actually resting his gun on my shoulder. It was one of the scariest times of my life and was glad when it was all over. But this was a time when the abnormal became the so-called normal. About an hour later we landed at my Ma's house and after a feed I went and had a bath. Later when I came down the stairs Leaf was fast asleep on the settee and I headed up to bed. The next morning after a good breakfast we headed back to base to see if anyone had called when we were away. There was always someone or something coming or going or looking.

After a few weeks the neighbours were getting annoyed about the goings on in their once wee respectable street. There was talk about a petition being signed to get us out and we decided to try and quiet things down and stop the late night drinking and singsongs but it was like flogging a dead horse metaphorically speaking. One day there was a bit of rioting and burning going on as we stood and watched as lorry after lorry was burned. As we stood outside the bookies next to the Long Bar we saw a lorry that was delivering meat to Leo Mc Courts butchers. Then some one threw a petrol bomb into the cab and the driver made good his escape running down Leeson Street. He left the district minus his load. It quickly burned out and as I went down to have a look I waved to Leaf to come down and have a gander. The meat was mostly intact in the back so I decided that it would be better in the Grumpy Rooms as sitting there. So between us we wrestled a front quarter of a cow of its hook. As I got my shoulder under it my we skinny legs buckled but Leaf jumped in behind me and as we ran up Leeson Street we got it around to our house and then thought, "what will we do now? ' It was decided after some debate with Leaf that we couldn't eat it all ourselves. So we came to the conclusion that we would share it out with our furious neighbours and it may just ingratiate us with them.

After some running about we got it up the stairs. We got a clean bed sheet covered the bed and then planted the meat on top of it on the bed. We then got the loan of a saw from John Manning who was a visitor to the house on a regular occasion and also lived across the street. We then set about butchering it, but we hadn't even got a knife. It was an old joiners saw and wasn't much good but the women of the street were glad to get some meat free of charge. Not all of them I hasten to add. Some were quite loath to accept anything like that. One wee woman, a great character I may add, organized who got what and then told the people that Docky and Leaf were great lads. That woman was one of the big names in the street, the one and only, Ena McKenna. After that the petition was torn up, if it ever existed and we returned to happy days in the now famous **Grumpy Rooms**.

The next week it was a sugar lorry that was burned belonging to Tate and Lyle and the house was coming down with sugar and our wee filing cabinet come larder was full of two pound bags of sugar so no one went short of sugar for a while. By the way none of our gang hijacked any of these lorries but there was always stuff coming into the house and when there was plenty it was shared around. But one night something new arrived. It was a few cases of Saint Brendan's Cream, a new liqueur that Lyle and Kinaghan's had become the agents for. It was like Bailey's but maybe not as good and it lay about and when there was nothing else it sufficed.

Another time it was Green Chartreuse and it was about ninety proofs and it literally blew the head of you. The best load of stuff we ever got was twenty five gallon plastic barrels of cider again old stock from McKenna and McGinley's, which was supplied by Eamon Walsh. The only condition was that he had to get the empty barrels back as they were worth a fiver each. You couldn't disagree with that and so the barrels arrived and where placed in the downstairs back room as we decided what to do with so much cider. It was great. The barrels had a wee tap and you just filled your cup, when you wanted.

After a few weeks the Grumpy Rooms smelt like the Spanish Rooms hence the name. It was terrible and try as much as we did with black disinfectant, the smell lingered on for months. So in actual fact it smelt and sometimes felt like a pub. Willie Norney, big Hugh McGrillen, Paddy Dillon better known as PD, Frankie Donnelly, Arder Carson, Joey Linton, Roy Smyth, Plum Duffy all frequented the *Grumpy Rooms* and there were regulars who were there most nights.

One such regular was JB who came in most nights but he didn't call the day he got his giro, one week and that was a capital offence. Everyone bought drink especially on giro or dole day. So we decided to have a court case to judge whether he was guilty or innocent. The first thing we needed was a judge who was neutral and a guy who popped in once with big Owen O'Neil came in just to kill five minutes and he agreed to be the judge. His name was Pat McAllister.

Pat thought it was all fun but he didn't realise that Leaf and me and some of the other gang were taking a sterner look at things. After everyone was sworn in on an old bible, I was appointed prosecutor and the case was led. JB had to explain why he held out as it was now called. Plum Duffy a regular visitor and one of the gang were appointed as his defender. Nugget, Linty, and Arthur Carson and some others, were appointed as the jury. It was one of those nights when we had no money and no pruck so in reality we were bored. After about an hour John Barrett or JB as he was known was found guilty and he was remanded in custody to the room were we stored the cider, which stank. He actually went in and sat there until we sent for him. I think JB took it more serious than any of the rest of us and that seemed to prove he was guilty. The first sentence that came to mind was to bar him but he was never out of the place and that would have been unfair and very difficult to enforce. After some deliberation we decided he had to sit in the cider room for two hours and JB took it on the chin. As he sat in the back room we all started to feel pity for him and it was decided to release him but I will never understand why he put up with it. The *Grumpy Rooms* was the focal point or meeting place for all the gang and if he had been barred he would have been out of the loop. After he came back in to the living room he just sat for an hour with the hood of his duffle coat up and said nothing. About an hour later he came around when the tea and toast was made and we all settled down for the night of, *The Court Case*.

Over the next few day things were getting tough and one night some one took a girl he had met in a pub up the road, down to the house. So we all went out to give him a bit of space and within an hour half the district were around all having a look and it became so bad that Marie Nugent and Ena McKenna were out with the holy water and the crowd dispersed. Leaf actually went in and ordered both of them out in a heated rage and told them it was his home and not to come back. Nothing really happened but it looked bad and that was the last girl to visit the house.

The few weeks later, John the Boy arrived out side with a car. He then carried in a large box of tools to show us and I went out and looked at the car and right away knew that John had made a big mistake. He was half drunk and I explained to him that if the owner found out who took his car he would be in big, big, trouble. I told him to carry the tools out to the car and I said I would dump it. We were in big trouble if any one saw us so I decided I would get rid off it but John with the drink in him was having none of it. He thought it was his car. After Leaf and myself explained to him, about the consequences if he was caught and giving him a bit of a telling off he handed over the keys. He then put the tools in the boot and I decided to get rid of the car. As I went out, looked around to see if the coast was clear I got into the car drove up Balkan down Cyprus and into Plevna Street. It was just my luck, or lack of it as I ran into a duck patrol of the green jackets. All I could think of was the Meehan sisters being shot previously and I looked at Major Lloyd and I floored the accelerator and it took of down Plevna Street so fast I near lost control. I had a few drinks in me and wasn't really a good driver then. The brits didn't open up but I dare say they might have, had they not shot the two Meehan sisters some weeks previously. As the car hurtled down the street I missed a gear and careered down Bosnia Street and hit a kerb. I jumped out and ran to the first door I came to but the door was closed in my face and I made my way down Servia and into Mc Donnell Street and walked slowly up the Grosvenor road and back up to the house.

After a while John sobered up and we both warned him that it might be best if he blew. After a bit of interrogation we learned that no one saw him and no one saw me except the Brits so we decided to sit it out nervously for about two weeks. The car was one that can be seen in the curfew film parked in Leeson Street and that's all I'll say on that matter. We kept a low profile for a while and the house became busier as guys from Andy town and other districts visited us and it was even called Crossroads for a while. That was the name of a television program that was popular around the same time.

One night big Owney O'Neil came in and he had brought his own bottle of brandy with him. He sat down and I think he drank it all in about three goes, straight from the bottle. His mate wee John Manning came over when he heard Owney was there and the stories flowed. There were more horses sold that night than ever sold at Belfast fair as we all talked about horses, be it trotters, welsh cobs, or Irish draughts. The next thing big Owney, who was the local coal man along with his Da Pope and his brother Pat, stood up fell back on the seat and flaked out. We thought he was dead but after some investigation we discovered he was completely drunk as a skunk. As we chatted on for a few hours he just woke up, shook himself, and walked out without a bye or a leave and was gone.

Sometimes the house was like Royal Avenue and other nights it was very quiet. We never went to bed early as we were all night owls and stragglers could walk in at all times.

One day about ten in the morning after going to bed about five o'clock Nugget came in and after a few words I told him what a cheek he had waking us up at this time of the day. There then ensued a bit of an argument and it got hot and heavy. I was half asleep and Nugget let go with a left hand and I slumped behind the door and he left. After struggling to my feet I went back to bed and slept it off. It took a few days to get back on talking terms but it was okay, it had to be. Marie did make our dinners, so everything had to return to normal. Time went on and things started to change and Leaf started going with Bernie who later became his wife and I went back to sleeping on Walsh's settee. *The Grumpy Rooms* had become unliveable and the smell of the cider never abated. It was at a time that we were all moving on in life, John The Boy had moved back to Wales and I was about to get married to Patricia. It was as if everyone was going in different directions or just growing up. The fun of the *Grumpy Rooms* was over and I was now married and it was as if I was to take on a whole new way of life but I didn't. I remained the same much to my shame and regret.

The morning I got married I had to sign on the dole. So it was straight out of the chapel into a taxi and down to Corporation Street and declared I was now a married man. I then went to the Long Bar met a few of the lads and we headed to my Ma's house. Chip, Joey Linton, Roy Smyth, Nugget, Patsy Carberry, John Barrett, Tommy Quinn who did best man and his cousin, Geraldine Short brides maid. That was all who attended, and that was it. I always remember Belle Clarke made the breakfast and then we got stuck into the carry out and Nugget started a singsong. I have to say I made it up to Patricia when I took her on our honeymoon to LA and for anyone that doesn't know were LA is, no its not Los Angeles, its Lenadoon Avenue. That was the beginning of another chapter in my life and all those around me. To all those who have passed away that I've met or mentioned in this book, this about memories some good some bad, but as the Beatles sang, obla dee obla da life goes on. But life was to change even more dramatically as it was now nineteen seventy-two, the year of Bloody Sunday. The war was beginning in earnest and it was the worst year ever. You can read about it in the next part of the trilogy.

* * *